T0330577

Routledge Revivals

The Civil Service in Commonwealth Africa

First Published in 1969 *the Civil Service in Commonwealth Africa* describes the changing role of the civil service in Africa from the colonial era, through the post-independence transition to the contemporary African situation. Mr Adu deals with policy and programme for reforming the machinery of government and the structure of the Civil Service to make them effective executive instruments of policy; he examines the organization of ministries and describes the policy making process. Africanization is seen as an urgently necessary phase in the process of nationalizing the public services and organizing a lasting and effective staff development policy. Mr Adu's rich experience in public administration covers the final years of British colonial era, the transition period of self-government and the post-independence period. This book is a must read for students of African studies, African government and politics, and public administration.

The Civil Service in Commonwealth Africa

Development and Transition

A. L. Adu

Routledge
Taylor & Francis Group

First published in 1969
by George Allen & Unwin Ltd.

This edition first published in 2023 by Routledge
4 Park Square, Milton Park, Abingdon, Oxon, OX14 4RN

and by Routledge
605 Third Avenue, New York, NY 10017

Routledge is an imprint of the Taylor & Francis Group, an informa business

Publisher's Note
The publisher has gone to great lengths to ensure the quality of this reprint but points out that some imperfections in the original copies may be apparent.

Disclaimer
The publisher has made every effort to trace copyright holders and welcomes correspondence from those they have been unable to contact.

A Library of Congress record exists under ISBN: 0043510256

ISBN: 978-1-032-52691-1 (hbk)
ISBN: 978-1-003-40788-1 (ebk)
ISBN: 978-1-032-52692-8 (pbk)

Book DOI 10.4324/9781003407881

The Civil Service in Commonwealth Africa

Development and Transition

BY

A. L. ADU

C.M.G., O.B.E., M.A. (Cantab.)

Deputy Secretary-General, the Commonwealth Secretariat; Sometime Regional Representative, United Nations Technical Assistance Board, East Africa; Sometime Secretary to the Cabinet and Head of the Ghana Civil Service; Sometime Secretary-General, East African Common Services Organization

London

GEORGE ALLEN & UNWIN LTD

RUSKIN HOUSE   MUSEUM STREET

PRINTED IN GREAT BRITAIN
in 11 on 12 point Pilgrim type
BY WILLMER BROTHERS LIMITED
BIRKENHEAD

To my Wife

PREFACE

My earlier book, *The Civil Service in New African States*, was written in 1963-64. By early 1966, it had sold out. When the publishers asked for a revised edition, I took the opportunity to write a new book, based very largely on the old, which takes into account the rapid developments in the political and constitutional fields which have taken place in so many African states.

In preparing the earlier book, I was operating under certain handicaps. Most Commonwealth African states were very newly independent or were on the threshold of independence. Their Civil Services were all in a state of transition and rapid changes in the political climate and ideologies in which they were operating were taking place. The euphoria and optimism that characterized the nationalist movements for independence were still very important factors in the attitudes of all those who had responsibility in the administration of any of the states. The authoritarian regimes which dominated some of the states and the restrictions on freedom of expression in a number of them made it difficult to write with complete frankness. In any case, the period of transition after independence brought so many unexpected developments, and created so many problems of adjustment and orientation for the machineries of government and the Civil Services, that I was conscious that what I had written in 1964 was out of date before publication.

An effort has been made in this new book, *The Civil Service in Commonwealth Africa*, to avoid most of the limitations of the past and to consider the problems of the Civil Service with a completely open mind and frankness. The fact that the period of transition in most African states is now giving way to a stage of steady development enables one to consider long-range policies to make the Civil Services suited to the development tasks of the new age.

The new book then is designed to overhaul the old and to make it more relevant to the developments that have taken place since 1964. I am conscious that I may not have been entirely successful as the pace of development is still very great.

London, April 1968   A.L.A.

ACKNOWLEDGMENTS

As is usual in all such cases, there are a large number of persons and institutions who in the course of one's career in the public service have made significant contributions to one's experience and ideas. It would be impossible to name them all. I should like, however, to acknowledge publicly the debt I owe to a number of individuals and Governments for the ideas and material on which this book is based.

The first real rethinking I ever did on the role of the Civil Service in a developing state was in 1953 when I served with Mr M. F. Dei-Anang, formerly in the President's office, Accra, and Mr D. A. Anderson, now Ford Foundation Adviser on Staff Development to the Kenya Government, on the working Party on Africanization of the Gold Coast Civil Service. To both these former colleagues I owe a debt of real gratitude for the courage, sense of responsibility and real intellectual integrity with which they tackled the assignment with me. It was an experience not easily forgotten. From Mr Anderson, on whose wealth of knowledge and rich experience I later was lucky to rely when, as head of the Ghana Civil Service, he was my head of Establishments, I learnt a great deal of what I know about general principles in the administration of the Civil Service.

I must mention also the Governments of Malawi and Tanganyika who did me the honour of inviting me to serve on two very important commissions – the Localization Committee in Nyasaland in 1960 and the Salaries Commission in Tanganyika in 1961. These assignments greatly enriched my knowledge and experience much of which is reflected in this book.

For twenty-five years I served in the Ghana public service and this period covered the most pregnant period of the recent history of that State. I have been lucky in being associated with some of the epoch-making events in the development of its Civil Service.

Since my earlier book appeared, there have been dramatic changes on the political scene in Africa. Among the notable events was the revolution in February 1966 that ousted Dr Kwame Nkrumah from power. His policies in the period after 1961 did much to undermine the integrity of the Ghana Civil Service, which he himself had done so much to inspire in the immediate post-independence period. Nevertheless, I still feel that the policies which were established during the pre-1961 period not only gave the Ghana Civil Service a firm foundation, but also sustained it through the period of transition so that, helped by structural reforms now being made, it is emerging as a viable instrument for political, economic and social change.

Finally, I wish to acknowledge the debt I owe to two former colleagues in Ghana, Mr E. K. Okah and Mr T. K. Impraim, reference to whom I unwittingly omitted previously, and also to all my former senior Tanzania, Uganda and Kenya colleagues in the East African Common Services Organization, 1962-1963. My association with them richly enhanced my experience and taught me much about human adaptability to change and opportunity which I had previously thought impracticable or risky.

CONTENTS

CHAPTER 1

Introduction

IN 1938, two West African university students attended, as observers, a conference in Britain on comparative colonial administrations. The principal participants were officials of the Colonial Offices of the United Kingdom, France, Holland and Belgium. In the course of the deliberations, representatives of each of the colonial powers described the pattern of the Civil Service in their overseas territories and the extent to which the indigenous people were participating in it. In all cases, the observers got the impression that good intentions had been translated into action only to a marginal extent. In some overseas territories, the indigenous people could join the Civil Services on the same terms of merit and competition as citizens of the metropolitan states, whilst in others the policy was to admit local people into the senior ranks of the services as and when they were deemed to be suitably qualified. There were no positive policies in any of the cases for creating their Civil Services on an indigenous basis suited to the needs of each overseas territory.

Even in 1947, after the great revolutions in many spheres brought about by the Second World War, the Civil Service development policies, certainly in relation to British overseas territories, were still passive although the proclaimed political policy was to lead these territories to independence and responsibility for managing their own affairs. Although the lower segments of the Civil Services in all cases were filled by local people (which in East and Central Africa included local Europeans and Asians), nevertheless the policy continued to be to use the machinery of the Colonial Office and the Crown Agents to fill posts in the senior administrative, professional technical and supervisory grades. It required special and extraordinary procedure therefore to fit in a local and suitably qualified aspirant to any responsible post in the service of his own country.

The post-war constitutional developments that led to rapid

political advancement in the British overseas territories did, in all cases, outstrip the development of the public services as local institutions. The Civil Services were therefore unable to respond to the national aspirations for self-government and independence and the progressive realization of these aspirations that eventually led to the independence of Ghana, Nigeria, Sierra Leone, Tanzania, Uganda, Kenya, Zambia, Malawi, The Gambia, Botswana, and Lesotho.

The main problems which all of them have had to resolve concern, therefore, the need to transform the Civil Services not only from a colonial pattern to a nationally orientated service, but also from being mainly controlled by expatriate senior staff to an indigenously based one.

The complexities of policies in all spheres of government which result from the establishment of new nationalist governments demand the fashioning and installation of a new structure and machinery of government. This could not help but have the profoundest influence on the Civil Services, their organization and structure. The changes that have had to take place have, unfortunately, had to be so rapid as to make carefully considered long-term planning impracticable. It was impossible to foresee the pattern that would be forced on the services by constitutional developments mainly because these were themselves forced on the colonial powers and because also of the rapidity of change.

The Civil Services were, therefore, compelled to make rapid and painful adjustments in their composition and structure. They have, however, shown considerable powers of adaptability and have. on the whole, served the new governments well. This would seem to indicate that the services were, in spite of their colonial origin, based on sound foundations and that the men who were in control were willing and able to reshape the machinery to serve the changing needs of the post-war era of rapid constitutional changes.

The task of matching the structure, composition and orientation of the Civil Services to the new political and constitutional situations has really only just begun. It is necessary, therefore, for the Africans who are now in the services, especially those who have recently joined, to understand the principles which have applied to the establishment and structure of the system of public service we have inherited as well as the policies which governments have adopted for its future development. With this understanding, they might not only be in a position to play a constructive role in the governments of their states but also might be influenced to work for the healthy development of the service into an instrument for effective participation in the evolutionary and revolutionary changes that are taking place in all African states today.

Such traditions of the colonial service as integrity, impartiality, efficiency of service, loyalty to the government of the day, and devotion to duty are worth preserving. How to preserve them at a time of rapid turnover of personnel in responsible positions in the service is the problem and challenge presented to all those with responsibility for building the new nations, and for shaping the new Civil Services in particular. Without these traditions, it would be impossible to preserve standards and pride of service, and the new states would be poorly served by those who are responsible for executing the policies of their governments. The task ahead is, therefore, tremendous, and the hope is that the men who are now responsible for shouldering this task will be able to measure up to the expectations of their people.

The era of transition covering self-government and the immediate post-independence period is virtually over for most of the African States. The main characteristic of the Civil Services in this era was the adaptation of their inherited structure and organization to meet the new demands that the responsibilities of independence placed on them. No fundamental changes in structure were possible while the Civil Services were taking on these additional tasks. Nor would it have been wise to contemplate major reforms while they were at the same time in a process of accelerated nationalization of their personnel. The new personnel could be effective more quickly when they were introduced into a structure which was well established and recognized, and they would have had difficulties in adjusting to a situation in which a reformed structure was being introduced at the same time as they joined. With the coming of the end of the era of transition in most states, thought is now being given to policies for reform in the machineries of government, the structure of the public services and the systematic reorientation of the public servants. Reform is essential if the Civil Services in particular are to become vehicles for change in an era of rapid political, economic and social change. This opens an exciting prospect for all those concerned with policy in the public services and is at least as exciting as any other responsibility in the total programme of development in any of the states. The Civil Services have the opportunity to exercise constructive initiative in this period of challenge but can do so effectively only if they are reorganized for the efficient performance of the new tasks assigned to them.

This book draws its inspiration from experience in Ghana and a few other states in West and East Africa which were formerly under British administration. It describes the problems and principles relating to the growth and development of the Civil Services in former British colonial territories which are now independent and self-governing. The material and ideas for the book have been drawn from these sources and no attempt has been made to describe the position in the former French, Belgian, and other parts of Africa of which the author has little experience.

CHAPTER 2

Historical Perspectives

THE Civil Service in Commonwealth African states had its origins in the creation of a machinery by Britain to consolidate her colonial administration in her dependent territories in Africa. The service was essentially one which was constructed to prosecute the imperial policies in Africa, and its orientation and personnel were, therefore, suited to this purpose. Initially, its main task was to pacify the areas which by conquest, cession or treaty, had come within the British sphere of influence. In nearly all cases, this involved compelling or persuading a number of hostile tribal states to live together in peace and consequently having the means to intervene in cases where peace was disturbed. The early Civil Service therefore grew out of military occupations and, in many cases, the first public officers were military personnel drawn from the colonial regiments and occupation forces.

The Civil Service in these African states in its early stages was therefore mainly concerned with collection of revenue and the maintenance of law and order. The main core of this service was therefore constituted by the Political Administrative service composed of Provincial and District Commissioners, the Police and, in some cases the Treasury officials. These branches of the service were closely related together functionally, and they maintained a country-wide grid around which operated all the administration of such services as existed. The chain of command was precise, clear and simple. District Commissioners or Officers were responsible for the peace, welfare, and good order of their districts or divisions, and supervised and co-ordinated the functions and activities of all local departmental officers including the Police and the Treasury. They maintained liaison with local traditional authorities, where these existed, or created chiefs where there were none, and helped to bring orderly administration to the people. In discharging their responsibilities, District Commissioners or Officers were answerable to their Provincial Commissioners (or Residents as they were designated

B

in some territorites). The Provincial Commissioners had general responsibility for, and supervision over, all government and local government activities in their provinces. The chain of command stretched upwards through Chief Commissioners or Regional Governors to the Governor and Commander-in-Chief at the apex. The Governor himself was answerable to the Colonial Secretary in London.

The Civil Service was, therefore, geared to the rather negative policy of preventing trouble and bringing the Pax Britannica to all the dependent territories overseas. It was not, until comparatively recently, concerned with economic and social development as a major objective of administration. Economic services were lacking in strength and purpose. Except where immigrant populations had settled, there were no developments towards industrialization. Economic activities were mainly in the hands of private trading companies from overseas—usually Britain. These were primarily interested in the sale of manufactured trade goods and the purchase of local agricultural produce. Such industries as developed were mainly concerned with the exploitation of mineral resources. A few companies established plantations for the supply of such products as rubber, palm-oil and other vegetable oils for their factories in the metropolitan countries. The central administration had no positive policy towards the promotion of these economic services except to create the conditions under which private enterprise could flourish, and to intervene where necessary to ensure fair play to the unsophisticated peoples of the territories.

Financial administration was on the basis of simple accounting of revenue and expenditure and the balancing of the budget. Revenue collection, mainly customs and export duty, was related to the necessity for raising funds to meet recurrent expenditure. Development expenditure, except in isolated cases such as the construction of harbours, railways, and telecommunications between main centres, was virtually unknown.

The initiative for promoting agricultural development came either from missionaries as in Ghana, or from immigrant populations as in East and Central Africa or from the reactions of the ordinary peasantry stimulated by the interest of overseas trading companies in purchasing produce, as in the cases of palmoil, rubber and cocoa in the West Coast territories. In very few instances was the Administration (which until the post-war self-government era was synonymous with the Civil Service) directly responsible for initiating the promotion of cash crop agricultural developments. Here again, it was principally concerned with ensuring that there was fair play on all sides. It was not until much later that Agricultural Departments were established to give attention to the preservation of the health of the cash crops, extension work on better husbandry and greater production, research into all aspects of the industry and the development of new cash crop industries.

In the social services, such as health and education, the Civil Service was not initially directly concerned with their development. The missionaries take most of the credit for this. Quite early on, however, Medical and Education Departments were established to provide some assistance and encouragement to the efforts of the missionaries and local traditional authorities, and ended by being mainly responsible for their respective services.

The Civil Service in its early stages was not required to deal with the complex responsibilities of the modern-day administrations in the political, economic and social spheres. Moreover, it was the effective government and even the later pre-war development of having representative, or partially representative, legislatures did not take away anything from the responsibility of the Governor to govern, acting through and advised by the Civil Service. The involvement of the service in the greater complexities of modern government came in slowly and did not become a major feature until the 1939-45 war and after.

Staff development in the Civil Service as a positive policy of governments was influenced by constitutional development which did not receive much impetus until during and after World War II. Before then, normal expectations were that independence, and even internal self-government, were out of the question for any of the African territories for a generation or more. Naturally, therefore, a positive policy of preparing the Civil Service for service in self-governing communities and, consequently, associating the indigenous people with it in policy determining positions, was out of the question until the postwar years. Lip service was paid to the ideal of appointing Africans when suitably qualified candidates appeared. But, as was once stated in the Legislative Council in the Gold Coast (now Ghana), if an African had the necessary qualifications, his application for employment in the Civil Service was turned down on the grounds that he lacked experience. If he had the requisite experience, he was said not to have the qualifications.

In any case, since all appointments to responsible positions were made by the Colonial Office, a local candidate had little chance of being considered. Such persons as got in were either fortunate or were picked under extraordinary arrangements made by the territorial Secretariats.

In most cases such appointments were made either to pacify the articulate but few educated Africans and Chiefs who clamoured for a place in the administration of the country, or to forestall the criticisms and agitation of liberal-minded parliamentarians in the metropolitan country.

Tribute must be paid, however, to a few British Governors and Administrators of vision who, against heavy odds, opened the door, albeit only a crack, for Africans of merit to squeeze in. One such Governor was Sir Frederick Gordon Guggisberg of the Gold Coast who endeared himself to the African by his liberal policy of educational development aimed at producing the future leaders of the country. He formulated an Africanization policy which had as its objective the filling of at least half the 'senior' service with Africans in the ten years ending in the middle of the thirties. Guggisberg expressed his faith in these words:

'Government has definitely adopted the policy of employing Africans in appointments hitherto held by Europeans provided that the former are equally qualified in education, ability and character. This, then, is our immediate task—the provision of teachers, instructors and professors from among Africans. . . . In no other way shall we keep them permanently the loyal and worthy members of our Empire that they now are. . . . No race can achieve full and permanent success under alien leaders.' Alas, his inevitable departure in 1927 brought in successors who regarded his policy as premature and impractical. Optimism languished until post-war revolution revived it.

If, then, there had been colonial administrators with the vision and foresight of Guggisberg in the inter-war years who were prepared to apply a progressive and continuous policy of staff development on an indigenous basis, there might have been a fair chance of sound foundations being laid for a stable Civil Service before World War II. Instead, we continued to have, until as late as 1948 and 1950, public services in British Africa which rested on a policy of automatic recruitment to senior posts from Britain and from the older Commonwealth countries of Australia, New Zealand, South Africa and Canada. As in-

dicated above, the responsibility for filling all positions in administrative, managerial, supervisory, professional and senior
technical grades rested with the Colonial Office which entrusted
to the Crown Agents the filling of certain of the posts. This
policy was so firmly entrenched that, in the few cases that
Africans were appointed to any of these posts, they were officially described as 'Africans holding European posts'.

In effect, therefore, the Civil Service in Africa was racial in
structure until very recently. In 1946, as a result of the work
of the Harragin Salaries Structure Commission, the racial basis
of the service in West Africa was abolished. In East Africa the
change came very late, in 1954, and happened as a result of the
Lidbury Commission recommendations of 1954; in Central
Africa, the final decision on this was not taken until 1960. The
pattern before the change was that Europeans filled all 'senior'
service posts, that is, responsible posts in the administrative,
executive, professional and technical grades. Local personnel
were recruited to fill the 'junior' service posts in the junior
executive, clerical, semi-skilled and unskilled industrial and
manipulative grades. In East and Central Africa, the situation
was further complicated by the intervention of the immigrant
European, Asian and 'Coloured' communities who filled intermediate grade positions between the expatriate Europeans and
the Africans. They occupied what in West African terms may
be described as the more junior of the so-called 'European' appointments and the more senior of the African appointments.
In a number of cases, skilled jobs for which no local personnel
were available were upgraded to senior posts in order to attract
Europeans. For instance, in one particular country, it was observed that the only typewriter mechanics were Europeans in
the senior service; and European railway engine drivers were
still to be seen in East and Central Africa in 1964—all holding
senior service posts.

The legacy of this structural system is still with us and has
had a disquieting effect on the service which will take a long
time to straighten out. One effect is the creation of a grave crisis
in all territories that achieved self-government and independence where the exodus of expatriate officers under compensation schemes left a vacuum which could not readily be filled
with Africans. Another effect is that the expatriates had all
along occupied the more responsible positions and their knowledge, skill and experience were not readily replaceable from

local sources. This is principally because, since Africans normally had no expectation of being appointed to these posts, they naturally did not aspire to qualify themselves for such posts. The West African had been accused of taking the easy way out in qualifying himself to become a lawyer or a doctor. But what could he do when he knew he had no career prospects in engineering, accountancy, education or administration? It was, on the other hand, always possible and lucrative for him to enter into private practice as a lawyer or a doctor. In East and Central Africa, where even junior executive and apprenticeship posts were not ordinarily open to Africans and were the preserves of the local Europeans and Asians, there was not even the incentive to complete secondary school education or undergo training in technical skills. In the result, when large numbers of local and African qualified personnel were required to fill gaps created by constitutional development, they had neither the training nor experience to meet the need. Either, therefore, under pressure from political agitation, the best available and usually unsuitable, persons were appointed and promoted, resulting in serious loss of efficiency, or else further recruitment overseas was resorted to, at very great expense to the State. Neither course of action has been really satisfactory.

Another effect of the colonial structure of the Civil Service is the distortion of the educational policies of the various states. In addition to the natural and expected desire of missions to train school teachers and church workers, there was also the need to produce clerks and other white collar 'junior' workers for the governments and trading houses. In Ghana up to the middle twenties, it was quite common to see, in the comparatively few middle schools, recruitment parties from government departments and mercantile firms endeavouring to persuade young men to accept clerical and similar appointments with them even before their final examination results were out. In these circumstances, there was no incentive to encourage the development of secondary schools, technical and trade schools, and institutions of higher education. Skilled tradesmen were obtained by recruiting and training illiterates, and the preponderance of uneducated Africans in these grades acquired for the technical class an unsavoury reputation, and made soiling of one's fingers taboo with men who had been to school. This aversion to taking employment as a technician or tradesman is breaking down among educated Africans only very slowly and is still not quite gone. Moreover, all the states in Africa are still suffering from the effects of the late development of secondary and technical schools and also of higher education institutions as we shall see later.

The exclusion of Africans from senior responsible positions also led to a feeling of a sense of inferiority among some of them, particularly among those who after many years of service still remained in very humble circumstances and had to take instructions very often from raw European recruits. Alternatively, they were filled with a sense of frustration and were inclined to be intransigent on the least provocation. In any event, there was engendered among Africans, whether within or outside the Civil Service, a sense of injustice and festering grievance. This has not been healthy for the service since even when Europeans were prepared to co-operate in schemes of African advancement and, later, when the policy of Africanization was being sincerely applied, Africans were still distrustful and unco-operative. They could not believe that a colonial government would be genuinely interested in creating an indigenous service to supplant expatriate officers.

The converse of the feeling of inferiority and injustice among Africans was the strong feeling of superiority and a spirit of arrogance displayed by the majority of European Officers, particularly the most junior European trades foremen who regarded themselves as superior to the most experienced African clerks and behaved accordingly towards them. There were very few cases of actual rudeness and maltreatment, but the mere existence of differences in status always in favour of the European emphasized a superior attitude towards the African Officer. This state of affairs complicated race relations, even in West Africa where there were no immigrant European settlers, and this remains with us to this day and is only just dying out.

Furthermore, the sharp division in status between the races reflected itself in separate housing arrangements, separate social institutions such as clubs, and separate social service facilities such as hospitals and schools. In East Africa, even toilet facilities in government buildings were separate for Europeans, Asians and Africans. When the barriers began to break down and locally qualified persons were increasingly occupying posts in the senior ranks, it was natural that they should adopt and expect from their Governments these status symbols in the facilities for housing, hospitals and so on. In this way, class consciousness in the service was introduced in a traditionally egalitarian African society. It is almost automatic that an African appointed or promoted to the senior service should immediately obtain a government loan to purchase a motor car, to give only one instance of this unconscious assumption of a distinct status. This status consciousness is so strongly entrenched that even when new service structures have abolished the distinction between the senior service and the junior service, officers have by an adopted convention drawn the line where it previously was.

It was inevitable that as local persons invaded the senior ranks of the service, their emoluments should bear a close relation to those of their expatriate colleagues in the same or similar posts. This has had a distorting effect on the whole of the salary structure. Even where an expatriation or inducement element was introduced, the gap between the lowest paid and the senior service officers of local origin was very wide indeed and still remains unhealthily wide. Moreover, since all Europeans, whatever their responsibilities, were in the senior service, their African replacements were also admitted into the senior service. This particularly evident in East Africa. All Immigration Officers, Executive Officers, senior clerks, stenographers were originally European and the posts were therefore graded in the senior service. They continue to be so graded for Africans now increasingly being admitted to these posts since it would be inequitable to discriminate against them. An example is a girl who spends a year, after receiving her School Certificate, obtaining proficiency in shorthand and typing, who can expect to be appointed to a senior stenographic post, though in West Africa all such appointments are in the lower segments of the service. Overgrading in relation to responsibilities is therefore a feature of the situation in East Africa which will be difficult to reverse, although it is recognized as a principle that it must be carried out if the service emoluments are to be related to the economy of the countries.

The change of policy on the racial structure of the Civil Service, as described earlier, was a by-product of the revolutionary approach to colonial administration in the post-war years, accelerated by the increased tempo of nationalist agitation for independence. All colonial governments, in the circumstances, accepted and formulated definite policies on staff development which placed emphasis on localization or Africanization. This inevitably influenced recruitment policies as well as the policies of governments toward creating a local field of recruitment through training and education. There was also a profound change of attitude towards the role of the Civil Service. It was recognized that the service could not continue to serve as an instrument of the imperial power but had a positive role to play in the development of the political institutions, and the economic and social development of the emerging independent states.

Unfortunately, this change of philosophy has come too late to change both the complexion of the service and its structure so as to ensure that it is orientated to play a positive role in independent African states. The problems thus created are formidable and their solutions will not be achieved for a number of years, particularly as the governments of the new states are in a hurry to achieve complete reconstruction and to revolutionize the whole economic and social structure.

It is fashionable to blame the British administrations for this lamentable state of affairs. No doubt they must accept a large part of the responsibility. But, it has to be remembered that, until the last war, no one – not even the most optimistic African politician – expected independence to come so quickly. Constitutional advancement has been so rapid as to outstrip the development of many national institutions including the Civil Service. Nevertheless, the solution to the problems affecting the Civil Service in new African states lies in this very situation. There would be no talk of accelerated Africanization or localization if there were no accelerated constitutional developments. All new African governments realize the need for a very sound, efficient, loyal and stable Civil Service, and are prepared to give very high priority to its reconstruction and development. The problems that face the service are therefore related to the general problems of transition and, given good sense and purposeful planning, they can be solved.

CHAPTER 3

The Civil Service Within the
Machinery of Government

ALTHOUGH everyone knows what the Civil Service roughly is and its position as the executive arm of government, it is appropriate that there should be a working definition of the term to avoid any misunderstanding of what is being discussed. Since the system being described derives its origin from the British connection and follows the British pattern, its definition necessarily is the same in principle as the British definition.

In Ghana, the definition is as follows: 'The Civil Service comprises all servants of the State, other than holders of political or judicial offices, who are employed in a civil capacity and whose remuneration is paid wholly and directly out of moneys voted by Parliament.' The term, therefore, covers all staff of Ministries and Departments, from Permanent Secretary to the daily rated employee; it does not include armed forces personnel, magistrates or judges. In treating the subject in the context of the title of this book, however, we are concerned principally with those positions in the service that have substantial responsibilities, the established part of the service. Daily rated employees are therefore excluded from any further discussion in this book.

As a servant of the State, the Civil Servant's first loyalty is to the State. Since the Government is charged, by popular choice, with the control and administration of the affairs of the State, the Civil Servant's loyalty is to the Government of the day, and he should appropriately feel a positive and consistent responsibility to prosecute the interests of the Government as his employer. Usually, the focal point of the Civil Servant's loyalty is the Head of State – the Crown in Commonwealth dominions and the President in republics.

In order to appreciate the role of the Civil Service in government, it is necessary to go over familiar ground concerning the basic constitutional structure of a State. The usual major divisions of the functions of government are the Legislature, the Executive, and the Judiciary. The Legislature has responsibility for making laws (Acts or Ordinances) under the Constitution for regulating the affairs of the State. It is usually a popularly elected body and derives its authority and strength from the people. In Commonwealth countries, the Legislature or Parliament is regarded as sovereign and is the only body that can alter the Constitution or, at any rate, initiate legislative action for amending the Constitution.

The Executive is charged, by the authority of the Constitution and within the Acts of Parliament, with responsibility for managing the affairs of the State. The Executive consists of the Head of Government, who is either the President or the Prime Minister, and Ministers of State who together constitute the Cabinet. In the countries whose Civil Services we are describing, Ministers are also Members of Parliament. They have collective responsibility in the Cabinet for the policy decisions of the government but are individually responsible to Parliament for the administration of the departments within their portfolios.

The Judiciary is responsible for adjudicating on disputes arising between individuals and other individuals, and between individuals and the State, on rights under the Constitution and the law. The Judiciary tries offences against the law, and is the final arbiter on all disputes arising out of the interpretation of any part of the Constitution. In order to carry out its responsibilities impartially and justly, it is generally agreed that it must have complete independence of both the Legislature and the Executive. Most constitutions define how members of the Judiciary should be appointed and how their terms of service are safeguarded so as to ensure this independence.

The Civil Service is part of the machinery of the Executive branch of government and exists to put into effect government policies. The effectiveness of the government, therefore, depends on the efficiency of the Civil Service and its ability to respond in practical terms to its policy decisions. It has been said, therefore, that the Civil Service is the custodian of the government's reputation since, if it is unable to carry out the government's policies faithfully and efficiently, it not only frustrates these policies but it might seriously undermine the government's position and stability. This emphasizes the special relationship between the Civil Servant and the government, and also underlines the sensitivity of all African governments to the attitude of the Civil Servants to their regimes, and their concern to ensure that attitudes and orientation in the services are in complete accord with the philosophy underlying the government's policies.

In recent years the British concept that the Civil Servant should not identify himself with any political party, in order to be able to respond to the policies of the party in power, has come under heavy fire in independent African states with a one-party system of government. The essential point, however, is not acquisition of a party card or lip service to the policies of the government in power, so much as a clear understanding of the policy of the government and the significant role the Civil Service has to play as the executive arm of government in the development of a country. Policy decision is the responsibility of Ministers and the Cabinet. The Civil Servant's essential role is to implement to the best of his ability decisions handed down to him by his Minister or the Cabinet, and provided the relative roles of Minister and Civil Servant are well understood, there need be no conflict between them. The most important feature of the Civil Service, it is firmly believed by many, is its non-political character. It is a permanent service and its members would not normally expect to take up or to quit office on a change of government. The Civil Servant must, therefore, be in a position to serve all governments of whatever complexion with equal loyalty, and obtain the confidence of Ministers irrespective of their political affiliations. This can only come about if Civil Servants, particularly those in the higher ranks, exercise special restraint in political matters, and are sensitive to the political climate so that they do not embarrass their Ministers by their actions.

At the lower levels, the definition of the responsibility of the Civil Servants as one of carrying out the decisions of his Minister fully describes his role. The ordinary clerk, executive officer artisan has to carry out instructions and although it is healthy for him to be able to appreciate the policy behind his instructions, he has no part in making that policy. It is his duty to carry out his responsibilities diligently and to the best of his ability. He can make, and often does make, suggestions for improvements in methods and results which are welcome, but he has no part in the formulation of political or administrative policies. His immediate loyalty is to his superior officer in the service, and this loyalty ultimately leads by the normal chain of command to the Minister.

The Civil Servant in the more senior posts of responsibility, however, has an important role in policy formulation. He is usually an officer with long personal experience and expert knowledge, and is able to bring that experience and knowledge to bear on policy matters which should greatly assist his Minister. This is particularly the case with such officers as Permanent (Principal) Secretaries, Heads of Departments and their immediate deputies and assistants. They have a normal responsibility of advising their Ministers over the whole range of their official duties. This advice is not only on the formulation of policy, but also on the execution and effect of any proposed policy. They also have the responsibility for interpreting to their staff the precise nature of their Ministers' policies. The topmost Civil Servants may therefore put forward policy proposals. The need for top ranking Civil Servants being sensitive to the political wishes of their political masters has already been emphasized. At the level of Permanent Secretary a realization of this need is the keynote to successful management and cordial relationship between Civil Service, Cabinet and governing party. The choice between alternative proposals rests with the Ministers, and once the Ministers have made their final decisions, it is the duty of Civil Servants to implement them in the best possible manner as if the decisions were their own.

The good Civil Servant studies his Minister's ways and saves him trouble. He has a special responsibility for preventing his Minister from making a fool of himself and this he must do in a tactful, quiet and unobtrusive way. He should at all times act in a manner to promote his Minister's general policy. In 1950, Sir Charles Arden-Clarke, then Governor of Gold Coast, reorganized the colonial secretariat into divisions that would be the nuclei of Ministries that would be established under the new self-government constitution that came into force in 1951. His instructions to the Permanent Secretaries-designate included the following admonition. They were at all times to study their Ministers' policies and their ways of approach to these policies, and do all they could to foster those policies and assist their Ministers in carrying them out. He would hold them responsible for major errors of procedure committed by their Ministers and it was their duty to prevent Ministers from committing avoidable errors.

But these special responsibilities of the Civil Servant to the government should be matched also by the special responsibility of the government to its Civil Servants. By the nature of their work, Civil Servants are often subject to public criticism in newspapers, in Parliament and on political platforms. The critical examination of the machinery through which the government gets its work done is a healthy and normal feature of a democratic community. The Civil Servant is, however, debarred from replying publicly to public criticisms since he has no voice but that of his Minister, and no authority save that which he derives from his Minister. The Minister is in honour bound, therefore, to defend his Civil Servants from criticism or attack in respect of acts which they carry out in their official capacities.

One of the matters which have caused anxiety to Civil Servants in new African States is the lack of appreciation on the part of Ministers of their responsibilities in this matter. Civil Servants have been attacked by politicians in and out of Parliament on acts performed by them in their official capacities. Sometimes even Ministers themselves have yielded to the temptation of passing blame for matters on which they have been criticized. This is usually a transition phase and, fortunately, the convention that Civil Servants are entitled to the protection of their Ministers is becoming satisfactorily established. In the meantime, however, the experience is rather painful for them. Experience has shown that very often criticisms by the public, especially in developing countries where the people have recently succeeded in throwing off their colonial bondage, serve as a useful outlet for letting off hot air and also for airing legitimate grievances. In the words of a politician, it is difficult for most members of the public to express a legitimate grievance without indulging in a little mud-slinging. The essential thing in these circumstances is for Civil Servants not to lose their balance and sense of humour and for the politicians not to allow the attacks to develop into a senseless quarrel.

Staff Associations and Unions can play a major role in establishing respect by members of the public and politicians for the role of Civil Servants. They can institute a public relations organization to provide a better image of the Civil Service to the public. They can organize programmes to ensure that Civil Servants respond effectively to legitimate grievances voiced by politicians and the public. And, where unfounded allegations are made, the Staff Associations can act in defence of the rights and reputations of their members. Unfortunately, the organization of effective Staff Associations and Unions has not been a strong feature of the Civil Services in African states in the past. In any reforms for the future, the role of Staff Associations and Unions in promoting and protecting the interests of Civil Servants should be given its proper place.

The importance of mutual confidence and loyalty between the Civil Service and the government cannot be over emphasized. The Civil Service holds the key to the effectiveness of the government and its ability to manage efficiently the affairs of the state. The morale of the Civil Service is, therefore, a matter of the greatest importance to the government and all governments realize this. Provided that members of the Civil Service carry out their duties diligently, loyally, honestly and to the utmost of their capacity, they should be afforded by the government the full measure of protection to which they are entitled.

CHAPTER 4

The Structure of the Civil Service

IN the Report of the Commission on the Civil Service of the Gold Coast under the chairmanship of Sir David Lidbury (1951), the structure of the service is defined as 'the arrangement of the component parts to form an organic whole'. This definition is used as the basis for the discussion of this subject that follows.

The structure of the Civil Services in former British Africa bears, as explained earlier, the stamp of its original racial sources of recruitment. The posts in the former 'European' appointments became what is now generally known as the senior service and the 'Asian' and 'African' appointments became the junior service. Even though this sharp division has been eliminated or blurred officially in new structures which do not draw a line between the so-called 'senior' and 'junior' services, the custom prevails of referring to certain grades as belonging to one part or the other of the service. Unfortunately, staff regulations or general orders still reflect the former divisions in the service. Allowances, leave terms, passages and travel arrangements, entitlement to houses and other conditions of service are applied on the basis of status, one set for the more senior branch and the other for the more junior branches of the service. Even where every effort has been made to revise the rules to avoid this invidious distinction, it still exists in the minds of officers and will take some time to eradicate.

Fortunately, a number of forces have been at work to influence a change in the old pattern of the service. One of these factors is the improved educational facilities in various countries, particularly at the secondary and technical school levels. The old educational system was good enough for the production of candidates for the most junior clerical and manipulative positions, but the establishment of increased facilities for secondary and technical education has resulted in opportunities for Africans to qualify for the more responsible posts. Furthermore, the establishment of higher educational institutions, including universities, as well as the introduction of large-scale scholarship schemes for the training of local persons overseas in professional, graduate, technical and managerial disciplines, have underlined the acceptance of the new policy of opening the door to Africans to attain all posts, even the highest, in the service. It has become possible, in the circumstances, to contemplate schemes for the advancement of officers in the lower ranks of the service into the highest positions of responsibility whilst, parallel with this policy, local persons with professional, technical and degree qualifications could be directly appointed to the more senior posts.

The most important single factor in shaping the structure of the service, however, is the transition of the countries from colonial status through internal self-government to independence. The role of the Civil Service since independence has undergone a fundamental change. Instead of being the Government, the Civil Service has become the executive instrument of government. The traditional colonial pattern of the Secretariat being the apex of the Government, with the field political administration and service departments working to it, has had to give way to a ministerial structure of government and a Cabinet system. The Governor as head of government handed over the reins to a Chief Minister or Prime Minister. This revolution in the philosophy of government could not help but have a very profound effect on the organization of the service as a whole, particularly in the higher echelons.

One effect of this change was to accelerate the process of Africanization or, as it is termed in some countries, localization. Few people would deny that an indigenous government should be served as soon as possible by an indigenous and local Civil Service. This implied a close and careful examination of the structure to find out in what respects it needed to be reformed to ensure that the optimum use could be made of locally available trained manpower as well as, of course, to ensure that it also operated in consonance with the policies of the new elected political governments which had been established.

It may be helpful at this point to describe the principal features of the old structure of the Civil Service. The usual pattern in all former British territories was to divide the service into the following main Divisions:

(a) *The Subordinate Service* This consisted mainly of daily rated or of monthly rated employees with either provident

c

fund terms or similar retiring benefit terms but not pensionable terms. They comprised office messengers, certain subordinate manipulative grades and equivalent grades in the technical and service departments. The members of this service were normally not required to be literate and the training for their responsibilities was as elementary as their responsibilities were simple.

(b) *The Clerical, Sub-Clerical Grades and Analogous Grades* These included posts of clerical assistant, typist, clerical officer and junior secretarial officer. They were open to candidates with elementary school education in the old days but in later years recruitment for the more senior of these posts was restricted to those with some secondary school education and to those who had been promoted on ability from sub-clerical grades.

(c) *Artisan and Technician Grades* For many years these grades did not attract men with literacy training, partly because of a shortage of candidates with education who were recruited into clerical or teaching posts, but also because the remuneration attached to these grades was such as to discourage those with even elementary school education from undergoing the apprenticeship or other training necessary for appointment. In some countries, these grades were on nonpensionable daily-rated or monthly-rated terms. In others, although personnel were on salary scales, they were not established Civil Servants. It has been said that educated Africans were unwilling to take on jobs which involved soiling their hands or manual work. In Ghana, the establishment of attractive terms of service and status for artisans and technicians (comparable to terms offered to clerical and executive grades) had the dramatic effect of attracting substantial numbers of literate young men into apprenticeship training. This clearly demonstrated that young men would be prepared to consider any job provided it offered suitable career prospects.

(d) *Executive and Analogous Grades* These included a varied middle group of posts which required specialized experience in the carrying out of responsible functions which were clearly defined. These functions required high standards of responsibility although they were of routine nature. Such posts as those in the Accounting, Customs and Excise, Office

Management, Postal and Storekeeping services were in this category.

(e) *Technical Grades* These were parallel to the Executive grades in levels of responsibility but were of a sub-professional nature. They included sub-professional posts in the Engineering, Medical, Agricultural, Forestry and other Scientific Departments.

(f) *Administrative and Professional Grades* The holders of these posts were in the Administrative Service or in such posts as Engineer, Doctor, Lawyer, Scientist, Architect, Surveyor, and similar professional grades. They usually required a basic qualification of a degree or membership of a professional body. Superscale appointments including headships of departments were drawn from these grades in the normal course.

The basic structure described above covered the whole service. The subordinate Service, Clerical and Analogous Grades and the Artisan and Technician Grades were generally occupied by local personnel. The other grades were filled by overseas officers and were automatically classified as senior service. The lines between the two levels were drawn for each country to suit the availability or otherwise of locally qualified personnel. For instance, in one country typewriter mechanics would be classified as technicians in the junior service because local personnel was available, whereas in another country they were technical officers in the senior service because European appointments were necessary. Again, in West Africa most immigration staff at ports were in the junior service whereas in East Africa they were all senior service officers because they were Europeans.

The structure was built around the main Government structure of the Governor at the apex with a supporting Secretariat, Field Administration and Service Departments. The Administrative Service formed the main framework of government. Members of this service manned the Secretariat and were the principal instruments of policy formulation. They also constituted the Regional Administration of Chief Commissioners, Residents, Provincial and District Commissioners, and District Officers who were responsible for the co-ordination of departmental activity in the Regions, Provinces and Districts respectively. They also operated the machinery of government at the Regional or local level working with local traditional rulers where these existed. The colonial Administrative Service was therefore the *élite* of all the Colonial Services. It had glamour but aroused the jealousy of officers in other departments. As the principle instrument of colonial rule, it was not the policy to appoint local officers to it. Until 1948, the view was held in the Colonial Office that it would be a mistake to appoint Africans to this service since, it was agreed that, with the attainment of independence, the Administrative Service would have to be dismantled. Indeed, it was thought that the few Africans who were in the service were likely to prove unacceptable to the new nationalist Governments because of their past associations with imperial rule. The change of attitude came about through pressure from the local public particularly in the Legislature, but also because it became gradually accepted that an indigenous Administratige Class would be needed, at the self-government and independence stages, for policy formulation and advice to the new Ministries.

As stated earlier, constitutional development and other factors have influenced changes in the structure of the Services. No attempt will be made here to describe the form the structure has taken in the different countries. Although they differ in detail, the adaptation of the colonial structure to a service to match the requirements of independence status has on the whole followed similar patterns. The principles on which this adaptation has taken place have been the same with only differences in emphasis.

The most important principle has been the need to reform the structure so as to make it efficiently responsive to the new political pattern and aspirations of the Government. The justification for this has been dealt with in other parts of this book. The most important application of this principle is in the Administrative Service. Its functions have radically altered from being the main machinery of government and the policy maker to being the administrative staff of Ministries charged with advising and assisting Ministers in carrying out their responsibilities. In some countries, like Ghana and Tanzania, field administrative officers – Chief Commissioners and Provincial Commissioners, District Commissioners and District Officers – were replaced by political officers – Regional Commissioners and new style District or Area Commissioners. In other countries, they have become Local Government Inspectors.

Where they have been retained in the field, their functions have radically altered.

To digress a little on this subject of political appointments to field positions, it has often been questioned whether this change of policy is not a retrograde step. To understand the attitude of the governments that have adopted this policy, one has to reflect on the former position of the pre-independence administrative structure. There was a complete chain of command from the Governor at the apex, through the Colonial or Chief Secretary at the head of the Secretariat, to the Chief Commissioners, Residents or Provincial Commissioners and District Commissioners in Regions, Provinces and Districts respectively. All these links, from the Governor downwards, belonged to the same service and shared a common loyalty. Authority reached down and up through the hierarchy and complete solidarity was maintained among all levels of the hierarchy. This solidarity was so strong that in some places, District Commissioners were referred to by their detractors as 'bush governors'. The introduction of an elected government meant that the Prime Minister replaced the Governor as the effective head of government and Ministers and Ministries replaced the Chief Secretary and the Secretariats respectively. As a result of the change the solidarity between the field administration and the centre of the line of loyalty became ineffective or at best obscure. In the circumstances, it was natural for the new Governments to find it impracticable to operate the old system and to seek, therefore, to replace it with a new arrangement. The appointment of Regional Commissioners and Area Commissioners was one way of providing the much-needed links which incidentally reflected the same pattern as the old chain of colonial command. In Ghana, the Government under the Convention People's Party unfortunately operated this system in a manner which resulted in the blatant exploitation of the government machinery for purely party political purposes; in the suppression instead of protection of the rights and interests of the people the Commissioners were supposed to serve; in the rigging of local and national elections and in systematic undermining of the liberties of the citizens. The experience of Ghana should therefore lead other governments to exercise extreme caution in considering policies for political appointments to key posts in the field.

To return to the main theme, another principle determining the reformation of the structure is the need to accelerate the policy and programme of Africanization (or localization where it applies). This implies, as explained earlier, having a structure which makes optimum use of available local, trained manpower. It implies also a complete review of the specifications of jobs so as to make possible their performance by available local personnel. In some cases, job dilutions were necessary and in the circumstances justified. The object it must be emphasized is not to lower efficiency or provide 'jobs for the boys', but rather to reconstitute the structure and composition of the machinery so that qualified local persons can carry out all the responsibilities attached to the posts efficiently and effectively. For instance, in Ghana, a review of the duties of Administrative Officers in Ministries made it possible for some of their former responsibilities which were executive in nature to be transferred to the Executive Class Officers to enable the reduced cadre of high-level administrative staff to discharge effectively their responsibilities with policy-advising content.

A further principle is the establishment of a close link between the educational system of the country and recruitment into the Civil Service, and to cater for the people who emerged from the various levels of the revised educational system. Thus the service structure should provide for recruitment at the terminal points of the elementary schools, secondary and technical schools, university and professional training institutions. This point will be developed below when describing the structure of service recommended.

Lastly, a reformed structure should provide for a full and satisfactory career for an individual in whichever class of service he belongs. Obviously, it is impracticable to provide for complete equality of career prospects for all. But everyone who joins the service, no matter in what humble position, should be able to advance to the highest position for his class provided that he is prepared to work for it. No one should be a prisoner of his grade. It has been possible for a messenger in a Secondary School in Ghana, to advance, by its own efforts and through the existence of a suitable career structure, to the position of Bursar of the School. In Tanzania, an African District Commissioner had in fact started his career as an illiterate office boy. These examples reflect cases in which the individuals had to overcome a number of obstacles which deterred others of equal ability although not of equal determination. A sound service structure, on the other hand, should make it possible for the talented to

rise from the more humble positions to the loftiest that the individuals are capable of attaining through ambition and an
ability to work.

When it comes to consider the best structure suited to the
conditions of the African countries, it is necessary to look at the
structure of the parent Civil Service, namely, the British Civil
Service. This is natural since the Civil Services in these countries
were installed by British administrations which adopted the
system they knew. Although newly elected governments have
their own approach to the type of government best suited to
their political philosophy and their development programmes,
nevertheless because of the nature of the educational system
and other factors which are not susceptible of quick changes,
the basic components of the structure would remain similar to
what had already existed. In the view of many who have been
concerned with the development of the public services in former
British Africa, the basic principles of the British Civil Service
structure are the best for these countries, at any rate, during
the period of transition. Admittedly, the main reason for this is
the historical association of these countries with Britain, but
this association has determined the pattern of government and
the sources from which recruits can be and are obtained for
the services.

Moreover, an adoption of the basic British pattern, with
adaptations to suit local conditions, would meet the tests and
the criteria mentioned in earlier paragraphs. It is, in the circumstances prevailing, the best that is able to assist in the process
of staff development and Africanization. It creates a ladder by
which a suitably qualified Civil Servant can climb from whatever grade he enters to the highest appointments. It provides a
link with the educational system so that the Governments can
recruit personnel into the service at the various levels at which
people emerge from the educational system. It provides also for
those who fail to pass the necessary tests for advancement from
one class of posts to a higher class – such as from the Executive
to the Administrative or Technical to Professional – to advance
to higher grades in their own class which provide increased responsibility and increased salary.

The pre-independence structure described in the early paragraphs of this chapter was no doubt the best that could be devised in the circumstances of the early days. Its main weakness
under present-day circumstances is that it is too rigid and does

not make the best use of staff available in the lower ranks of the service. The divisions between the classes and the tests for promotion from one class to another are, because of their racial origins, too rigid. In a number of countries, special devices, such as the creation of Training Grades, have been adopted to enable promising staff in the junior service to qualify for senior service appointments. Such schemes are, however, necessarily *ad hoc* and temporary. Today's structure should ensure that the gifted and dedicated officer in the lower grades is given increasing responsibility to qualify him, eventually, for a position in the senior ranks.

The basic structure commended can best be described by the General Services Branch of the Civil Service. This Branch should be divided into four Classes as follows:

Class	*Educational Level for Entry*
(i) Sub-Clerical Class	Elementary School after 8-10 years of education.
(ii) Clerical Class	General Certificate of Education 'O' Level or local equivalent.
(iii) Executive Class	General Certificate of Education 'A' Levels or equivalent or at least Grade I and II School Certificate.
(iv) Administration Class	University Degree or equivalent.

There would be corresponding Classes in the Technical, Professional and Industrial branches as follows:

(i) *Auxiliary and Minor Technical Class*,
to correspond with Sub-Clerical and Clerical Classes.
(ii) *Technical Class*, to correspond with the highest Clerical and Executive Classes.
(iii) *Professional and Scientific Classes*, to correspond with the Administrative Class.

In addition, there should be a separate Secretarial Class which would form part of the General Services Branch, but concerned with typing, stenographic and secretarial responsibilities only. A diagrammatic presentation of the Service structure is given in Appendix I.

The main features of the structure proposed, which are different from the old structure, are, *firstly* emphasis on the Executive and Technical Classes. Inherent in the old structure, and perhaps in its racial origins, was the comparatively high status placed on middle-grade responsibilities in the administrative and technical/professional fields. Executive and serious technical responsibilities did not apply to grades below those of the 'senior service'. The structure proposed gives emphasis to the importance of these classes which are intermediate between the Clerical/Sub-Technical and the Administrative/Professional Classes. They should relieve the higher Classes of all responsible functions which do not call for the exercise of policy formulation or professional knowledge and experience. This might result in a reduction in the cadre of Administration and Professional staff. In Ghana, the introduction of a more clearly defined Executive Class with properly assigned functions enabled the Government to avoid the expansion of the Administrative Class which the introduction of a major development plan would have made necessary in the past. This was important since the supply of graduates was, in general, insufficient. In East Africa, the Posts and Telecommunications Administration has been able to manage with a small cadre of professional engineers as a result of the emphasis placed on careful selection and concentrated training given to supporting cadre of technical staff.

Secondly, it is proposed that the Executive and Technical classes should extend downwards. The main purpose of this would be to ensure that those who are likely to exercise high executive and technical responsibility later in their careers are selected at an early stage and given training and experience in the appropriate fields to prepare them. In some countries, notably Nigeria and Sierra Leone, the Executive and Technical Classes start at least a grade higher than is proposed here. The purpose stated here is, however, taken care of by the allocation of functions to the higher grades in the Clerical and Sub-Technical Classes so as to prepare the officers for higher responsibilities of their Executive and Technical Classes. The difference is therefore only a matter of classification and not of principle.

Another innovation proposed is the establishment of a separate Secretarial Class. In the old structure of most of the countries, except for the senior posts of Stenographer/Secretary and Personal Secretary, most of the typing was carried out by clerical staff. Here again, the status of the posts of Stenographer/Secretary and Personal Secretary tended to be overgraded because they were filled originally by European women. A separate Secretarial Class would ensure that more economic use is made of clerical staff by using personnel who are specially trained in typing and stenography to carry out normal secretarial duties. It would also provide a normal progression for typists and stenographers to the senior secretarial posts of Personal Secretary.

The main features of the proposed structure will now be discussed.

THE ADMINISTRATIVE CLASS

The Royal Commission on the British Civil Service (1929/31) defined administrative work as:

'that which is concerned with the formation of policy, with the revision of existing practice or current regulations and decisions and with the general administration and control of the departments of the Public Service. For the effective performance of those duties officers of the highest qualifications are needed'.

The functions performed by Administrative Officers in Ministries, that is, by Assistant Secretaries through to Permanent or Principal Secretaries, should conform broadly with the definition of administrative work stated above. Where it still applies, most of the administrative work in Regional Administrations would conform with this definition.

Administrative work calls for the highest qualifications, mental discipline and intellectual training and a university course, therefore, offers the best guarantee that these qualities will be forthcoming. In Britain and the older Commonwealth countries a first or second class Honours degree is insisted upon for direct entry into this class. In Africa, however, where there is a shortage of graduates of all types it would be unrealistic, at any rate until much later, to refuse to consider graduates of all classes. Also, initially in Africa, written competitive examinations are dispensed with and instead competitive interviews are adopted as a means of selecting for appointment those graduates who have the very high personal qualities required for this class. Any graduates who are found to be unsuitable for the Administration Service could, for some time to come, be placed in other posts requiring degrees, and so there is no need to waste good graduate talent.

Direct entry into the lowest grade in the Administrative Class is therefore normally restricted to graduates. In time – and this is happening already in Nigeria – there will be the need to introduce written competitive examinations in addition to competitive oral examinations or interviews. A proportion of the vacancies in this Class, normally one-fifth, should, however, be reserved for deserving officers in the Executive Class who demonstrate the qualities of mental discipline and intellect necessary for efficient performance in policy formulation and advisory posts. These qualities could emerge after considerable experience in the Executive Class, and there should always be provision for the normal promotion of long service officers in very senior executive positions into the Administrative Class if they merit such advancement. Normally, however, the scheme of service for this class should provide for a written competitive examination for members of the Executive Class who have served for a minimum period of years and are confirmed in their appointments. The minimum period should be not less than the time it takes a candidate with the School Certificate – the normal entry qualification into the Executive Class – to obtain a university degree. The examination, which should not be a test of academic ability in normal university subjects, should nevertheless be such as to select the candidates who have attained an intellectual standard normally expected of university graduates. The examination should be followed by interviews of the same standard as are required for normal graduate entrants.

Where Institutes of Public Administration have been established successful completion of a carefully planned course should be a condition for permanent appointment to the Administrative Class. Officers promoted from the ranks to the Administrative Class should also be required to attend a modified course in order to ensure that all officers appointed to this Class receive adequate training in professional management and the techniques of planning and decision making.

The Administrative Class is divided into a number of *Grades*. The highest is usually the Head of the Civil Service termed differently in different countries as Chief Secretary to the Government, Secretary to the Cabinet, or Permanent Secretary, or Secretary to the President or Prime Minister. At the lowest level is the grade of Assistant Secretary or District Officer in Regional Administrations. A typical system of grades would be:

(a) Secretary to the Cabinet, who is Head of the Civil Service,

    (b) Permanent/Principal Secretaries, who are heads of Ministries, or similar offices of Government.

(c) Under Secretaries	responsibilities at progressively higher levels for blocks of work in Ministries, and other similar offices of Government.
(d) Principal Assistant Secretaries	
(e) Senior Assistant Secretaries	
(f) Assistant Secretaries	

Countries, however, adopt gradings and designations suited to their individual systems.

In many instances, the management responsibilities of the top grades of the Executive Class, say, above the Senior Executive Officer level, are not easily distinguishable from those of the lower grades of the Administrative Class. For this reason and also in order to pursue a policy of blurring the class distinctions between the Administrative and Executive, some governments have proposed a merger of the two Classes at these levels. Thus, there would be automatic opportunities for promotions from the higher grades of the Executive Class into the Administrative Class. Further promotion, thereafter, would be based purely on merit in performance. This policy of merger does not undermine the scheme for encouraging accelerated promotion into the Administrative Class from the lower grades in the Executive Class through competitive examinations which have been described below.

THE EXECUTIVE CLASS

Executive work has been defined as work in which a code of law or administration is applied in order to obtain results. To quote again from the Royal Commission on the British Civil Service (1929/31), the following is the definition of the work assigned to this Class:

'To this class we would assign the higher work of supply and accounting departments and of other executive or specialized branches of the Civil Service. This work covers a wide field and requires in different degrees qualities of judgment, initiative and resource. In the Junior ranks, it comprises the critical examination of the scope of approved regulations or general decisions, initial investigations into matters of higher importance, and the immediate direction of small blocks of business. In its upper ranges, it is concerned with matters of internal organization and control, with the settlement of broad questions arising out of business in hand or in contemplation and with the responsible conduct of important operations.'

In a number of departments of Government, the duties performed by all but the highest grades of officers are executive in nature. Departments such as those concerned with accounting, audit, labour, co-operation and personnel are in this category. In the higher levels, of course, policy formulation responsibilities would apply, and grades at these levels would be comparable with the higher grades in the Administrative Class. As stated earlier, the proper use of the Executive Class is of the utmost importance in ensuring that government business is carried on effectively without the use of high grade Administrative staff on routine duties however responsible these may be. It provides also for the optimum use of the experience and abilities of local staff who in the past could rise no farther than the higher clerical grades. With training and experience, such staff could be used for the performance of the highly responsible but routine functions in Ministries, Departments and Regions and thus save the time of Administrative and Professional officers who should apply themselves to formulation of administrative policies, advice on political policy matters, and purely professional responsibilities.

Like the Administrative Class, entry into the Executive Class should be both by direct recruitment of candidates who are suitably qualified, and also by promotion of officers in the Clerical Class. The majority of vacancies in the entry grade should be reserved for the direct entry candidates who should ideally have at least the Higher School Certificate qualification or its equivalent. In Africa, such candidates are in short supply and they are probably best encouraged to undergo degree, professional or higher technical training as the best use of the countries' political talent under the existing circumstances. Until there is an adequate supply of candidates with this qualification, therefore, it is expedient to open the competition for direct entry to candidates with good School Certificate qualifications, or their General Certificate of Education equivalents.

Experience in Ghana has shown that, even at the School Certificate level, most of the bright candidates who secure

Grade I, or II at the School Certificate examinations continue to the Sixth Form to prepare for the universities, and are least attracted to the Civil Service. In order to overcome this difficulty and ensure a steady flow of good quality officers into the Executive Class, intensive in-service courses organized by the Training Branch of the Estabishment Secretariat have been launched to prepare experienced and intelligent clerical officers for advancement to the Executive Class. This ensures that all the vacancies not filled by direct recruitment of candidates with the School Certificate or equivalent are made up by promotions from the Clerical Class.

The most effective method of selection is by a Competitive Examination in English, Mathematics or Logical Thinking, and General Knowledge papers followed by an interview. Where the number of candidates is small, however, it may be possible to rely on interviews only. Even in the latter case, a written examination is useful in sorting out those who have the intellectual capacity at the level required and who would therefore be able to train to exercise the judgment and responsibility of the Executive Class.

Entry by promotion should also ideally be by a competitive written examination and interviews at the same standard as for the open competitive examination, drawing on the Clerical and analogous grades for candidates. The candidates should be confirmed officers with ages within prescribed limits. A proportion of the vacancies, usually about one-third, should be reserved for this means of entry. In suitable cases of older officers, promotion could be made on the recommendation of Heads of Departments but this method of entry should be used with circumspection.

Because it is necessary to recruit into the entry grade of the Executive Class from the School Certificate level, it is necessary also to start the Executive Grades at a much lower status than in the United Kingdom where it is normal for graduates even to compete for entry. In such countries as Sierra Leone and Nigeria, the entry grade into the Executive Class is higher and carries greater responsibility than in Ghana and Tanzania. In the former countries, the upper grades of the Clerical Class are used for the responsibilities assigned to the junior Executive Grade, for instance, in Ghana. Furthermore, recruitment into the Executive Class is through a special training grade for candidates with School Certificate or by competitive selection of suitably qualified officers in the Clerical Class. It is not necessary to be dogmatic about the best pattern for the Executive Class. The most important consideration is that there should be nothing in the pattern to inhibit the flow of talent from the lower to the higher grade or class and that the duties of each grade or class are defined clearly and applied effectively. It is seriously contended, however, that given the present output of the secondary schools, it is a much tidier and perhaps a more effective pattern to reach down the Executive grades in order to start the regular School Certificate entrant on the beginning of the responsibilities which would come to him in the higher grades. Certainly, experience in Ghana has demonstrated that good results are obtained by this pattern.

The Executive Class is also divided into a number of grades varying from five to seven depending on the status of the lowest grade and the levels of responsibility assigned in each country. The designations of the grades are usually, starting from the lowest grades, Junior Executive Officer, Executive Officer, Higher Executive Officer, Senior Executive Officer, Principal Executive Officer, Chief Executive Officer and Executive Secretary. Minimum salaries range from £300 per annum to £600 per annum and in the higher grades salaries are comparable with the lower superscale salaries in the Administrative Class with equivalent responsibilities. There are departmental designations also. In the Accounts departments for instance, designations such as Junior Accounting Officers, Accounts Officers or Assistants, Assistant Accountants, Accountants, Senior Accountants and Principal Accountants are applied. Similarly, there are Tax Officer grades in the Income Tax department, Customs and Examining Officers and Collectors in the Customs and Excise department, and so on.

CLERICAL CLASS AND SUB-CLERICAL CLASS

The Lidbury Report on the Civil Service of the Gold Coast (1951) defined the duties of the Clerical Class as follows:

'The work of the class may be defined as comprising all the simpler clerical duties not assigned to the sub-clerical class and in addition the duties dealing with particular cases in accordance with well-defined regulations, instructions or general practice; scrutinizing, checking and cross-checking straightforward accounts, claims, returns, etc., under well-defined instructions; preparation of material for returns, accounts and statistics in prescribed forms; simple drafting and précis work, collection of material on which judgment may be formed; supervision of work of members of the sub-clerical class.'

The higher grade of the Clerical Class is mainly used for supervisory duties over numbers of Clerical Officers and Clerical Assistants.

The work of the sub-clerical class is defined by the same Lidbury Report as:

'routine clerical duties up to and including the preparation, verification and scrutiny of straightforward documents, statistics, records, etc.; the preparation of other documents, etc., subject to check; simple arithmetical calculations with or without the aid of office machinery; the simpler forms of registry work, simple correspondence of the stock letter and printed form type under well-defined general instructions; the operation of office machines where convenient. This is a description rather than a rigid definition and other similar duties may also be assigned to the class. The higher ranges of Clerical Assistant duties overlap with the lower ranges of Clerical Officer duties.'

Entry into the Clerical Class is by direct recruitment of candidates with the School Certificate or equivalent or those who have completed a well-defined stage of secondary education such as Standard X in East Africa or by the promotion of deserving members of the Sub-Clerical Class. Competitive examinations may be used for both methods of entry. Entry into the Sub-Clerical Class is by direct recruitment of boys and girls who have completed the elementary school education.

The usual division into grades are as follows:

Clerical Class	Sub-Clerical Class
Clerical Officer	Clerical Assistant
Higher Clerical Officer	

In some countries, there is no grade of Higher Clerical Officer and its duties are merged in those of the most junior of the Executive grades. In others where the Executive Class starts at a more senior level, the higher clerical grade is used for junior executive work as well as supervisory responsibilities and is thus a fruitful recruitment ground for the Executive Class.

SECRETARIAL CLASS

As stated earlier, a Secretarial Class is necessary to take over responsibility for all typing, stenographic and secretarial duties. It is bad policy to use clerical officers, as in some places, for copy-typing duties. It is a most inefficient way of utilizing the services of such a grade of officer.

The grades in this Class are usually:
Typist
Stenographer and Audio Typist
Stenographer/Secretary
Personal Secretary
Reporter

Most copy-typing work in large offices and in small stations should be able to be performed by officers in the Typist grade. Officers in the Stenographer and Audio Typist grades could either be used in stenographic pools or be attached as personal assistants to senior officers ranking below heads of large divisions or small departments. The Stenographer/Secretary and Personal Secretary grades should provide personal assisants to heads of Departments or Ministries or officers of equivalent or higher ranks. Reporters are used for verbatim reporting in the Legislature, the Courts or at conferences.

Typists need be selected from those with elementary education only. Proficiency in copy-typing and an intelligent understanding of the English language are all that is required for efficient performance in this grade. Stenographers and higher grades, however, require education of School Certificate or equivalent standard, or, at least a knowledge of the English language at G.C.E. 'O' level. Progression from the lower to the higher grades in this Class is related to proficiency in shorthand and typing, and the attainment of the appropriate educational levels, particularly in the English language. The salary scales attached to grades in this Class are related to those in the clerical and executive classes.

The highest grade of Personal Secretary or Reporter is usually well below the level of the highest Executive grade. It is normal in some countries, therefore, to provide further promotion outlets for officers in this class into the Executive Class. A stenographer/Secretary or Personal Secretary, in discharging the duties

D

of personal assistant to a top official, is in fact doing the very responsible work of managing his affairs and his office. These responsibilities are not unrelated to some of the functions of the lower levels of executive work. Promotion into the Executive Class is therefore not as inappropriate as it might seem.

EXAMINATIONS

In the preceding paragraphs, prominence has been given to the use of examinations for the selection for entry into various classes of posts. It may well be asked whether it is necessary to make such a fetish of examinations. It is well known that there are some persons who are bad examinees and who, nevertheless can perform duties of posts of greater responsibility. Where the number of competing candidates is relatively few in number, it may be possible to dispense with a written examination and use the method of interview or recommendation based on a carefully planned system of staff reporting. Where numbers are very large, however, interviews become a tedious and cumbersome system and recommendations become unreliable since the recommending officers do not observe the same standards. In these circumstances, written examinations are the most convenient means of making a fair, equitable and objective selection. Moreover, the examinations could be designed to encourage the flow of persons of ability from the lower into the higher classes, and the individual should be encouraged to sit for the appropriate promotion examination. Thus, an ambitious junior officer who is prepared to work hard to improve his intellectual standing should be able to attain to the highest class of the Civil Service. Any system of class to class progression should, however, make provision for the mature person who was never able to pass examinations, or never had the chance to, but who nevertheless has clearly demonstrated suitability for advancement to a higher class.

The Class to Class examinations should be designed to test intellect, logical thinking, general knowledge of the country, Africa and the rest of the world, current affairs and the standard of the English language appropriate for entry into each class. They should not be designed to test the knowledge of particular school or college subjects nor should they be a test of proficiency in the duties of the Class to which the officer belongs For instance, for entry into the Administrative Class, an Executive Officer should be required to pass an examination to indicate that he is of the same standard of mental discipline, intellectual calibre and command of English expected of a university graduate. A test of proficiency in the performance of the duties of an Executive Officer is irrelevant for this purpose, although no officer should be allowed to compete unless his record of work is satisfactory. When he has been accepted for promotion into the higher class, he would then be trained in the performance of the duties of this class in the same way as direct entry candidates are trained.

Examinations may also be used for promotion from one grade to a higher grade in the same class, for instance from Executive to Higher Executive Officer or from Junior to Senior Accounts Officer. These may be necessary where officers serve in many departments of Government but are on a common seniority list. In this case, there is no means by which a uniform objective reporting can be provided as a means of selecting on merit for promotion. In other cases, training schemes or levels of proficiency require tests as a means of selecting the most deserving of promotion. In such grade to grade examinations, the test should be on the actual duties of the grades, or the next higher grades, since merit should be measured by the efficiency in performance of duties in that particular class.

It is the responsibility of the Public or Civil Service Commission to arrange the proper conduct of these examinations and to lay down the rules therefor. The standard and syllabus for each examination would be provided for in the scheme of service for that particular class. The Commission may conduct the examination itself, but it is more usual for it to contract with an examining body, such as a statutory Examinations Board or Council, or a Departmental Examinations Board in the case of promotion tests within the same Class.

PROFESSIONAL CLASS

The posts in this Class are those requiring recognized professional qualifications or university degrees or scientific qualifications of university degree level. These posts include those in the Legal, Medical, Engineering, Architectural, Agricultural, Forestry, Veterinary and Education services as well as in a number of scientific posts such as Geologist, Entomologist, Chemist, Physicist and Meteorologist. Professional officers are the specialists of the Civil Service, whose qualifications are equal to or better than, the normal entry qualifications for the Administrative Class. The salary structure is the same, usually, as for the Administrative Class but it is also usual to set a premium on these professional posts and give them enhanced salaries or higher points of entry.

The highest posts in the Civil Service, such as heads of Ministries, are usually in the Administrative Class, and in a number of countries there is a tendency to reserve these posts for members of this Class. This gives cause for resentment among professional and departmental officers who see the door closed to them for attainment to these chief policy formulation and advising posts, which are also usually the highest paid. There is no reason in principle why these posts should not be open to any, of whatever Class, who demonstrates the qualities of administrative ability, sound political judgment, ability to work in consonance with political Ministers, and the highest integrity. If this were done, the optimum use would be made of professional staff whilst removing causes of friction and jealousy from the Service.

As the description implies, for entry into the Professional Class, a candidate must have the appropriate degree or professional qualification. Unlike the Administrative Class entry into it by promotion from a lower Class is most unusual, unless the professional qualification is somehow obtained. There are cases, however, where persons are able to prove, after long experience in the sub-professional grades, their competence to undertake professional responsibilities. In these exceptional cases, promotion into the Professional Class is permissible.

The Professional Class also has grades parallel with the grades in the Administrative Class, the highest posts being those of Directors or Specialists.

TECHNICAL CLASS

This Class is parallel with the higher grade of the Clerical Class and the whole of the Executive Class. In the lower grades, the Technical Officer is concerned with minor technical functions where responsibility and initiative do not have the same importance as technical competence. In the higher ranges, however, they should be able to relieve professional officers and scientific officers of all routine but responsible functions and be able to supervise field operations where they would exercise full responsibility for the success of these operations.

This Class includes such posts as Medical Assistant, Health Officer, Laboratory Technologist/Technician, Engineering Assistant, Draughtsman, Survey Assistant, Veterinary Assistant, Agricultural Assistant and Superintendent, Forest Ranger and Forester, and Scientific Assistants of all types.

There is no uniform method for entry into this Class since there is such a wide variety of them. In countries with a good supply of secondary school candidates recruitment is usually from this source with post-school technical training lasting from two to five years – either full time or on a sandwich part-time basis. In other countries, technical training is given to those without any or the full secondary education. Since a basic knowledge of science and mathematics is necessary in most cases, it is obvious that some secondary school training in these subjects is also necessary. This can be, and is in fact, provided as a preparatory course to the main technical training course where the trainees have had no previous school training in these subjects.

Whilst it is not impossible to obtain the training for the Technical Officer Class on the job, the normal policy is to provide special training institutions or courses. Thus there are special schools in all countries for the training of Technical Officers in the Agricultural, Forestry, Veterinary, Survey and Health fields, whilst Technical Colleges or Institutes provide training in other fields such as Engineering and Laboratory Technology.

AUXILIARY AND MINOR TECHNICAL CLASS

This Class is composed of a large number of auxiliaries and others who work either in the field or in laboratories in support of technical and professional staff. Included in this Class are Field Assistants, Laboratory Auxiliaries and Microscopists, etc. Their responsibilities and consequently their remuneration are parallel to the sub-clerical class. They frequently provide a useful field of recruitment for training for the Technical Officer grades since their duties give them some knowledge of the basic scientific principles necessary for technical training.

ARTISAN CLASS OR INDUSTRIAL CLASS

This has not been included in the classification described so far because, in principle, the members of this class should not be established Civil Servants. The duties are industrial in nature and they are not, and should not be, subject to the same code of discipline and conduct as for Civil Servants who work in departments with policy responsibilities. In the higher ranges, however, there are supervisory posts such as Foreman, Works Inspector, and Superintendent, who because they have responsibilities of management, are established Civil Servants. In some countries, therefore, most of the Artisan Class are in the established Civil Service. The criterion applied is that they are permanently required for construction, installation and maintenance functions, whereas those required for development work of a non-permanent nature are taken on and discharged according to the works programme.

The main distinguishing feature of the Artisan Class is that entry into it is by a specific and regular apprenticeship training. This takes the form of progressive training on the job combined where necessary with the teaching of the theory and principles of the skill required, or two or three years' training in a Trade School or Technical Institute followed by a shorter period of apprenticeship. In both cases, a trade test is required to be passed before qualifying as a skilled Artisan. The Artisan Class includes Carpenter, Bricklayer, Mechanic, Electrician, Boilermaker, Millwright, etc. They form a very important group since much development construction and installation as well as the provision of a wide range of services depend on their skill and efficiency. For this reason a good educational background, preferably not less than eight to ten years' attendance at elementary school, is essential.

REMUNERATION

Closely tied up with the structure of the Civil Service is the salary structure and it is necessary to consider at this stage the principles on which remuneration for the various classes and grades in the Service should be determined. In African circumstances, the main principle that should determine levels of remuneration is that the salary structure should be consonant with the general economic circumstances of the country, and should be related to the general level of income of its people. The *per capita* incomes of the African countries under consideration range from £15 to £90 per annum, with most of them in the lower part of this range. In these circumstances, it may appear that top Civil Service salaries in the region of £2,000 per annum, or higher, may be hard to justify. If this were the only consideration, it would not be difficult to apply this principle to depress the present levels of top salaries. There are other factors, however, which have to be borne in mind.

The Tanganyika Salaries Commission of 1961 had as part of its terms of reference 'the need to devise a salary structure for the Local Civil Service constant with the general economic circumstances of the country'. The Commission spelled out in its Report the considerations that guided it in arriving at its proposals for remuneration in the Service – and these are so much the result of a thorough examination of Tanganyikan economic circumstances that apply with equal force elsewhere, that it is worth examining its conclusions.

The Commission took the view that the costs of administration, that is, the cost of the emoluments of salaried and daily-rated staff, should be less than forty per cent of the total Government expenditure in its regular budget. If the costs exceed this percentage, then it is necessary to examine the situation to see whether staff numbers are not too high in total or in particular grades; or qualifications might be unnecessarily high generally or in particular posts, that is where the jobs could be done at a lower level at a cheaper cost; or officers might be employed on duties of a lower standard than those for which they are qualified or remunerated; or Government organizations might be over-complicated or involve duplication.

The Commission set out the principles which should determine the salary structure as follows:

(i) Remuneration is only one of a number of factors in the conditions of service of Civil Servants. In fixing remuneration due regard must be paid to other factors, notably security of tenure, prospects of promotion, leave and sick leave privileges and pensionability. It might still be true of the Civil Service that a strong element of vocation might play its part.

(ii) Ministries must have sufficient suitably qualified staff to carry out the tasks demanded of them and to ensure the maintenance of a Civil Service recognized by the community as efficient.

(iii) Civil Servants and the community they serve must feel that levels of remuneration are fair.

(iv) In prescribing rates of remuneration and other conditions of service which are considered to be fair, it is necessary to ensure that:

(a) they are not out of scale in the sense that they are so low as to affect adversely the quality and numbers offering themselves for employment;

(b) alternatively, that they are not unduly high which would have the effect of elevating Civil Servants into a privileged class and so doing an injustice to the community.

(v) The community must feel that it is getting an efficient service and that it is not being asked to pay an excessive price for it. On the other hand, levels must be adequate to ensure the retention of efficient Civil Servants and a salary structure that could endure.

(vi) The recruiting procedures for admission to the established Civil Service are more formal than those in Commerce and could not, or should not, be changed at short notice. A corollary is that the salaries of all posts in the public service should be public knowledge and not be susceptible to arbitrary variation. It follows from this that there must be a high degree of standardization in pay and conditions of service. Subject to certain limitations Government cannot improve conditions for new recruits or any selected Civil Servants without applying such change simultaneously to all members of the grade or class concerned. To this extent the Civil Service salaries structure is not as flexible as that which can be applied by commercial/industrial organizations.

In applying these principles, other factors might govern the situation. In particular, in African circumstances, there is the need for some time yet to retain or attract the services of expatriate personnel. This has the effect of enhancing the market value of local candidates of similar qualifications, experience and competence. Market value is, therefore, of significance in fixing remuneration, especially in the case of graduates and professionally qualified men where governments are in competition with commerce and industry. On the other hand, there are others whose services are equally essential but who might not enjoy the same competition for their services. The danger in this situation is that the gap between the lowest rates and the highest might be too wide.

Another factor is the cost of living. Governments have a duty to pay a living wage, enough for a man to maintain himself and his family in adequate housing, food and other necessities of life. Any consideration of salary terms must therefore have regard to costs as well as the standard of living appropriate to the various classes of officer.

Another factor to be borne in mind is the need to relate salaries to levels of responsibility. This is one of the most difficult principles to apply since there are no easy criteria by which relative weights of responsibility of different jobs can be measured and salary levels attached. There is or should be, a section of every Establishments or Personnel Office concerned with job analysis and inspection in an attempt to determine these relativities, among other purposes. A fair attempt can therefore be made and injustices can be avoided. In the ultimate, the fair salary level is the one which attracts and retains staff of adequate qualifications and efficiency.

No attempt will be made here to state what the actual salary levels should be for the various grades and classes of posts. These are dependent on general levels in the particular country and they may also change with time. In Appendix II may be found examples of salary structures applying in a few of the countries.

GENERAL REMARKS

The Civil Service structure described above is hierarchical in principle. This has often been criticized. Most people would agree that those who should fill the principal posts which concern management and the making of policy should be men who have had the best education the nation can provide, that is a university education. There are, however, those who say that there should be provided for those in the lowest ranks the opportunity to advance to the highest offices in the service. Obviously any structure which insists on rigid horizontal divisions with no available means of a break-through for those in lower levels would tend to create castes and classes which would be unhealthy for morale and for society generally. The structure re-commended fortunately avoids this rigidity.

In new countries, the two principles stated above should not conflict since shortage of university candidates necessitates a policy of encouraging the use of talent from the lower ranks. A progressive policy of training should enable non-graduates to bring themselves up to the level normally expected of graduates. The situation may change, however, with time, and the hierarchical principle may tend to create classes in the community where none existed before. This should be resisted and steps should be taken to counteract it.

Some of the things which can be done to avoid the danger are, firstly, that university education should be open to all on merit rather than on the ability of parents to pay. This is already the adopted policy in all new countries as part of their man-power development policy. So long as this policy continues to be applied, there is no danger that a particular social class would arrogate the best and influential jobs to itself. Secondly, post-entry training should be exploited to reduce the hierarchical rigidities. As will be stated later it is the duty of government as employer to provide training facilities for its staff, and the schemes of training should ensure that all officers of ability have access to them and are able to advance to administrative and professional ranks. Once the facilities have been provided, normal human ambition should ensure that advantage is taken of them. The kind of training facilities envisaged should not exclude opportunities for university and professional education either on full-time or part-time basis.

Another special step that should be taken is to bring pro-fessional and scientific Civil Servants close to the sources of policy decision so as to provide an increased reservoir of recruits for top administrative posts. This problem has been touched on earlier from its negative aspects of jealousy and resentment. It is, however, undeniable that some of the best administrators have come from the professional and scientific fields. This is fully recognized in America and other countries. In Africa the finest Governor that the Gold Coast (now Ghana) ever had, in the opinion of many, was Sir Frederick G. Guggisberg who start-ed in the Royal Engineers. It is therefore in the interests of all countries that these useful fields be tapped to increase the top administrative manpower resources. This would also have the healthy effect of reducing the rigidities between the professional and scientific group and the administrative class. It may be represented, of course, that it is wasteful to use professional and scientific men on pure administration. This is surely a matter of point of view and, in any case, what is proposed here is the judicious use of a proportion only who have the ability and the experience for this other field of professional responsibilities.

Another principle governing the Service structure outlined is that there should be a unity of the Civil Service with freedom of movement between grades, classes and departments. Some argue that the application of this principle leads to inefficiency and waste and that a more efficient approach would be to retain any special experience within Ministries and Departments. For instance, the retention of an Administrative Officer in, say, the Ministry of Finance makes him more useful with time. If he were posted to another Ministry, his experience might not be fully utilized and therefore he is inefficiently used. In older countries, Ministries are usually large enough to provide satisfactory lifetime careers for staff without unnecessary cross-posting. Even in these countries, however, it has been found that it is good policy to improve the quality and usefulness of promising officials by posting them to other Ministries. They are thus enabled to broaden their experience and so qualify for higher service more quickly.

In new countries, and particularly in those undergoing a period of transition which all African states are passing through, it is a great advantage to be able to move staff around so as to make optimum use of available trained manpower. Even in normal conditions this practice is desirable, and it should consequently not be regarded as making a virtue of necessity. It is a recognized training technique that an officer is moved from one type of experience to another to improve his range, competence and understanding of the complex situations he may have to deal with in the future. Compromise arrangements are, however, possible to preserve specialist experience in Ministries and Departments whilst ensuring that the best men are used in the best positions.

One way in which this can be achieved is that promotion to the highest positions should draw on the whole service for the best talent. As explained earlier, this should include the professional and scientific men. This implies, for instance, that in filling posts of Permanent Secretaries, not only the Administrative Class but also senior heads of Departments, should be regarded as a proper field to select from. If this principle is applied, then it may be good policy to retain special experience in a Ministry or Department for considerable periods: at any rate, until officers in this category are eligible for consideration for high administrative posts.

Another way is to make appointments to a 'Service' rather than to a Department or Ministry, for instance, the Administrative Service, Executive Service, Scientific Service and so on. Experience of officers in a Service should then be arranged to be as wide as possible so as to ensure that specialization at later stages in their careers should not disqualify them for promotion to the highest positions elsewhere. Thus an Administrative Officer who specializes in labour relations or as an economist, would, if his early years have included experience over a wide range, qualify to be considered on merit for promotion to a Permanent Secretary's post in any Ministry. Subject to this policy of making use of the best material in the topmost positions, however, the objective should be to maintain continuity in Ministries and Departments, and to retain specialists where their experience and training could be most efficiently exploited. A sensible policy is using men in the jobs they are best qualified to do whilst maintaining reasonable flexibility in the deployment of the manpower available. In the long run, the most efficient use of man power is not necessarily keeping them in very narrow specializations.

The structure described in this chapter would not apply in all details to all circumstances in all countries. It is basically the structure adopted in Nigeria, Sierra Leone, Ghana and Tanzania. The principles are accepted in the other countries although the patterns are not exactly as described. Moreover, any service structure has the role of providing the 'building' material with which the whole executive machinery of government could be organized. A realistic service structure should be such as could be applied to a wide variety of government organizations in differing political circumstances. It is in this sense possible to adapt during the period of transition a structure which is basically British to the developing political and constitutional systems of government in those African states which belong to the Commonwealth.

POLICIES FOR POST-TRANSITION ADMINISTRATIVE REFORM

There is now a movement to introduce administrative reforms in many African states. The need for this arises out of the fact that the period of post-independence transition is at, or near, its end and that the evolving responsibilities of governments require more effective executive instruments than could be had through continuing tinkering with the Civil Services inherited from the colonial past. A close investigation of the whole system is now taking place in a number of countries and policies for reform are being considered which are aimed at complete nationalization of the machinery of government, and at a restructuring of the Civil Services (as well as other public services) to make them more effective vehicles for the political, economic and social changes which all governments are endeavouring to bring about.

The principal objectives for such a policy of reform are, firstly, accelerated economic and social development requiring more efficient mobilization of resources – financial, natural and human. This requires that advantage should be taken of the knowledge accumulated in the more advanced states in the disciplines required for development including the results of the tremendous progress made in science and technology. Secondly, all states in Africa have the problem of the integration of peoples of different ethnic or tribal groups, geographical regions, religions and even races. A primary task of all governments has therefore been to stimulate the process which in time could result in a growing sense of real nationhood, with all the spiritual and emotional commitments and loyalties that go with the acceptance of the existence of a united nation. Thirdly, it is being increasingly recognized that planned change, whether political, economic or social, should have as a principal objective bringing development to the grass roots level in the rural sector and not just in the urban centres. Also, for African states to be more effective in the process of international relations, their Civil Services should be more adequately prepared for their tasks. Lastly, a great deal of attention needs to be given to training and orientation policies so that Civil Servants, instead of being concerned mainly with observing regulations and routine procedures, do become, collectively and individually, the machinery for bringing about dynamic change and, the source of initiatives for advancing priority policies for progress.

POLICIES FOR STRUCTURAL REFORM

No programme for structural reform of the Civil Service can be complete unless considered in relation to reforms in the machinery of government as a whole and also to the programme of training and orientation. These matters will be discussed in the chapters on the Structures and Functions of Ministries and Departments and Staff Development respectively. It needs, however, to be said here that the new Civil Service structure should fit as nearly as possible into whatever new government machinery is established and should exploit all training resources for making itself quickly effective.

The traditional colonial structure, as has already been explained, provided for an elite Administrative Service which was the main instrument of control and policy formulation of the whole of the colonial system. The other branches of the public services – the Professions (doctors, engineers, agriculturists, scientists, etc.), the Technical Services, the Executive/Clerical Services and the various auxiliary units – were generally regarded as being subordinate services. In an era in which policy was dictated from the metropolitan capital, and when the main concern was to maintain law and order, this system was effective. The adaptations brought about by self-government and independence have served their purpose adequately so far, but are beginning to show signs of inadequacy.

We are now in an era of development and technology and the new elite in the Civil Service are, or should be, those possessing the skills required for determining development and technological strategy. This implies that the emergent skills in the various areas of economic and social planning, in engineering, in science, in education, in health programmes, in management, and in other fields of the new technology, now come to the front. A new policy for structural reform in the Civil Service should therefore recognize that the 'old' administrator has no place in this new order unless he can be transformed into becoming the 'new' administrator with management and planning skills of the same level of competence within the development policy and programme as the economist or the technologist. This implies that, in future, there should be, as in commerce and industry, a proper definition of the role and responsibilities of the administrator as manager in relation to other professional disciplines, the selection policy to be pursued, and the training and allocation of progressive responsibilities calculated to bring about the best results.

Again, like commerce and industry, the policy for reform should provide that advancement to the top should be so organized that the highest directing positions, whether they be in Ministries, departments, provinces or districts, are open to members of all professional disciplines and not kept as a preserve for administrative officers. This implies that for each professional discipline, including administrative management, there should be a normal career structure below the level of the highest directing positions within which most Civil Servants would expect to satisfy their normal career aspirations.

Increasingly, the tasks of governments at the centre and in the fields are being organized on a project basis. The new structure of the Civil Service should consequently be organized as task forces, or project teams, each containing the appropriate combination of professional and technical skills for the particular project in hand. Moreover, there is an increasing tendency for a number of public sector responsibilities formerly run by government departments to be organized and operated by para-statal bodies. Thus, in many states, such activities as water supplies, railways, harbours, radio and television services, posts and telecommunications services and electricity generation and distribution services, have been assigned to autonomous statutory bodies outside the Central Government machinery – and not staffed by Civil Servants. Any structural reform for the Civil Services should take this trend into account.

On the other hand, there is an opposite trend in the direction of bringing the Education Service and the Local Government Service into the main stream of the Civil Service. The Education Service used to be partly within the Civil Service but was hived off to constitute the Unified Teaching Service outside the Civil Service. Local Government Service has not, however, usually been within the Civil Service in the past. Neither the Education Service nor the Local Government Service has succeeded in acquiring the status and prestige of the Civil Service and they have not therefore been able to attract and hold their fair share of trained manpower and professional skills. And yet, they are responsible for very important areas of the development policies of government. The conviction is growing that they should now be brought within the Civil Service so that they may be made more efficient instruments of policy particularly since they are the public services with most to do with the people in rural areas and with the public in the urban centres.

Structural reform should also pay particular attention to the question of mobility of personnel not only within the Civil Service but also between it and other public services, para-statal organizations – and even the private sector. There should not just be the removal of obstacles in the way of mobility, such as a more flexible policy for pensions and superannuation schemes, but there should also be purposeful programmes designed to encourage the movement of persons from one part of the economy to another where their experience, knowledge and speciality could best be exploited to increase productivity and efficiency. There are, however, definite risks in operating unplanned mobility. There could be wastefulness through loss of continuity, experience and expertise in particular areas of activity and through too rapid a turnover of personnel. These risks can however be overcome if a policy of mobility is pursued with circumspection and on a planned basis. For instance, appointments could be made for, say, five-year periods and movements without specific agreement before the end of the period could result in forfeiture of benefits. This would ensure stability for known periods and provide also for continuity.

These and other ideas for reform of the structure of the Civil Service emphasize the importance of manpower development planning and programming together with an imaginative and purposeful staff development policy. They also call for the establishment or strengthening of machinery, on a permanent basis, for the management, the control and the review of the Civil Service. There is also the need for strengthening the policy for Research which would make the whole system of administration take advantage of new ideas for pursuing a programme of consistent planned progress and development. Research into the machinery and institutions of government, administrative systems, training material and programmes and the promotion and growth of administrative knowledge should be promoted by the machinery responsible for administering the Civil Service.

It has been emphasized that the principal objective of structural reform is to make the Civil Service a more effective instrument for bringing about planned economic and social change. Central planning is now part of the policies of all African governments and the central planning agency is one of the most important motive forces for bringing about change. But the process of planning should not be the prerogative of the central planning agency only. The whole machinery of government and the Civil Service should be planning conscious and Civil Servants whether in Ministries, Departments, provinces or districts, should be actively brought into the process of planning. The implication of this should be that all Civil Servants handling policy matters and management responsibilities should be planners by orientation and training and this should be an integral and conscious part of all the policies for administrative reform which may be pursued.

CHAPTER 5

Administration of the Civil Service

THE ESTABLISHMENTS OFFICE

THE Civil Service is a permanent government service. Like all services of the government, it is subject to the scrutiny of the Legislature in respect of its establishment arrangements, recruitment programmes, promotion and transfer policies as well as disciplinary procedure and policy. It is also a single unified service, but its members serve under various Ministries and Departments with a very wide variety of functions and duties. The Civil Service is usually one of the biggest single organizations in any country. In each of the States under consideration, the Government is the largest single employer. It is necessary in the circumstances that such an organization should be managed under uniform policy rules and regulations whilst making provision for adaptations to suit the wide variety of circumstances under which the different parts function.

There consequently has to be a central organization responsible for the management of the whole service on behalf of the Government. This staff management organization is termed in the Civil Service, the 'Establishments' department or office. In business, the same organization would be called the 'Personnel Management' Department. The Establishments organization is the main instrument by which the Government exercises control of the Civil Service and ensures that it is in good shape to serve as an efficient and effective machinery for executing the policies of the Government.

The functions of the Establishments organization may be described in the words used by the policy paper issued by the Ghana Government in 1960 – *A New Charter for the Civil Service*: 'to supervise the day to day administration of the Civil Service, to provide an advisory service for Ministries and Departments on Civil Service matters, to ensure that the Civil Service is designed to do its job with the maximum of efficiency and economy, to have regard that salaries paid are adequate to attract Staff of the requisite calibre but that they do not absorb an excessive proportion of the country's revenues, and, above all, to see that the Civil Service is one balanced smooth running integrated machine and not an aggregation of independent units pulling in different directions'. The importance of the Establishments organization is thus seen to be very great and its effectiveness can make a major contribution to the operational efficiency and economy of the whole of the executive machinery of government. On the other hand, an inefficient Establishments organization would result in the whole machinery running down, with consequent lowering of morale in the whole service and the involvement of the Government in needless expenditure. Because of its importance, its place in the whole government set-up and the government portfolio that controls it are matters of major policy consideration.

LOCATION OF THE ESTABLISHMENTS OFFICE

In the United Kingdom, as is well known, the Establishments Organization formed part of the Treasury and this until recently was the traditional home for the controlling organization of the Civil Service. In all but one of the African Commonwealth states, Establishments are *either* a separate department under the Prime Minister or the Head of Government *or* under a Minister of Establishments. In Ghana and Tanzania, the Establishments Division is part of the President's Office, in Sierra Leone, Uganda, Eastern and Northern Nigeria it is part of the Prime Minister's Office, and in the Federal Government of Nigeria there is a Minister for Establishments. In the former Western Nigeria, however, Establishments were part of the Treasury although there was a close link with the Premier's Office through the Chief Secretary to the Premier who was Head of the Service.

The justification for placing Establishments under the Treasury is said to be, firstly. that the cost of the Civil Service makes it a matter of high finance, and, secondly, that the Treasury has the best knowledge of the work being done throughout the service because of its functions in the control of other expenditure. It is true that Treasury control over estimates and expenditure involves it in the consideration of such matters as staff complements and grading since these involve the outlay of funds. Moreover, all the matters that come under the general heading of 'Conditions of Service' have substantial

financial implications. It is a matter of great convenience, therefore, that the Treasury should, in exercising its general responsibility of expenditure control, also control the administration of
the Civil Service.

There is, however, a major factor that has particular relevance
to the situation in new African States, and that is that all these
countries are in various stages of transition, not only in constitutional development but in all the attendant adjustments
and changes including, in this particular context, the development changes in the Civil Service. This factor makes it necessary
to consider whether in all these countries, it is appropriate to
adopt the United Kingdom policy of placing establishments
under the Treasury or the Finance Ministry, at any rate in the
early stages of self-government and independence. It is seriously
contended that it is inappropriate to let the logical view prevail
but that a more important consideration is the political one,
namely, that the administration of the Civil Service should be
very closely associated with the fount of power, that is, with
the Prime Minister or President, whoever is the effective Head
of Government in the particular case.

Associated with this main consideration are others. Africanization or Localization is always a political issue, and in all
countries is a subject of constant public and political interest.
Certainly, it is always a matter of much ventilation in Legislatures and more heat is generated on this subject than many
others of equal or greater importance. And yet the integrity,
efficiency and effectiveness of the Civil Service are matters of
prime importance to the orderly administration of the state
services and, more important, to the execution of the Government's policies. There is need, therefore, to adjust the accelerated progress of Africanization to the higher interests of State.
This is best determined by the Head of Government who is
ultimately responsible for stating the priorities of government
policy.

Furthermore, the Civil Service is much too important to risk
making it a tool of factional politics. It is important, therefore,
that there should be a practical guarantee that its administration, including the policies for appointments, promotions, transfers and discipline, is not subjected to political interference. If
the administration of the service is in the hands of a Minister
who is organizationally not closely tied to the Head of Government, there is serious risk of irresponsible day to day applica-

tion of policies undermining the health and morale of the service. It is not inconceivable that the Service could, in certain circumstances, be used as one of the counters in a political game from which it may not come out unscathed. These fears may be unfounded in some cases, but the risk that there may be grounds for fear makes it necessary to consider playing it safe by leaving it under the supervision of the Head of Government.

There is another consideration which has relevance and that is that the Treasury, by its nature, is cautious and deliberate in its functions. And yet, in the special circumstances of a developing Civil Service in a period of transition a dynamic approach to the shaping of the service to bring it into consonance with the other measures of development – political, economic and social – is essential. Until more stable conditions have been established, therefore, it might be difficult for Treasury administration of the Service to carry out the wishes of the Government. It might be argued that, due to these major and rapid developments, it is essential to keep the service conservative in order to introduce an element of stability in the affairs of the State. On the other hand, one runs a risk in not shaping the service to keep pace with other developments. It might find itself left behind by a political Government that is not going to wait for a ponderous machine to creak along. The lesser risk would therefore appear to be to arrange for a conscious development of the service in step with other developments in the Government.

The arguments developed here therefore support keeping the administration of the Civil Service under the close control of the Head of Government, be he the Prime Minister or the President. He might decide to have a Minister of State or Minister of Establishments to assist him in this responsibility since his other work might make it impracticable for him to give the day to day policy directions to the affairs of the service that are usually necessary. It is important, however, that the President or Prime Minister should retain a firm grip on major policy so that the integrity of the service is never in danger of being undermined. There is no need, however, to be dogmatic here. Each State would have to decide for itself what is the best arrangement for its peculiar circumstances. These circumstances might include the personality of the Head of Government who might have no special aptitude for handling the affairs of the Civil Service. The most important consideration, however, is that all proper and necessary steps are taken to safeguard the integrity, efficiency and morale of the service, and that its administration and development respond effectively to the demands of policy.

In recent years, some African states which have come through their period of transition have considered the question of the machinery for administering the Civil Service in relation to the whole question of administrative reform. The view has been promoted by some experts that there is a need for setting up a permanent machinery which combines the functions of the Establishments Office with those of the Public (or Civil) Service Commission. If this policy were adopted, there would, as in the case of the Public Service Board in Australia, be a central authority with responsibility for all matters affecting the administration of the Civil Service, for recruitment, promotions, training and discipline, and for all programmes for the progressive development of the Service so that it keeps abreast at all times with government policies for development and expanded services. The central authority would include in its responsibilities such matters of current concern as administrative reform, staff development within the national manpower development plan, administrative research, pay research as a basis for periodical salaries reviews and the organization of policies for achieving planned mobility.

A policy along these lines would have far reaching consequences and the political climate in any particular state would have to determine whether it would be wise to adopt it or not. The appropriate location for the central authority would also need to be determined in each case according to the local circumstances. It would have to be clothed with a high degree of autonomy if it were to function satisfactorily and its relations with the Government would have to be carefully formulated. The persons appointed to the authority should have a development consciousness and be progressive in outlook. They should be prepared and able to organize the Civil Service as an instrument for executing the government's policy for planned economic and social change. A conservative, cautious and unprogressive authority would prove disastrous and would risk undermining the integrity of the Civil Service.

THE ORGANIZATION OF THE ESTABLISHMENTS OFFICE

Establishments control divides broadly into

(a) staff complements and grading; and
(b) pay and other conditions of service.

Staff complements and grading relate to the actual numbers of persons necessary for the efficient functioning of each department or division, the numbers in each grade and class of posts, and the determination of the appropriate grading required for each post in relation to the duties and responsibilities of that post. This responsibility of determining complements and grading by the Establishments organization is necessary if it is to fulfil its task of ensuring that the service is designed to do its job with the maximum of efficiency and economy. This responsibility is shared with the Treasury since complements and grading are closely tied in with its budgeting responsibility. Indeed, it has been argued that they are more nearly a Treasury responsibility than the Establishments organization's. It is, however, tidier to have these and other personnel management matters in the Establishments Organization, provided that suitable co-ordinating machinery is set up between the two organizations. In Ghana, budget hearings on departmental estimates were carried out by the Treasury in association with the Establishments Office.

The Establishments Office or department should be organized to provide for divisions or sections dealing with :

(a) Staff Complements and Grading Policy
(b) Salaries structure
(c) Staff Inspection and Job Analyses
(d) General Conditions of service
(e) Recruitment and Training Policies and Programmes
(f) Pensions and Allowances
(g) Organization and Methods

In some countries, Organization and Methods and Pensions and Allowances are handled in the Treasury. In a few others, Recruitment and Training policies, because of their close tie-up with the policy of accelerated Africanization and Localization, are placed under separate organizational control. This is, however, a transitional arrangement and the proper place for these subjects is with Estabishments control. Their importance during the post-independence period is such that they are discussed in separate and subsequent chapters.

The size of the Establishments office or Department depends on the size of the Civil Service and the degree of delegation of establishments control made to Ministries and Departments. In a strongly centralized system, all decisions are taken by the Central Establishments office. The opposite extreme is when a small compact Establishments Office is responsible only for formulating policies, taking decisions on major policy matters, providing advisory services for Ministries and Departments, and ensuring that policies are uniformly applied except in so far as it is necessary to respect peculiar situations in Departments.

Generally speaking, the ideal system is one in which decisions on establishments matters and on matters affecting the personnel interests of individual officers are taken as close to the operational level as possible, that is, in Ministries and Departments. This system is more in harmony with the management and administrative responsibilities of Heads of Ministries and Departments. Certainly, Departmental and Ministry heads resent any remote control imposed by a central organization in day to day matters affecting their staff. It is obvious, however, that for such a system to be practical, the rules on which it is to be operated should be clearly defined in order to achieve the maximum possible degree of uniformity of application in the different departments. It has happened for instance, that in cases where Heads of Departments have responsibility for determining the granting of allowances, some have been more generous in their treatment of their staff than others. This inevitably has led to complaints which, if not effectively handled, have led to lowering of morale or, alternatively, to a situation in which all Heads of Departments have tended to be too generous in order to appear to be treating their staffs with equal justice.

In the more stable Civil Services experience and circumstances have determined a substantial degree of devolution of establishments control in accordance with rules which have been found to ensure reasonable uniform application. In most African countries, however, the services are in a state of transition; policies are still being formulated and establishments rules and conditions of services are subject to periodical reviews. In these circumstances there is need to retain central control in varying degrees of detail. A reasonable compromise arrangement is to create a cadre of Establishments Officers as part of the staff of the Establishments Office some of whom are outposted to Departments and Ministries. They would be functioning as

Ministry or Departmental Establishments Officers responsible to the Head of the Ministry or Department for the discharge of their duties. They would, none the less, be operating on the policies and rules laid down by their parent Establishments Office to which in the normal course of the postings programme, they would return for spells of duty. This arrangement would ensure that the Heads of Ministries and Departments exercise reasonable control over the affairs of their own staffs, whilst allowing for experts to apply rules and policies laid down by the centre for the good and efficient administration of the service as a whole.

INSPECTION AND GRADING

Regardless of the degree of delegation adopted in any particular set of circumstances, it is essential that a staff *Inspection Unit* be established in the Central Establishments Office. The functions of the unit would be to carry out a comprehensive review of posts in all departments of government with a view to determining whether the staff complement on the establishment is adequate for the tasks of the particular department or, alternatively, whether it is extravangant in size in relation to these tasks; to check that each officer is correctly graded in terms of the duties he is actually performing or is expected to perform; to ensure that the department is following the policies and rules laid down by the Central Establishments Office; and generally, to make sure that the staff disposition and grading are the best for efficiency and economy in performance and administration. The Staff Inspection Unit is to Civil Service administration what the Audit Unit is to financial administration. Indeed, in some countries, staff inspection is termed personnel audit.

The Inspection Unit should be staffed with Establishments Officers in the Administrative and Executive Classes who are experienced in or trained in job analysis. Job analysis is the principal instrument of their trade since they have to know the actual content of the duties of each post under examination, the level of responsibility discharged, and how the post fits into the general pattern of responsibilities of the section or division. On the basis of this information, they would be able to determine the relative rating of the post in terms of grade and class and the appropriate level of remuneration for it. Since policy application is involved, the Inspection Unit should be headed by an Administrative or Professional Officer with a clear understanding of the administrative task: policy analysis and decision-making. The other members of the team would be Job Analysts who might be drawn entirely from the Executive Class or, in large units, partly from the Administrative/Professional Class and partly from the Executive Class.

CONDITIONS OF SERVICE

The other main responsibility of the Establishments Office is to administer the policies and rules relating to general conditions of service. When a person is offered appointment to a post in the service, the first thing he does is to scrutinize his letter of appointment before he writes to give his formal acceptance. He is interested to know the remuneration of the appointment he is offered and the prospects of further advancement. He is anxious to know also what provisions are made for allowances, housing, leave and passages, medical treatment, pensions and other retiring benefits, and the hours of work. These and others relating to the terms of appointment constitute the material that determines very largely the relations between the Government as an employer and the Civil Servants as employees. Conditions of service which are not only realistic but also seek the interests of the staff are a most important factor in the maintenance of the morale of the staff and in providing the healthy climate within which optimum efforts can justly be expected from them. Staff relations principally concern conditions of service and they constitute the matters on which negotiations usually take place between staff associations, unions and the government. The importance, therefore, of ensuring that the machinery exists for the review of conditions of service cannot be underrated. On the one hand, the public interest must be safeguarded and the government should not be saddled with avoidable expenditure which serves no purpose other than to benefit certain classes of officers. On the other hand it is important that the staff is assured of reasonable and fair terms of service, and relieved of unnecessary anxiety.

Remuneration and pay have already been discussed in a previous chapter. Brief descriptions will now be given of the principles and practice relating to the more important of the other conditions of service.

STAFF HOUSING

This subject has caused more controversy and difficulty in the relations between staff and governments than any other condition of service. In all the countries whose services are under review, the provision of part-furnished housing accommodation was part of the terms of appointment of all expatriate staff. Since, until comparatively recently, the senior service was staffed entirely by expatriate officers, it became accepted that all senior officers were entitled to government housing. The only local officers who had houses provided for them were those who were attached to institutions such as schools and hospitals, those who were in the disciplined forces and had to live in barracks, those who were required to be on call such as certain categories of telephone, hospital and power station employees, and those who were posted to remote stations where suitable accommodation would otherwise not be available.

As local officers were admitted into the senior branches of the service, it became the custom to provide them with houses on the same basis as their expatriate colleagues, except that the policy had always been that they were not entitled as of right to them but only eligible for them if any were spare. It has been the constant agitation of all local staff associations to have their members of the same status as expatriate officers treated in this matter on exactly the same terms.

The provision of houses for local officers cannot really be justified. They are living in their own country and they should not expect to be housed by government merely because they are government servants. There are exceptional circumstances, which will be dealt with later, which may justify the provision of houses. Generally speaking, however, Civil Servants should expect to take their place in the community like any other citizen. They should not expect to be treated as a privileged group.

It is right in principle, however, that governments should accept responsibility for the housing of expatriate staff. Since they are not normal residents of the countries they serve in, they are not in the position to make their own arrangements, nor indeed can they contemplate owning their own houses as local officers can. To attract them for service overseas, therefore, it is necessary for governments to include provision of housing as part of the terms of their appointments.

The main reason why local officers expect to be housed is that they are nearly always unable to find suitable houses to hire in the general market at rents within their means. In some places, the situation is acute. A good example is the situation in Ghana and Tanzania in the years following independence. The influx of diplomatists, new businessmen and other visitors, as well as the increased recruitment of expatriate staff for development and technical assistance programmes, resulted in acute shortage of housing of all types. In these circumstances, considerable hardship was caused to those African officers who were unable to qualify for government houses. The long-term solution is the provision of more housing units for the people as a whole to enable Civil Servants to rent them at a level they can afford.

The government should provide accommodation for the following categories of local staff, however:

(a) those who must be available at all times and who must therefore live in tied houses. These may be termed duty-post houses. Included in this category are Medical Officers and nurses attached to hospitals, Police Officers and District Administration staff, staff of boarding schools and training institutions with extra-curricular responsibilities and Prison Officers.

(b) those belonging to disciplined forces who are therefore on 'short call' such as police and prison staff including those in the rank and file.

(c) those who are posted to isolated or remote stations where suitable accommodation is not available.

(d) in present circumstances in many countries, it is necessary also to provide houses for those holding the highest positions such as Heads of Ministries and Departments to ensure that they are able to live in reasonable dignity and can discharge their social responsibilities in a manner that would do credit to their governments.

If there is likelihood of acute housing shortage persisting for a number of years, then, rather than build more houses for the purpose of accommodating local officers, governments should spend the funds available for this purpose in pump-priming schemes for home ownership for these officers. In any case it is inevitable that governments should be reluctant to invest large sums of money in housing when there is such a heavy priority call on the countries' resources for economic development. To give an idea of the magnitude of the capital sums involved in housing Civil Servants: in 1961, Tanzania government housing represented a capital investment of the order of £9 million. The East African Railways and Harbours Administration in 1962 had £15 million tied up in 26,300 staff houses. Government houses are normally let at heavily subsidized rents. In East Africa, rent charges per house range from £6 per annum for a one-room unit to £102 per annum for the largest houses for topmost senior officers. In Ghana in 1962, rent charges ranged from £90 per annum for officers with salaries of £650-£830 per annum to £225 per annum for the highest salaried officers. The rent charges are seen to be very heavily subsidized. Since those not entitled to government houses have to face the prospect of paying economic rents on houses in the open market, it is no wonder that there is a demand for access to government houses. The subsidized rent system has other serious consequences. It distorts officers' ideas as to what is a reasonable standard of housing. If they were paying economic rents, they would have more modest ambitions in their housing ideas. Furthermore, the system concentrates demand on the limited supply of higher standard accommodation and the governments are brought under strong pressure to provide more of such accommodation so as to extend the privilege of occupying them.

There is a good case therefore for charging economic rents for government accommodation. As a corollary, the salary levels should reflect the incidence of economic rental payment in the budgets of officers. The enforcement of such a system would result in

(a) the encouragement of officers to seek cheaper accommodation which might not necessarily be that provided by government;

(b) incentive to own houses so that the amount that might otherwise be paid over as rents would contribute towards the instalment payments on houses;

(c) the prevention of the isolation of Civil Servants in special residential areas and, conversely, the possibility that officials would lose their separate identities in the general population such as happens in Europe and America; and

(d) the avoidance of a privileged class complex among Civil
Servants.

It was a principle of the old colonial terms of service that leave
was a privilege, not an entitlement. Nevertheless it is now recognized as a fundamental principle that a Civil Servant should,
both for rest and recuperation and also from the point of view
of efficiency of the public service, be required to take a break
away from duty every now and then. The period of leave entitlement is usually the subject of negotiation between Governments
and staff associations and unions, and it varied under former
arrangements from between 1½ days leave for every full
month of service for the lowest ranks of Officers to 7 days for
senior expatriate staff in West Africa.

Leave rates have always been generous compared with the
rates obtaining in countries like Britain. In West Africa until
recently, African officers in the senior ranks were entitled to
five days for each full month of service. Thus, after only twelve
months' service, they were entitled to sixty days' leave. This
very generous leave rate was justified by reference to the seven
days for each full month's service enjoyed by expatriate officers
of similar status. Consequently, although the leave rates enjoyed by officers in the lower ranks were scaled down, yet they
were comparatively generous.

It is now generally accepted that vacation leave rates should
be related to the conditions in the country, should be long
enough to achieve the purpose of giving the officer rest and
recuperation away from work, and should be rated according to
the broad limits of the relative burdens of responsibility borne
by differing classes of officer. The limits in rates now usually
recommended are from 14-18 days per annum for the lowest
grades of established staff, to 42 days for the highest. This leave
entitlement has to be taken within the twelve months of the
leave year.

It is desirable that vacation leave should be taken every year
and not accumulated from one year to another as was the case
in the past. In countries with large distances to cover and poor
communications, annual leave arrangements are not always
convenient for some of the staff. It should, in such circumstances be accumulated over a period of two years so that

officers may enjoy a reasonable period of vacation in their own home areas if they wish. In such cases, it is still advisable that officers should be compelled to take a short break during the year in which they choose not to travel to their homes. As stated earlier, a break away from work is necessary for efficiency in the long term and this break should be at least once a year. Moreover, leave taken annually is necessarily of short duration and there would generally be no necessity to provide leave reliefs since other officers should be able to cover up.

Any leave not taken in the year, or biennial period, as the case may be, should be forfeited. It was, and still is in some countries, the practice to accumulate leave over a number of years. There were a number of reasons for this. In some cases, officers accumulated leave so that they might have a long period of study leave overseas. In others, officers were prevented from taking their leave by their heads of departments on the grounds that they could not be spared or, otherwise, that the exigencies of the service demanded postponement of their leave. During the war, it was impracticable, for many reasons, for officers to have regular leave. There were many cases where officers preferred to defer as much leave as possible until after their retirement so that they might enjoy a long period of retirement leave. Some officers have been known to have as much as twelve months' leave due to them when they retired and consequently to continue to draw full salaries for a long time after they left the service.

With the introduction of government-sponsored training courses locally and overseas, officers need no longer accumulate leave for their studies. If vacation leave is necessary for efficiency and recuperation, then Heads of Departments should encourage their staff to go on leave. If leave not taken is forfeited, they would find it difficult to justify, even owing to exigency of the service, depriving their staff of their earned rights. It is also not right that officers should accumulate leave earned when their salaries are lower to enjoy it at a much higher salary, which is what happens when accumulated leave is spent after retirement.

In exceptional circumstances permission to accumulate leave may be given, but this should certainly not extend beyond the leave period following the one in which leave could not be enjoyed. In Ghana where the annual vacation leave system was introduced in 1958, its strict enforcement without permission to accumulate compelled Heads of Departments to prepare and rigidly observe leave rosters for their staff.

LEAVE TRAVEL ARRANGEMENTS

It was and still is, part of the conditions of appointment of expatriate officers and other officers whose homes are outside the country of service to provide travel expenses by sea or air to their homes every vacation leave. To economize on the cost of travel, the normal tour of service was, and is, more than one year. In West Africa, the expatriate officer's usual tour is 18 months, although older officers or those with many years of service are allowed to shorten their tour to 15 or even 12 months. In East Africa the length of tour was formerly three years but this period was reduced to between 21 and 27 months in 1961.

Because overseas officers had their leave passages to their homes paid for by governments, it was considered equitable to provide travel expenses for local officers to get to their homes also for their vacation leaves. The situation of overseas staff should have no bearing on the terms of service of local officers in this particular regard and, consequently, travel assistance of this nature is outmoded. The normal practice should be for officers to save from their own salaries to pay for their leave travel to any destination of their choice. The salary levels should consequently be determined on this basis. This is the normal practice in most independent countries and it should apply normally in African states as well.

SICK LEAVE

It is the normal practice of governments to provide leave terms for established staff who are sick and unfit for duty. The usual entitlements are sick leave on full pay for three months and thereafter sick leave on half pay for three months. Shorter periods of entitlement apply to unestablished subordinate staff. Besides being a commonsense humanitarian policy for a government to set an example to other employers, it is the desire of governments to retain the services of trained staff who might be difficult to replace and who should therefore be given reasonable periods of paid leave during illness. Sick leave terms are therefore justifiable on sound economic grounds. If an officer after exhausting his full entitlements for sick leave is still not fit to return to duty, he can have further leave without pay, though a Medical Board would determine whether he should be retired from the service or be given further leave to enable him to recover.

MATERNITY LEAVE

Most countries grant leave to expectant mothers in the Civil Service. The aim is to encourage African women to seek employment in the public service and so lessen the strain on the limited number of trained men.

ALLOWANCES

Civil Servants all over Africa are said to be 'allowance' conscious and to tend to look upon allowances as non-taxable hidden emoluments. This is obviously unhealthy and there is need for rationalization and control to avoid waste of public funds. Allowances are a normal feature of any Civil Service structure, but they should be restricted to cover circumstances not common throughout the service and circumstances which cannot be covered by the general levels of remuneration of Civil Servants.

Civil Service Allowances fall into two main categories:
(a) those relating to responsibility or additional work; and
(b) reimbursement allowance to cover abnormal expenses necessarily incurred in the performance of duty.

ACTING ALLOWANCES

These are an example of the first category and are provided in recognition of additional work or responsibility. It is the United Kingdom practice that such allowances 'should only be given where an officer is regularly required to carry responsibilities conspicuously superior to those of the most senior officers of his grade'.[1] This principle is sound and should generally apply to African countries also.

In a number of such countries the system of acting allowances is much abused. It is automatically applied to all cases of

[1] Estacode.

F

temporary absence of officers where more junior officers assume their responsibilities or where posts are vacant and their functions are temporarily discharged by junior officers. In the form of a duty allowance, it is payable in cases where an officer is 'doubling up' for an officer who is absent, or where an officer assumes some of the responsibilities of a higher class post in which he is normally not qualified to act. An extreme form of absurdity is found where the absence of a top rank officer sets up a chain reaction and acting allowances are paid all down the line to the most junior officer at the base of the hierarchy.

It is debatable whether a wholesale system of acting allowances is justifiable and can pass the test of the definition stated above. It is the considered view of most people that the system should be severely restricted and should apply only to cases where officers are required to act as Heads of Ministries, Departments or large Divisions, or where it is statutorily necessary for someone to act in a particular position. For instance, there should normally always be provision for someone to act as Permanent Secretary of a Ministry if there is no substantive holder or if he is temporarily absent. It is necessary also to provide for an Acting Commissioner of Police or Acting Attorney General or Acting Solicitor General. There is a statutory requirement for the Registrar of a Court, and although he is not head of a Department, a temporary vacancy requires to be filled by an acting appointment.

In other cases, temporary absence of the substantive holders of posts should be covered by other officers in the same unit sharing the tasks. Even where officers are made to discharge the full responsibilities of higher posts, they have the opportunity to demonstrate their ability in these higher responsibilities and so qualify themselves for promotion.

Acting allowances vary in rate from the full difference between the substantive salary of the acting officer and the minimum of the salary scale of the higher post, or the salary of the higher post if this is fixed, to twenty-five per cent of the difference. The usual practice is to pay the full difference, reduced amounts being payable only if the full responsibilities are not being discharged. The allowances are non-pensionable but are taxable. They are paid if the acting period covers, usually, a period of more than a month.

Reimbursement allowances are those payable to officers to cover the cost of goods or services they require for the performance of government business. They include allowances for official entertainment, for subsistence and transport, transfer and detention, outfit, uniforms, tools and disturbance. There is a tendency to multiply the incidence of allowances, in some cases, to a point of irresponsibility. Allowances in these circumstances come to be regarded as additions to emoluments.

The general principles that should govern all these allowances should be, firstly, that the salary of a Civil Servant should normally constitute the full remuneration of the performance of the services attached to his post. Secondly, factors such as discomfort and unpopularity should be taken into account in assessing salaries but should not be regarded as justification for additional remuneration by way of allowances. Thirdly, the salary of a Civil Servant should be based on the understanding that his full time is at the government's disposal. Where, however, he receives permission to perform work, either for the government or for an outside agency, which is not within his normal duties and which is performed outside normal working hours, he should be permitted to accept and keep the remuneration for the work.

If these principles are applied to the policy for determining allowances, justice will be done not only to officers but also to the public interest. Abuse of the system of allowances is bound to induce its own reaction in that they may be curtailed to such an extent as to cause unnecessary hardship.

RETIREMENT BENEFITS

The usual retirement benefits for the Civil Service are:

(a) Non-contributory pensions
(b) Provident Fund Schemes
(c) Contract Gratuities
(d) Widows' and Orphans' Pensions

NON-CONTRIBUTORY PENSION

It is usual in the Civil Services in the African States for career officers to be assured a pension based on length of service and final salary on retirement. The salary structure of the Service is based on the principle that the officers' pensions would be paid for under a separate arrangement. A pension is to be regarded as a reward for a life's service under the Government, and its level should be such as to enable an officer who has served the Government honourably, efficiently, loyally and with satisfactory zeal to live a life after retirement in reasonable comfort.

It is usual for Governments to set a limit to the length of an officer's service by age. In the colonial days the age at which officers were compulsorily retired was fifty-five. This was based on the principle that in tropical conditions the health of officers usually deteriorated after fifty years of age, and their efficiency decreased. With the improvement of health and environmental conditions in Africa, this theory no more applies, and there is therefore a strong case for raising the compulsory retirement age limit. In Ghana, this has already been raised to sixty years of age, and Government is therefore able to retain the experience and ability of those older men who wish, and are able, to continue serving their country.

It is recognized, however, that there are occasions when it may be desirable to retire an officer earlier, or to enable an officer to retire voluntarily earlier than the compulsory age of retirement. On the part of the Government it may be desirable to dispense with the services of an officer whose efficiency has fallen off or who, for disciplinary reasons, should be retired early. On the other hand, an officer who, after many years' service, wishes to retire because there are no further prospects of promotion should, in certain circumstances, be permitted to do so on pension. If there is no provision for retirement of this nature, the build-up of a sense of frustration may seriously impair the officer's efficiency. It is not to be expected in these circumstances that the incentive to maintain a satisfactory output of work can be sustained. Premature voluntary retirement may enable the officer to seek employment in another sphere where his experience and ability can be more usefully exploited. Since, however, a pension is to be regarded as a reward for a lifetime of service to the Government, and because actuarially the cost of a free pension scheme would become prohibitive if the retiring age is too low, the age limit for voluntary retirement should be reasonably high. The former lower age limit of forty-five is, in present circumstances, too low and the age of fifty is to be regarded as more realistic. This is the figure adopted by Ghana, Tanzania and the East African Community.

Most free pensions in the Civil Services under discussion are calculated on the basis of 1/600 of the average salary for the last three years of an officer's service multiplied by the number of completed months of pensionable service. Usually an officer is permitted to commute a proportion of this pension entitlement (normally one-quarter) as a lump sum gratuity, the commutation factor being for the present 12.5. There are of course, rules governing entitlement to pensions, covering the classes of posts covered by the pensions scheme, the minimum age below which service does not qualify for pension, the treatment of non-pensionable service for pensions purposes, the effect of breaks in service, and other conditions. These rules are normally embodied in pensions legislation which also guarantees the payments of pensions. Pensions are a statutory charge on the consolidated funds of the States which means that their payment cannot be stopped by the Appropriation Acts of Parliament.

On the basis of the pension constant of 1/600, it has been actuarially calculated that the pension payable requires that a little over twenty-five per cent of the officer's aggregate emoluments should be set aside. In other words, if a pension fund were to be created, twenty-five per cent of the personal emoluments of officers, at least, must be paid into this fund. Most Governments, however, prefer to make pensions a charge on normal revenue. In Ghana, an attempt was made before independence to fund the pensions. The East African Community operates pension funds for each of the Administrations, the reason being presumably because it has no taxing powers and therefore it should insure against the possibility of current revenue not being able to meet pensions liabilities indefinitely. The State governments in East Africa meet pensions charges out of the normal revenue allocations and provision is made in each year's budget accordingly.

PROVIDENT FUND SCHEMES

Such schemes where they exist, cover officers in posts which are not part of the normal career structure, such as daily rated employees, temporary officers and other classes of posts which are excluded from the normal free pension scheme. In the Provident

Fund Schemes, the employee makes a monthly contribution which is matched by a contribution from the Government. The retirement benefits – whether by way of lump sum payments or monthly 'pension' payments – are calculated on the basis of the contributions made by and on behalf of the employee so that the whole fund is kept actuarially viable. Provident fund schemes are useful because of their flexibility. An employee retiring at any time may benefit at least from the contributions he has himself made and, subject to satisfying the permissible retirement rules, also from the contributions made by Government on his behalf. The penalty for a break in service is thus not as drastic as for the free pension scheme.

Provident fund schemes are uncommon in their application to employment in Civil Services. In West Africa, they in fact do not exist. Instead, employees outside the free pension scheme receive ex-gratia gratuities, and/or retirement allowances which are based on a factor somewhat lower than the 1/600 applied to the free pension scheme. Where, however, provident fund schemes exist for certain classes of posts, the emoluments for these posts should, in principle, take account of the fact that they should carry contributions to the fund.

CONTRACT GRATUITIES

Contracts are usually the basis on which non-local officers are employed in African Civil Services. It is not usual to employ local officers on contract terms although this is permissible where at the time of their engagement their ages are such that they could not qualify for pensions. If the minimum period of service qualifying for pensions is ten years and the compulsory retiring age is sixty, then it is obvious that a person engaged above the age of fifty could not qualify for a pension. In such circumstances, a contract appointment is appropriate. Since as stated earlier, the hypothetical cost of a career officer's pension is calculated to be about twenty-five per cent of his pensionable emoluments, it is equitable that the contract gratuity should also be twenty-five per cent of the contract officer's pay.

This principle assumes that the emoluments of the contract officer are the same as for a pensionable officer of the same status and seniority. Some countries, however, prefer to make the contract salary more attractive by making a percentage addition, of the order of 10, 15, 20 or even 25 per cent, to the pensionable salaries. The rates of contract gratuity paid in these circumstances are necessarily lower than the twenty-five per cent stated earlier.

WIDOWS' AND ORPHANS' PENSION SCHEMES

It was compulsory for European officers in the Colonial services to contribute to a Widows' and Orphans' Pensions Fund. As its name implies, this fund was applied to the payment of minimum pensions to widows and orphans of deceased officers. African officers were neither required nor permitted to contribute to the fund. The contributions were paid normally into revenue and payments were made from expenditure voted in the annual budget.

There has been from time to time in the past agitation to have similar schemes applied compulsorily to local officers to ensure that their widows and orphans also had minimum provisions made for them if the need arose. There were serious impediments, however, to the application of the scheme to Africans. In all African countries, polygamy is permissible, and the application to such a scheme in the circumstances would either be cumbersome to operate or prohibitively costly for the officer with more than one wife. Moreover, there was never any widespread enthusiasm for the scheme among African officers. In Ghana a Widows' and Orphans' Pension Scheme was introduced before independence, but was subsequently abandoned under pressure from the staff associations and unions.

It seems that in African circumstances, a better approach to the problem of safeguarding the future of widows and orphans is to encourage staff to take up life insurances. It should be possible for staff associations and unions to negotiate favourable and suitable endowment or life assurance schemes for their members.

HOURS OF WORK

The number of hours a Civil Servant should work in a week is one of the conditions of service which frequently feature in discussions or negotiations between staff associations and governments. In general, it can be said that weekly hours of work in Africa are fairly short: as low as 36 hours and the longest is 42 hours. For technical and manual workers, however, it could be as high as 44 hours although this would appear to be exceptional.

The tendency in newly independent African countries is to raise the weekly hours of work. In Ghana, the number was raised to 42 in 1962 from 39, and in Tanzania from 37 to 40 in 1963. It is understood that in Nigeria, the Civil Servants themselves agreed voluntarily to increase their hours of work as an act of patriotism and in the interest of greater output. The general world trend, however, is to reduce the hours of work and even to aim for a five-day week in order to give staff time for recreation. The main considerations in African conditions should, however, be the need to make the optimum use of available experience and talent, at present in short supply, and to ensure that overwork does not mean inefficient work. For the present, therefore, there is good reason to maintain hours of work at at least 40 per week and this may be reduced when there are more people with ability and experience to meet all the national requirements.

MEDICAL BENEFITS

It was the normal policy in the pre-independence era to provide free medical and dental attention for all Civil Servants and their immediate dependants. This policy has usually been maintained by Governments after independence. It has been challenged, however, on the grounds that medical benefits enjoyed by Civil Servants place them in a privileged class in relation to the general public, and could be regarded as being in the nature of hidden emoluments. In countries in which medical and health conditions were, and still to an extent are, not very good, it is necessary for the Government to provide for the fitness of its officers and so maintain efficiency and satisfactory productivity. This is sound commonsense since the Government has invested emoluments in these officers and has a duty to the taxpayer to ensure that this investment is being efficiently managed and exploited. All large employers of labour in corporations, commerce and industry provide medical facilities for their employees in order to cut out wastage and absenteeism resulting from illness. The Government, however, has a duty to the general public in this respect and its policy should be to bring the public service and the general public on to the same plane.

This is in fact the trend in the development of Government policies in health matters.

POLICY OF MOBILITY AND SUPERANNUATION

As has been discussed earlier, some states are giving consideration to a policy which encourages movement into and out of the Civil Service as a means of ensuring that available trained manpower could be deployed to meet the priority demands of the economy and society.

The non-contributory pension schemes now adopted for all established Civil Servants are not flexible enough to permit such a policy of mobility to work. Any state that seriously considers such a policy would therefore have also to consider appropriate changes in the pensions legislation. In some cases already, a degree of mobility is possible and Civil Servants are able to transfer into other public services or academic institutions in circumstances which preserve their accrued Civil Service pensions entitlements. If transfers into para-statal bodies and the private sector are to be encouraged, and *vice versa*, then a more drastic approach to pensions legislation would be required.

One such approach has recently been proposed by the Public Services Structure and Salaries Commission in Ghana (1967).

The proposal is that all Civil Servants – and other public servants also – should be brought into the national social security pensions scheme, subject to the preservation of existing accrued rights in the existing pensions schemes. This is along the lines of the usual contributory schemes where both the employee and the employer make monthly payments into a fund. The suggestion would need very careful consideration since its adoption would mean a radical departure from one of the main features of the Civil Service which has proved so attractive to potential candidates.

Where this suggestion cannot be pursued and where it is still proposed to pursue a policy of mobility, it may be necessary to give consideration to other approaches for a flexible pensions policy. A great deal would depend on local factors, the terms of whatever pensions legislation exists and whether it would be feasible to integrate the Civil Service in a national comprehensive superannuation programme.

CHAPTER 6

Staff Development—Recruitment and Training

As has been stated in an earlier chapter, the development of a national public service which is indigenously based has in every case not kept pace with constitutional development. The reasons for this situation have been explained. The major problem facing all African Governments, as far as the public service is concerned, is therefore the establishment of a progressive programme of staff development. This presents a formidable task since, parallel with it, is the urgency to mount a programme of economic and social development and expansion of services in order to satisfy the needs of the people. The two programmes are related since a sound, stable and effective administration properly staffed is essential to the carrying through of any major programme of development.

COMPENSATION SCHEMES FOR LOSS OF CAREER

And yet, just at the time that self-government and independence came, the Governments were faced with the exodus of expatriate staff under premature retirement schemes. The expatriate officers belonged to the Colonial Service or, as it was later designated, Her Majesty's Overseas Civil Service. They were recruited by or on behalf of the Secretary of State for the Colonies who controlled the Service and guaranteed security of tenure. With the accession of a country to internal self-government, the control of the whole of the Civil Service, including the expatriate element, passes into the hands of the Government of the country, and the Secretary of State for the Colonies ceases to have any functions in relation to the expatriate officers. These officers have suffered a loss in that the terms under which the Secretary of State safeguarded their careers no longer apply. In these circumstances, an agreement is always concluded between the United Kingdom Government and the Government of the newly self-governing country, as part of the constitutional settlement and conditions of self-government, granting to expatriate officers who are designated as qualified under the agreement the right to opt to retire with accrued pension entitlements and lump sum compensations calculated actuarially on the basis of age, length of service and emoluments at the time of retirement.

These compensation schemes started with India and Pakistan when they became independent and they set the pattern for other former British territories that became independent subsequently: Ceylon, the Sudan, Ghana, Malaya, Nigeria, Sierra Leone, Tanganyika, Uganda, Zanzibar and Kenya. The maximum payable as a lump sum under the schemes varied from £8,000 in the cases of the countries that became independent prior to 1959 to £12,000 for other cases. A later development has been that the United Kingdom Government has been willing to enter into technical assistance agreements with the Governments of the countries concerned under which half the amount of compensation is paid by the United Kingdom. This has applied to Sierra Leone, Tanzania, Uganda, Kenya, Zambia, The Gambia and newer states. As a further relief, the compensation has been made payable in six instalments, except where an officer has his appointment terminated, in which case he is paid his full compensation in one lump sum.

The expectation of the Governments, and indeed one of the main arguments used to support the scheme, was that the agreement to compensate officers for loss of their Overseas Civil Service careers would serve as an inducement for them to be willing to remain as long as their services were required. Why this view was ever put forward at all is difficult now to understand when the situation is reviewed in retrospect. In the event, what has happened is that the compensation schemes have rather hastened the departure of expatriate officers. The reasons for this are not far to seek. A number of the officers were unwilling to work under the new regimes either because they were not in sympathy with them or because they could not adapt themselves to becoming advisers instead of, as formerly, being the policy deciders. It is obviously in the interests of all that those who are unwilling or unable to adapt should go. A more serious reason, however, is that many officers felt that since there was no further assurance of a lifetime career – which was the basis on which they entered the service originally – it was in their interests to take steps to start a new career elsewhere as soon as practicable. This applied especially to those who were young enough to make a fresh start, but it weighed also with the older officers. In any case the indigenous Government itself would be bound to adopt a policy of Africanization which might mean the displacement of some of the expatriate officers to make room for local personnel.

The effect of all this is that expatriate officers become 'foot loose' and are able to leave the service at a time to suit themselves, without the deterrent of loss of pensions which under ordinary circumstances would have applied to premature retirements. This has made it extremely difficult for the Governments of all the new states to organize and develop a realistic programme of staff development. It is difficult to resist the temptation of criticizing in the strongest terms British Colonial policy in this regard. At a time when the newly independent countries needed breathing space to develop and stabilize their administrations they were compelled to face a real crisis over the loss of essential staff. The British Government could not be absolved entirely from blame for the weakness of the administrations in these states. As the administering power which had stated as a principle of its colonial policy the preparation of all the countries for independence, it had a responsibility to prepare the administrative machinery of the colonial territories for independence, and the process of carrying through this policy should have started a number of years before nationalism and the post-war climate of world opinion accelerated the pace of constitutional development. Since this was not done and independence could not be held back until it had been done, Britain had a responsibility to devise a scheme which could have given the new countries access to the staff essential for efficient administration until they had had the chance to develop an indigenously based staff.

From time to time, proposals were made to place Her Majesty's Overseas Civil Service on a permanent basis with careers, emoluments and pensions guaranteed by the United Kingdom Government. Members of this Service could then be seconded, on request, to the new independent states to help them maintain existing services at an adequate level and to promote new development programmes. Technical, and no doubt what appeared to United Kingdom eyes to be sound, reasons were advanced against the establishment of such a scheme. One cannot help feeling, however, that if the United Kingdom had adopted a more progressive approach to its responsibilities as an imperial power, a constructive and realistic solution would have been found. The imposition of the existing compensation schemes on new countries is, in the view of many, an abandonment of responsibility and an imposition of an intolerable financial burden on new states at a time when they need all their resources to give impetus to their development. A more enlightened policy is the one adopted by France. The French Overseas Service was kept in being with salaries and career prospects guaranteed by France. The staff were then offered under technical assistance to the newly independent states. Whatever the criticisms one may levy at the French approach to their former overseas territories, it must be admitted that the responsibility for enabling the new countries to maintain government services going at the previous level of efficiency is fully accepted. Former British territories, however, face constant anxieties regarding the maintenance of the health, engineering, research, scientific and technical services because of heavy losses of experienced and specialist expatriate personnel who cannot be replaced easily either locally or by further overseas recruitment.

It must be stated, however, that within the limitations of policy laid down for it the new United Kingdom Ministry of Overseas Development has been doing a magnificent job in assisting the new countries to find essential staff from the United Kingdom and elsewhere, and the Ministry can claim a fair measure of success in satisfying the requirements of the new states. Without the help provided by this Ministry, it would have been difficult for a number of the states to manage. It would have been better for all concerned, however, if the Ministry had had the responsibility for the management of a permanent corps of United Kingdom-based service available for placement on request to meet overseas demands instead of giving it the invidious task of liquidating one service and at the same time attempting to recruit in a scarce market fresh personnel to replace those who are being liquidated.

There is another factor, however, which bears on the problem of the exodus of experienced expatriate officers. The Governments of the new African states themselves adopt a policy of displacement of non-African staff to make room for Africans as part of a policy of Africanization. The policy and programme of Africanization will be discussed in a later chapter. In the context of this problem, however, it has to be said that very often the lack of detailed planned programmes of displacement has made it difficult for expatriate officers to determine the length of time for which their services might be required. In the circumstances, they have preferred to determine the timing of their departure under the most convenient arrangements for themselves rather than wait to be required to go under terms and at periods which might not suit their interests. It is likely that if a planned and progressive programme of Africanization is prepared in each state it would be possible to secure the conditions of certainty and limited security which would have the effect of retaining a satisfactory number of experienced expatriate officers until at a pre-determined time they have to give way to Africans.

LIMITING FACTORS

Against the background of what has been said above, the main problem facing the African Governments is the need to maintain an effective administration which is efficient, loyal, and in tune with the political spirit of the time. This problem is aggravated by the need to re-orientate and transform the Civil Service, in its structure and objectives, from a colonial service into a service which is in resonance with the highly nationalistic independent states. This is a very difficult adjustment to bring about even under the most favourable staffing conditions. In the circumstances in which there is a heavy loss of experienced staff the task becomes much more difficult to manage.

Furthermore, the period immediately after independence is accompanied by an accelerated pace of economic and social development and expanded provision of government services in response to the people's expectation that independence means greater economic well-being for all. At the same time, there are financial difficulties which might have arisen out of the need to adjust policies to the new situation or, as is more often the case, the shortage of financial resources. This means careful planning to provide for the husbanding of resources at a time when experience in the administrative machine is dissipating or being diluted. This situation leads to a failure to take bold action in economic and social matters and so leads also to the risk that government action might not match the expectations of the people deriving from promises made to them in election manifestos and nationalist party pronouncements.

Another source of strain is brought about by the staffing of the foreign relations machinery. The new states enter, for the first time, into direct relations with other independent states and international organizations. Necessarily experience in this sphere is lacking; and the process of building up an indigenous Foreign Service and putting it to work is made no easier to regulate in the face of a serious scarcity of experienced personnel in the 'home' services.

All these sources of strain impose a very heavy responsibility on those charged with the tasks of staff development in the new states. They have to be able to mobilize all available resources to create, develop and maintain effective administration of the services of the states and of their development programmes. The mobilization of resources, however, is severely limited by the educational facilities available, the increased demands on these resources by expanded services and development projects, the need to maintain reasonable standards of efficiency and integrity, the competing demands of other priority programmes and the private sector, multi-racialism and regionalism and, above all, the availability of finance for staff development programmes or, rather, the insufficiency of it.

The limitation imposed by the educational system is now fully acknowledged. At the time of self-government of all the African states, such university institutions as there were were in their infancy, and their output was woefully inadequate in relation to the demand for high level trained manpower. The use of scholarships to stimulate an increased supply of graduates, professional personnel and technical staff through training courses overseas helped, but not sufficiently to make a real dent in the problem. Below university level, there were also inadequate facilities for secondary and technical schools. Indeed, the output of secondary and technical schools constituted – and still constitutes – the main bottleneck in the whole manpower development programmes of governments. Without an adequate supply of secondary school graduates, the university system cannot be developed. Lack of personnel trained at a technical school has created a major problem in filling the essential middle grade posts, the backbone of any professional and technical department. Moreover, trade training and apprenticeships were not properly organized to give the kind and volume of training needed to meet requirements for technicians and artisans. Much of the resources of the new governments are therefore necessarily devoted to accelerating the whole programme of education at all levels, and this inevitably means that a considerable time elapses before the output of the educational and training institutions rises to meet adequately the staffing requirements of the public and private sectors. In the meantime, crash programmes and makeshift arrangements have to be resorted to with the inevitable risk of falling standards.

At the same time as governments are endeavouring to cope with this problem, they are faced with the major task of coping with a very great expansion of government activity in response to the demand of the public for improved amenities and services. Furthermore, all new governments embark on major economic and social development programmes. These programmes, together with expanding services, inevitably make very heavy demands upon resources in capital and manpower, and create in their wake, maintenance services and ancillary projects requiring trained manpower. For most countries, if not all, a temporary solution to the manpower problem created by this factor is found in recruitment of personnel from overseas, but this solution is expensive and, because of its short-term nature, tends to be inefficient.

Another limiting factor in the programme of staff development is the need to maintain standards of performance and efficiency as well as of integrity. It is easy to make a fetish of standards and the attempt to maintain the standards of efficiency which prevailed before independence under mainly expatriate direction and management has caused more controversy and discussion whenever Africanization and training are in issue than almost any other subject in this field. There is the general criticism that unrealistic standards are being set which have the effect of impeding the progress of recruitment of local persons for high level positions, and that it is more realistic to relate standards to the needs and requirements of Africa and not to those accepted or acceptable in Europe or America. At the same time, the public has grown used to certain standards of service which it is reluctant to abandon. People complain vigorously if the standards of telephone services, water supplies, roads, attendance at Government offices and treatment in hospitals tend to drop. There are also bitter complaints against the fall in the standard of integrity in public officers.

There is an obvious need to reappraise the whole subject of standards so as to ensure, on the one hand, that standards which are not required for local circumstances are reviewed and made realistic and, on the other, that proper standards are maintained to safeguard the public interest. In 1953 a Working Party of officials on Africanization in the Gold Coast (now Ghana) examined this whole problem and arrived at conclusions which have now been widely accepted. The following formulae were recommended for deciding policy on the question of standards:

(a) As far as concerns integrity, the standard required of all Civil Servants is absolute integrity and there should be no departure from this rule.

(b) As regards levels of efficiency, in all spheres of activity where the safety of the public is a major concern, the standard should be maintained at a level which would be accepted in more highly developed countries, that is, the standard should be that accepted internationally.

(c) In all matters concerning the collection of major revenue (Customs and Excise and Income Tax), standards of efficiency should be maintained at a level necessary to ensure that the collection of the country's revenue is not endangered.

(d) In all other spheres, the standards should be compatible with the rapid conversion of the service into one which is locally based and with the general welfare of the people of the country. In these spheres, it is for the government to decide, if the occasion should arise, whether or not these two interests are in conflict and, if so, which should have priority.

The competing demands of other priority programmes and the private sector also have their impact on staff development for the public service. The demand for trained manpower for this sector is legitimate as being equally essential to the balanced development of the economy of the country and must be taken into account by the Government when formulating its manpower development policies. The private sector is usually able to outbid the Government when it comes to competing for exceptional talents. The need to formulate policies which take account of the necessity for coming to terms with the private sector, is, therefore, self-evident.

In East and Central Africa, multi-racialism is a factor to be reckoned with. Whether by deliberate policy, or by the process

G

of natural development, the educational system and employment in the public service placed the European element in the population at an advantage over the others, and the Asian and Coloured elements over the African. Staff development programmes in these places must take account, therefore, of the need to redress the imbalance in numbers of the different communities – European, Asian and Coloured, and African – in all the levels of positions in the public service, particularly in the higher ranks – so as to make it reflect, broadly speaking, the general complexion of the population. Unless the obvious inequity of placing minority communities in privileged competitive positions is redressed, there could be no contentment or stability. Quite apart from the obvious strain this imposes on the whole programme of staff development, there is the probability that trained manpower is ineffectively used or is even not used at all. In East Africa, the policy of Africanization has been deliberately resorted to in an effort to redress this imbalance. In the process, however, some Asians who are citizens are being displaced to make room for Africans, not all of whom could be regarded as equally efficient; and, furthermore, Africans have superseded Asian citizens of greater merit. This is the inevitable consequence of a policy of remedying injustices of the past; and this policy, and the need to apply it, must be accepted as unfortunately necessary but only in the short term. A related problem is the need to have all regions or states within a federal or quasi-federal service fairly represented in the service. Thus, in Nigeria, all parts of the federation should be equitably represented in the federal public service. Similarly, the East African Community has to adopt a recruitment policy which ensures that Tanzania, Kenya and Uganda citizens are all reasonably well represented in its services. Frequently it is possible to obtain an excellent supply of candidates for particular vacancies from one of the constituent countries, but it becomes necessary to provide for the appointment to some of the vacancies of candidates from the others even if these are of lower abilities and merit.

The limitation of finance is so obvious that it requires little discussion. The chronic nature of this problem is familiar and would be accepted with equanimity if it did not have such serious consequences to the whole programme of staff development. The demands on the limited financial resources are great, and outside aid, in some cases even in substantial amounts, is not enough to resolve all the problems. Only time can resolve them and, unfortunately in all countries, time, too, is scarce.

All the factors discussed above, in varying degrees for different states, determine the size of the staff development programmes as well as the volume and pace at which they can be implemented. In some cases, they even determine the policy to be applied in the critical period before and after independence. For instance, the magnitude of the economic development programme in Ghana before and immediately after independence compelled the Government to ensure that there was no weakening of the administrative machinery necessary for the servicing of this programme. This consequently determined the nature of the whole policy and programme of staff development. On the one hand, training and education for the public service was given priority. On the other, there was no wholesale replacement of expatriate staff with African until the massive investment in training and education had yielded local personnel adequate for the purpose in quality and numbers.

To forge a realistic staff development policy in this critical period is made all the more difficult because this is also the period in which advice and offers of aid pour in from a number of sources: overseas governments, international organizations, universities and private individuals. Many of these offers are genuine and well intentioned, but some are actuated by ulterior designs. Difficulty is created because the range and volume of offers tend to confuse and so make orderly planning impracticable. To take an instance again from Ghana, the Government accepted so many offers of scholarships from overseas Governments and international organizations that orderly planning of the use of the output of secondary schools became impracticable, and local university institutions were starved of students even though the facilities were more than adequate to handle those who were being sent overseas to undertake courses in alien environment not all of which were compatible with the local situation.

NEED FOR POLICY FOR STAFF DEVELOPMENT

The need for a systematic and planned policy for staff development is, in all circumstances, vital to the new African states. It is of importance because these countries have a compelling need to ensure that the available manpower is used to the best advantage, and there must be as little waste as it is humanly possible to avoid. This principle is so obvious that there would seem to be no need to emphasize it. Indeed, all governments accept it as a policy and attempt to implement it. The need to emphasize it is because Governments have to be induced to devote adequate resources to implement this policy, and ensure that the impetus is never lost. A well-defined and systematic policy of staff development which is also fully backed by the Government in any particular state should ensure that proper and economic use is made of available manpower resources and that distracting and vested interests are cut to size and not allowed to interfere unduly.

MANPOWER PLANNING

The first essential step in the carrying out of any such policy of staff development is to establish a Manpower Survey programme. The object of such a survey would be to assess the need of the public sector as well as the private sector for trained manpower, the types of training required to meet the various requirements of the state, the ability, or otherwise, of the educational and other training institutions to produce the various types and levels of training required, and an estimate of future requirements for trained manpower in terms of development plans, industrial development and expanding services. A realistic manpower survey, which is systematically and scientifically conducted, should form the basis of a manpower development plan. Under this plan, the development of manpower training would be fitted into the overall economic development plan as an essential part of it. It would identify what the bottlenecks are, or are likely to be, in the production of the types and levels of trained personnel required with a view to preparing a realistic programme of education and training to match, as far as possible, future demands. Since, in all new African countries, high level and technically trained personnel is in very short supply, the manpower development plan should lay down the priorities for the use of scarce types of personnel by creating the necessary incentives for the channelling of such personnel into priority occupations.

Manpower survey programmes should be continuous, and there is the need therefore to provide a permanent machinery for carrying it out. In view of the close organic relationship be-

tween economic development planning and manpower development planning, the manpower survey organization or bureau
should be closely associated with the development planning
organization of the Government if not an integral part of it.

In Ghana, a major manpower survey programme was carried
through in 1960 under technical assistance arrangements with
the Ford Foundation. The report and recommendations of this
survey have had the most profound influence on the policies of
the Ghana Government in the fields of university, technological,
technical and secondary education, in the deployment of the
output of the educational system at the different levels, in the
programme of manpower development in relation to the
country's development planning, and in the determination of
the priorities for the use of scarce high-level manpower both in
the public and private sectors. There is now a permanent Manpower Bureau within the Central Planning agency. Similar manpower survey and planning programmes have been established
in Nigeria, Tanzania, Uganda and other states.

Having established an overall manpower priorities programme it is now possible to give consideration to the limited
sector within this programme relating to the public service.
Staff development policy for the service is essentially one of
making the best use of available trained manpower and, where
there is a shortage of suitable manpower, of instituting a programme of training on as comprehensive a basis as is necessary
to provide the skills, knowledges and experience required for
the public service.

In new countries, it is not often practicable to wait for the
long period of training necessary for some of the posts in the
existing structure to be occupied by local personnel. In these circumstances, another important aspect of staff development is to
undertake the exercise of examining existing standards of qualifications and efficiency of the service. Where possible, these
should be modified to suit the prevailing conditions and circumstances. This might imply a considerable review of the structure
of the service to permit the optimum exploitation of such
trained manpower as is available. For instance, the East African
Posts and Telecommunications Administration has over the
years so shaped the structure of its telecommunications services
and standardized its equipment, that it is able to delegate to sub-
professional engineering staff much of the installation and maintenance of the system. On this basis, only a relatively small

staff of professional engineers is required throughout. It is possible to envisage a more rapid process of training local staff for the sub-professional posts whereas it would take some years before local professional staff became available in adequate numbers. In most of the states, a similar exercise has been carried out in the administrative and professional departments which has had the aim of keeping administrative and professional class officers on policy formulating and purely professional responsibilities whilst delegating to executive and technical class staff such routine but responsible functions as can be efficiently discharged by them. The latter class of staff could be more easily found locally.

Now the application of the principles set out on p. 97 should enable an exercise to be carried out so as to establish a realistic review of the standards of qualification necessary for effective performance in the various classes and grades of posts in the service. This would make it possible to provide a basis for the proper definition of policy in regard to the replacement of such trained manpower as is available to the optimum extent, and for the training necessary to meet the terms of the modified qualifications. For instance, where previously possession of a university degree, or appropriate accountancy professional qualification, was compulsory for all appointments into the higher ranks of the Audit, Income Tax and Accounting services, a reappraisal of the qualifications needed has resulted, in most places, in lower qualifications for entry being established in association with well-defined training programmes, designed to raise staff recruited on this basis to the level necessary for carrying out efficiently most of their responsibilities.

TRAINING

Another most important element in staff development is Training. It can be defined as any form of instruction designed to improve an officer's capacity in his present job or to enable him to perform a more responsible job. Training also implies formal instruction in theory and practice to prepare a person for the performance of a specific task. A most essential and important part of training, especially for serving officers is directed experience, that is, training a person while he is actually at work. This definition of training thus covers all aspects of the shaping of the abilities and talents of a person required for this performance of specific tasks.

Training understood in these terms becomes important as a permanent feature of the staff development machinery for the Civil Service. A policy decision in this sense is essential for the health of any service. It is the responsibility of the Government to provide this permanent machinery and the means for a purposeful, comprehensive training programme, and to give all staff access to facilities for training so designed as to improve efficiency in their existing jobs as well as to equip them for assuming posts of higher responsibility. All officers are entitled to receive training as a right and it is the duty of the Government to provide adequate facilities. This principle is important because training, as described above, must be viewed as an instrument for creating efficiency; and a planned investment by both sides, Government and staff, in training should yield rich dividends.

Training for the public service has to be organized on a systematic basis and geared to the needs of the service. This is not incompatible with the right of the staff to receive training. If the training requirements at all levels are properly defined, that is, if systematic and comprehensive *Schemes of Training* are prepared and established, then programmes of training naturally flow from this. In this way, the staff know what training they should take advantage of to improve their efficiency or to advance themselves. The training establishments of the departments also are able to organize instruction and other forms of training to meet the requirements of their departments. The establishment of comprehensive Schemes of Training for each department and division of the Government is therefore an essential part of the programme of staff development since this would define clearly what forms and levels of training is necessary.

FORMAL EDUCATIONAL QUALIFICATIONS

Training for the Civil Service takes different forms. In the first place training can lead to formal educational or professional/technical qualifications. Government has the general responsibility for promoting educational institutions of all kinds for the general public and the Civil Service would expect to obtain its personnel requiring formal qualifications from the university, secondary, technical and primary institutions of the state. There is generally no need for separate educational institutions to be set up to feed the Civil Service only, although there are cases where training in Service institutions is necessary because the public system does not provide for the specific forms of training required. An example is provided by the technical schools maintained by Railways Organizations to provide for specialized railway technical training.

Unfortunately as explained earlier, the educational system is not geared to supplying the requirements of the Civil Service in all the new countries. Those responsible for training for the Civil Service cannot escape commitment therefore for stimulating the expansion of the facilities for general education and the provision of facilities for as many persons as possible to qualify for posts in the service. An assessment of the needs of the service for qualified personnel is a help to those who plan the public education system, and the readiness of the Civil Service to sponsor scholarships and bursaries for training leading to formal qualifications would also stimulate the development of institutions of education. While local educational facilities are being steadily expanded, and until they are adequate for all the requirements, it is the normal practice of Governments to award scholarships – or, as is often the case, sponsor overseas technical aid scholarships – for the training of personnel. It is good policy that such scholarships, whether for local or for overseas courses, should be made available also to serving staff. An investment in the training for formal qualifications of persons who have already demonstrated interest and aptitude in a chosen career and have proved their loyalty is more likely to yield better returns in terms of efficiency, stability and morale.

POST-QUALIFICATION AND POST-ENTRY TRAINING

A second form of training is post-qualification or post-entry training. Persons recruited from the general educational system have to be prepared for the effective performance of the duties of the posts which they have entered. This may take the form of training on the job, formal instruction in institutions or a combination of both. Where institutional training is unnecessary or inappropriate, it is nevertheless important that care is taken that every new officer is given an induction training and a properly regulated on-the-job training. The normal technique resorted to here is that of directed experience under the close supervision of an experienced officer. The old system of leaving the new officer to find his own feet by trial and error is obviously inefficient and wasteful of resources and valuable manpower. This is so well understood now that it does not need emphasizing.

It is now generally accepted that there is a need to organize courses of training for new entrants to all grades in the service. A typical example is the *Induction Courses* for new Clerical, Executive and Administrative Officers. It had been the practice for the induction training to be given invariably on the job. It is, however, now generally agreed that directed experience on the job is more efficiently conducted if the new officers have had basic institutional instruction in the general principles of the duties of their posts. These courses may last from two to three weeks for Clerical Officers to two or three months for those Administrative Officers who have received no training at an Institute of Public Administration. The training schemes for all classes of new entry posts should give details of the syllabuses required for the induction courses, and should define quite clearly the nature and purposes of such additional practical training on the job as might be necessary. Indeed, the policy should be that the departmental training establishments should be responsible for the supervision of the training of new entrants to the point at which the whole process of training is complete.

Another example of post-entry training is the training provided in post-graduate *Institutes of Public Administration*. In some countries, this may in fact be pre-entry training. In most new African countries, however, this training is provided for graduates already selected for appointment. The programmes of these institutes provide for the training in the general principles of public administration as well as specialized training in branches of administration designed to introduce officers to particular careers, as for instance, in public finance, foreign relations, local government, personnel administration, and social development. The usual period of such training is one academic year which may lead to the attainment of a diploma in public administration. In some countries, the need to put graduates to work as soon as possible is paramount and the courses may be shortened to six, or even three, months. The value of such training is to give the officer a professional approach to his responsibilities and enable him to evaluate more readily the experience he gains on the job when he starts. Institutes of Public Administration are usually attached to universities, but there are some which are separate autonomous institutions as in Ghana and Kenya. The charter of the Ghana Institute of Public Administration provides for close association of the institute with the University of Ghana and other institutes of higher learning. The object of making the Ghana Institute autonomous is to provide for a reasonable measure of autonomy in the direction of the Institute as compared with the status of an academic department under the authority of a University Academic Board. The curriculum of the Institute is therefore primarily a professional curriculum aimed at equipping officers with the basic tools of administration and management, and their application.

As part of the policies for administrative reform, consideration would need to be given to the format and content of courses given at Institutes of Public Administration. In an era of accelerated economic and social development, emphasis should be placed in the curriculum on development economics, planning (including sectoral planning techniques, implementation and evaluation), development administration, social development and communications techniques. The objective should be to provide the administrator, in particular, but others also, with the basic professional skills needed for evaluating his role in whichever branch of the government he is assigned to. It should also be the objective to provide for a degree of specialization, for instance work in the Economic and Finance Ministries, Social Service Ministries, Political Ministries, in professional/technical Departments, or in provinces and districts. The era of the peripathetic generalist administrator may be coming to an end.

DEPARTMENTAL TRAINING SCHOOL

This is really a form of post-entry training and is needed where the public education system does not provide the types of training required, or where the training necessary is peculiar to the needs of a particular department. Examples are post-secondary courses in departmental institutions for sub-professional or technical posts of the Posts and Telecommunications, Broadcasting, Civil Aviation, Public Works, Water Development, Roads and Electrical and Mechanical Engineering Services.

These courses are run by departments only because the technical schools and institutes do not provide them. In cases such as Forestry, Agriculture, Survey, Air Traffic Control, Meteorology, Postal Services and several Branches of Railway Services, it is more convenient and more efficient to have the courses under departmental control.

IN-SERVICE TRAINING

In-service training is probably the most important of the forms of training but is usually the one that is left to take a haphazard course. Properly and systematically organized, in-service training gives the most immediate results in improved efficiency and confidence in the officers. Even after the post-entry training or training in departmental institutions, further in-service training within the departments should be regarded as an essential and continuing process. For some cases, in-service training is the only form of training necessary or possible, and it would then combine the elements of induction as well as proficiency training. The object in all this is to improve efficiency of performance on the job. Training for promotion can only be regarded as a by-product of the main objective as far as in-service training is concerned. The training unit of every department has a special responsibility therefore to ensure that all tools of training – extra-mural, institutional, supervisory and others – are exploited to make the officer so effective as to earn his pay and so qualify him eventually for assuming positions of greater responsibility. For this purpose, programmes of training must be properly planned and established and not left to chance.

APPRENTICESHIPS

Apprenticeship training is most important for industrial departments. In most African states, apprenticeships were not established as a regular system until recently, and when they were introduced, there was a slavish adoption of European apprenticeship schemes without much thought being given to whether they were in fact suited to African conditions. It is now being recognized that this form of training can be streamlined, and the traditional period of five or six years reduced. Also, part of the training can be provided in Trade Schools with a topping up of industrial experience. Since in most African states industrialization is still in its infancy, it is necessary to give special emphasis in the public service to this form of training so as to ensure that the necessary skills are made available to the departments that need them. This is now accepted in most states, and all the industrial departments like the Railways, Public Works and Electricity and Mechanical engineering services now pay a great deal of attention to the training of their skilled artisans and technicians.

TRAINING FOR SUPERVISION AND MANAGEMENT

In the British-type Civil Services which apply to the States being discussed, not much attention was given to the training for supervision and management. In the past, there were stable conditions which enabled the system to select almost automatically the most experienced persons with qualities of leadership and management abilities for the key supervisory and managerial positions. A new and developing Civil Service should, however, lay emphasis on training to fit relatively inexperienced and untried personnel for these important assignments. It has become necessary therefore to establish training courses for all levels of supervisory and managerial staff, and special programmes and techniques have been developed for this purpose. For instance, the Training-within-Industries scheme developed in Britain has been adapted in a number of countries to meet their requirements. This form of training is justified by the need to have supervisors who are able to get the best output from their staff and to ensure that the staff are getting the right kind of training, either through directed experience or through in-service training. Moreover, it is only right that those who are charged with the management of blocks of the nation's business should have been given the right kind of training. Supervisors and Managers are key personnel in any government organization; on them depends the proper running of the operational services without which the public does not receive efficient services whatever the intentions of the Government. Effort expended in ensuring their proper training is therefore a good investment.

PREPARATORY TRAINING

There is one form of training which is purely of an interim nature and this is preparatory education of low level personnel in the Civil Service. Until the educational system is geared to produce all the personnel required for the public service, it is necessary to consider upgrading serving officers in subordinate positions. This applies particularly to the need to fill the gap left by the inadequacy of the secondary school output. Experience in Ghana and Tanzania has demonstrated that a tailored course in appropriate subjects releases talent for training in technical and executive responsibilities which would not otherwise be available. For instance, the Ghana Government has for years provided a one-year's intensive course in English and Science for girls with elementary school education, which has enabled them to take the State Registered Nursing course side by side with girls with secondary school education. The Tanzania Government has planned preparatory courses for serving officers for entry into clerical positions or into department training institutions.

The curriculum for each preparatory course would depend on what the persons are to be trained for and their previous training. For all training objectives, a course in the official language – English in practically all states – is essential. Arithmetic, general knowledge, or current affairs may be necessary in courses leading to clerical and executive responsibilities, whereas mathematics and science would appear to be necessary for entry into technical training courses. The essential considerations here are that the courses are tailored to the immediate particular purposes; that the aim is to make use of talent and intelligence in the subordinate ranks of the service or elsewhere which would otherwise be unexploited; and that this is an interim measure until the secondary schools output is enough to meet all requirements. It has to be borne in mind that most of those who would be rescued by this policy would have the ability to have benefited by secondary school education if sufficient facilities had been available in their time. Therefore it should be possible so to organize this scheme that there is no loss of quality in the staff prepared for the more responsible positions.

ADMINISTRATIVE STAFF TRAINING

It is now recognized in all the developed countries that staff training in administration for high level responsibilities is vital if those who are charged with the functions of formulating high policy and advising Ministers in the whole range of matters which fall within their portfolios are to be prepared for their assignments. Administration has become complex to match the complexity of all government operations. The proper assessment of all the factors of national and international significance and also of the advice of experts is important if the right policies are to be recommended for action. New situations arise constantly which would not ordinarily have counterparts in the previous experience of those top officials who have to formulate policy. Development administration is, for instance, now a major responsibility charged to all senior administrators in Ministries, in Departments and in the field. It has been recognized therefore that administrative staff training is essential in cases where people are likely to be appointed to top policy formulating and advising positions in government or in business. Thus, institutions such as the Administrative College at Henley and the Imperial Defence College, both in Britain, and their equivalents in Europe and America have been established. There are also a large number of other institutions catering for specialized staff courses below this level.

In Africa, the need is further accentuated by the fact that persons appointed, or likely to be appointed, to high-level positions, such as Permanent Secretaries of Ministries or Heads of major Departments, would not have had the lengthy experience of officers similarly placed in the older countries. Moreover, they assume office in situations of great political dynamism and ferment when ability to work in consonance with the situation, whilst maintaining a sound policy and balanced approach, is an asset of great value. It is more important in these circumstances even than in the older countries that such officers should be given the high-level staff training mentioned above. And yet, in fact, this does not normally happen. In a few instances in Ghana and Nigeria, advantage has been taken of places at the Imperial Defence College in London, and in East Africa a Staff College has now been established. Other countries have followed suit. One of the main obstacles to promoting such courses is that governments are so pressed for high-level personnel and supply is so desperately short, that officers cannot be spared for courses lasting more than a few weeks. Partly, however, there is the operation of the factor of ignorance since most of those who have to advise governments on the need for such courses have usually no knowledge or experience of them.

That administrative staff training is essential in all programmes of staff development is now generally accepted. The training can be organized in institutions which are established in association with universities, as has happened in East Africa, or in autonomous institutions, as in Ghana. In any case, the courses should be organized to provide facilities for training officers who have reached fairly high ranks in their careers and are likely to advance to the top as heads of Ministries or major Departments of Government. The courses should make room for high level personnel from the armed forces, police, commerce, industry and any major activity in the state in which staff are required to take high-level managerial decisions on policy. The courses should be organized to provide for all participants an intimate appreciation of all the normal factors that bear on national policy, including internal politics, finance, the economy, military strength, industry, world politics, security and national tradition and history, so that they prepare themselves for the handling of the problems and affairs of their high office of the future. They should be confronted with actual practical problems and projects in the national life which require intelligent and responsible solutions, and be made to provide their own practical programmes for action. These exercises should result in policy papers which could be of immediate use or interest to the Government while at the same time providing the participants with valuable training in methods and approach to the handling of matters of major policy. By bringing together persons from as many branches of national life as practicable, experience is shared, and the importance and relevance of the different types of national activities as factors of national policy is more readily appreciated. The value of this, and the influence of a well-organized course on the quality of intellect and responsibility brought to bear on policy examinations subsequently, are bound to become evident when participants return to their respective occupations.

SPECIALIZED COURSES

What has been discussed in the previous and earlier sections relates to various levels of training for officers in the Civil Service. An important level which should not be forgotten is the middle-range administrative and departmental officer. Induction courses – whether institutional or in-service – are provided for these officers when they first enter the service, and mention has been made of administrative staff courses for them when they are near the top of their careers. Somewhere in the middle, normally when they have had five to ten years in the senior service, they would be in charge normally of important blocks of responsibilities as heads of units or divisions. In the old colonial service, the senior of the Devonshire courses – the Colonial Service Course 'B' – was available for such officers. They were able to study their chosen fields of activity in depth against the background of the operation of general Government policy. They were also able to evaluate their past experience and consider how this experience could be projected into their future responsibilities. And they were able to acquire training in specialized fields to make them effective staff operators.

There is need in any well regulated staff development programme to provide for this type and level of training which is valuable for the responsible middle range operational personnel in the professional, departmental and administrative services. The sort of persons envisaged are those processing policy matters at fairly high levels in such subjects as labour relations, agriculture, forestry, public works and utilities, internal security, treasury control and budgeting, establishments, recruitment and training, economic planning and staff work in Ministries and departments. This could be additional responsibility for the Staff Colleges, or where the numbers warrant it. Junior Staff College courses could be organized to provide this type of essential training.

SCHEMES OF SERVICE

An essential pre-requisite to all programmes of staff development is the preparation of schemes of service for all branches and departments of government. A Scheme of Service is a plan showing how entry to a particular class of post in the Civil Service is made, the training facilities provided after entry, and the method by which, and the posts to which an officer may obtain promotion at various defined stages in his career, and the salary structure for the classes of posts available to him. The preparation and publication of schemes of service lead to a clear understanding of the recruitment, staffing and training policy in the various departments, and officers are clearly informed of the posts to which they can aspire and how they can attain them, either through training schemes provided for them which are clearly defined or through their own efforts.

Schemes of service are also a valuable aid to recruitment since prospective candidates are enabled to see clearly what the career prospects are in any given branch of government. They are essential also to the Africanization programme and to the construction of an efficient local service and a healthy promotions policy. It is important, therefore, that in all Civil Service staff development programmes, Schemes of Service for all departments are prepared, are approved by all the competent authorities, including the Public Service Commission, and are then published. Once they are published, it is important that they should be applied to all cases that arise within the policy rules laid down without variation unless and until they have been amended by the approved procedure.

The introduction and publication of Schemes of Service in the Ghana Civil Service in the period 1953 to 1957 had a profound effect on the whole programme of recruitment and training, the quality of entries into the various branches of the Civil Service, and, therefore, eventually the quality of the whole Civil Service, and the general morale. The policy left very little to the discretion of line officials, and where discretion was to be exercised, the nature of it was clearly understood. The experience in Nigeria has been similar and the need to establish schemes of service is now recognized in practically all the states.

ORGANIZATION FOR TRAINING

The importance which has been attached to training in the public service, the comprehensive and all-pervading nature of the training programme, and the fact that training has to be a permanent feature of all staff development programmes, imply necessarily that there must be a permanent organization for formulating policy and programmes and managing the programmes when prepared. Training as stated earlier is a tool of efficiency, improved performance and increased output, and an integral part of recruitment policy and of conditions of service. This is fully recognized by all big commercial and industrial undertakings which invest substantially in elaborate machineries for promotion of comprehensive training programmes. The need to invest in an organization for training in the public service is now also fully recognized, although much has still to

H

be done in many states in giving it adequate resources and man-power for effective performance.

A realistic machinery for training should provide for a central organization which is part of the office of the Ministry, Department or Division responsible for the overall administration of the Civil Service described in Chapter 5. Its head should be an officer of very high rank, keenly interested in training, preferably an officer at or near the Permanent Secretary level, who should have direct access in policy matters to the Head of the Civil Service and the Minister responsible for the administration of the Civil Service. He should be given the necessary staff and resources in finance and physical facilities. He should in fact be the Director of Recruitment and Training who is referred to in the next chapter.

The central training organization would have overall responsibility for defining training policy which should apply generally to all government departments; for co-ordinating training in all departments; for general oversight of the training arrangements in all departments; and for running central training schemes, such as central schemes of training for administrative, executive, supervisory and secretarial staff.

There should also be in each Department a Training Division with responsibility for organizing, operating and superintending all training required for the needs of all sections and classes of posts in the Department, including departmental training institutions where these have been established. The Departmental training division would be responsible also for indenting on the central training schemes to meet departmental training needs. The scope and size of the departmental training division would vary from department to department according to the complexity and size of operations. The Ministry of Works, for instance, would have an elaborate training organization as would also the Railways and Harbours administration and Posts and Telecommunications administration. On the other hand, the set-up in the Legal Department would be a comparatively simple one. Whatever the size and scope of a departmental training division, its responsibilities are essentially the same, and it should ensure that all necessary training programmes are formulated, defined and applied, so that all grades of staff that should receive training do in fact get it.

Although the head of the central training organization has overall responsibility to the Government for the formulation of training policy and the co-ordination of all training, the responsibility of a Head of Department or Ministry for training in his organization must be firmly recognized and enforced. Training is part of his managerial functions which he cannot escape nor be deprived of. As has already been implied, he needs training as an instrument for efficient operation and increased output. A recognition of this fact by all concerned with training policy at all levels would lead to greater smoothness in the operation of the whole policy and programme for training. The Head of Department or Ministry, once policy has been agreed, should be left to get on with his responsibilities in the field of training subject only to the need to maintain reasonable co-ordination from the centre. At the same time the Head of Department or Ministry should accept the fact that he has a responsibility for training and that he should honestly and sincerely accept this and promote it to the optimum extent necessary.

TRAINING RESEARCH AND CONSULTATIVE SERVICE

The training requirements described above may be recognized by all concerned with staff development as necessary for application over the whole range or in different combinations. There is, however, a need to base the policy adopted on what is known to be required and how and in what form it is to be applied. An important part of the staff development programme is, therefore, to undertake research and investigation into the problems of training needs and effectiveness, the development of training materials for application, and the development of training methodologies which take account of the cultural, social and economic patterns of the country. The research and investigation are best carried on in established institutions such as Institutes of Public Administration, Administrative Staff Colleges and the Political Science Faculties of universities. The important consideration in this matter is that so much is being invested in training by all governments that it is essential that this investment is economically and relevantly applied to the problems of each state in this field. One of the essential functions of Institutes of Public Administration is research and consultation. Research Sections of Institutes of Public Administration usually undertake studies of some fields of special interest either for training purposes or to help government agencies. In the latter case the research is usually undertaken at the request of the governments and in most African States Organization and Methods groups and the Research Sections of Institutes of Public Administration deal with immediate and practical problems arising in various departments.

The need for research is particularly urgent now because of the requirements of the era of planning, development administration and the application of science and technology to development. Training in the Civil Service should be given the material for providing efficient performance of these developing functions. Research would become important also in places where new policies for administrative reform are introduced.

CHAPTER 7

The Africanization Policy and Programme

THE most important short-term problem of staff development is one relating to Africanization. The discussions in the previous chapter lead naturally to the consideration of this problem. It is treated separately because, although relatively short-term, it is usually the subject of intense political activity and it generally evokes so much passionate agitation and discussion as to become sometimes unreasonable. This passion only dies down when in the process of time the application of a progressive Africanization policy has resolved the problem. In any case, the problem is important for discussion in its own right since it constitutes one of the most important stages in the evolution of the Civil Service in any Sate.

In East and Central Africa, a policy of 'localization' has sometimes been advocated. This is because of the multi-racial nature of society in this area and it is intended that the Civil Service should reflect the racial complexion of the States. On the other hand, there is always racial imbalance in the Civil Services of these States in that the minority racial communities occupy the majority of the posts in the senior ranks. A policy of 'Africanization', rather than 'localization', usually comes to be adopted in these places owing to the need to achieve a proper balance between the races, reflecting as nearly as practicable the racial composition of the population. In any case, it must be expected that any non-African, who assumes citizenship of the State of his adoption becomes African in the continental sense and the use of the term 'Africanization' should apply to him so long as it is just and equitable to all minority groups. It must be recognized, however, that it is wrong in principle to discriminate in appointments and promotions in the Civil Service against citizens on grounds of race only and, therefore, as soon as the inbalance in racial composition of the Service is remedied, the policy should be one of merit being the only consideration in these matters.

DEFINITION

Africanization can be defined as the process of transforming a colonial type Civil Service into a national service. In the short-term, Africanization implies the control of key policy advising and formulating posts by citizens. In the long-term, of course, all posts in the Civil Service would be filled from national sources. At this final stage of progression, Africanization as such merges into the normal problem of staff development and training which has been discussed earlier. Africanization as a policy in the long-term must be qualified, however, by the need at all times to borrow talent from other countries where it is necessary to apply new knowledges and techniques not available locally. The most advanced countries constantly recruit talent from other countries in specialized fields and there is nothing wrong with this, nor is it incompatible with a policy of complete Africanization.

The replacement of expatriate officers by local personnel is not, however, the sum total of Africanization as a policy. This merely results in putting Africans into an existing structure which may have suited a past colonial era but which is certainly not fully adapted to the new constitutional status of African countries. An important aspect of Africanization is, therefore, the creation of a national Civil Service which, in structure and spirit, works in consonance with the policies of new independent Governments in Africa which are attempting to transform their national societies into prosperous communities which project the African personality.

JUSTIFICATION FOR AFRICANIZATION

Although Africanization as a policy is generally accepted by all as necessary, it is important to examine some of the motivations behind the policy. The first and most burning issue is one of politics. It is natural that the political urge for independence should be reflected also in the urge to create a national Civil Service. Political independence not matched by an administration which is African in complexion would eventually result in disharmony. African Ministers inevitably realize that they would prefer to work with Africans in policy advising and directing positions even though this might result in some measure of loss of experience in these positions. Any expatriate officers retained for a time after independence in these sensitive positions should be regarded as a temporary expedient until Africans are ready and available to take over from them.

Furthermore there are some posts which are really sensitive from the national security point of view and key posts such as those in the Police, Armed Forces, in the Ministries of Defence, External Affairs and Interior, should be taken over by Africans as soon as they can be trained or are adequate to fill them. Even in the so-called non-sensitive key posts, it becomes increasingly uncomfortable politically when an independent state is represented at negotiations with representatives of foreign states (in for instance, trade, agricultural, finance and civil service matters) by non-nationals.

If as happens quite often in all the new States, trade agreements are being negotiated with, say, Germany, there is always the suspicion that the British official acting for the government might not sincerely represent the interests of the State and, in any case, the other side might feel uneasy in discussions with him and might not be willing to confide their business intentions to a person whose own parent country might have rival interests. In any event, national pride demands that as soon as possible – and the sooner the better – relations with foreign states, at whatever level, should be conducted by the citizens of the State. Moreover, the African official can be expected to be in tune with local psychology, character and attitudes and, therefore, after training and experience, should be more effective in the conduct of relations with other States. Politically, therefore, it becomes a matter of national necessity and honour that an African front is demonstrated in all key policy posts in the Civil Service, and in all sensitive posts affecting the security and foreign relations of the State.

Although politics is the main emotional impetus behind the application of an accelerated Africanization programme, the more important and, to many, the real justification for Africanization is based on reasons of economy. It is obviously more economical to employ local rather than expatriate personnel. The markets from which these two sets of people derive are different, and the expatriate market is invariably more expensive than the local African one. In addition, in any case, to having to pay more for an expatriate officer for the same quality of experience and training, it is necessary also to provide additional inducements in cash and kind since otherwise it would not be worth his while leaving his own home unless he is the adventurous or the missionary type. In some African countries now, the British Government, under the Overseas Service Aid Scheme, meets the overseas element of the salaries of those expatriate officers recruited through its agencies. This is a considerable help since it enables young African countries to have the time in which to train their own personnel while still having access to experience and expertise from overseas without the extra heavy cost of purchase.

Even so, employment of expatriate personnel is still not as cheap as having Africans. Whatever one might say, the fact that overseas officers are working side by side with African staff does have a distorting effect on the local salary levels. The Governments set up commissions to devise salaries structures which are related to what the local economy would be capable of sustaining and which would reduce the gap between the lowest paid Civil Servants and the highest paid. These commissions can only have limited success in this task so long as there is a large element of expatriate staff in the senior ranks. One of the reasons for this is that, to begin with, Africans in the senior ranks are initially in a minority and they find their normal social life with expatriate officers with whom they work. This is all the more so since, in the early stages, most of these Africans have themselves been trained in Europe and America and have assumed the patterns and standards of life of these materially more advanced countries. It becomes unrealistic, therefore, to attempt to pitch their salary levels too much below those enjoyed by their expatriate colleagues. In equity, all salary commissions and governments must take this factor into account. It does mean, however, that, in terms of the real value of services provided by these local persons and of the economy of the country, far too big a slice of the resources of the State is applied to the emoluments of what might be called a privileged few.

Moreover, it is normal to guarantee housing for staff recruited from overseas. And there are a number of other additional items of expenditure such as leave passages – by sea or air – for officers and their families, and the cost of leave salary for long periods of absence from duty. But taking housing alone, each Government has had to build and manage large housing estates for its expatriate staff. In addition, governments have had to lease additional housing or to pay substantial housing allowances. African officers have come to expect, as stated earlier, that they are also entitled to housing privileges and this is one of the most intractable problems relating to conditions of service there is in Civil Service administration. All governments state that they accept no responsibility, in principle, for the housing of local staff, but this principle is usually observed in the breach rather in its application. Ghana appears at last to have broken with the past and decided to charge economic rental for all houses occupied by local staff. It is too soon, however, to judge how effective this policy is. As an indication of how costly this factor can be, an example can be given of one country in East Africa which has been spending nearly £1 million on housing allowances alone each year.

Africanization is justifiable also by the fact that it ensures stability in the staffing of government services. Employment of staff from overseas can be regarded as a short-term expedient in any case, but the period after independence is particularly difficult in maintaining a stable expatriate staff structure. The incidence of the inevitable compensation schemes becomes a most unsettling element in all staffing programmes. Replacement by recruitment from overseas on contract terms is useful but it is not the permanent answer to the problem. To ensure stability, the only answer is to build up a local cadre of officers whose careers and fortunes are tied up with those of the State and who are bound to their jobs by ties of pensionability and national loyalty. If the main core of the staff is African, then such reinforcements in experience and expertise as may be necessary from overseas can be applied with economy and good sense.

A minor factor is the drain of money out of the country caused by the employment of expatriate officers. This may not be a very large sum compared with other factors in the balance of payments position of a state but it is still substantial. A high proportion of the salaries paid to expatriate officers is spent in the country, but it is natural that savings should be remitted to their home countries overseas. Later, when they retire to their home countries, gratuities and pensions are paid to them overseas. This is a price, but admittedly a relatively small price, a country has to pay for having to rely on overseas staff for its development and the maintenance of its service. But, obviously, it is in the country's interest to reduce this price to the absolute minimum necessary to ensure efficiency by employing local staff to the optimum extent that can be managed by a progressive Africanization policy.

Another factor justifying Africanization is the importance of the experience of retired officers to the State. It is sad to see the wealth of experience and expert knowledge which is acquired by overseas officers who have had a life-time career in Africa being wasted in their home countries to which they naturally retire. In a few cases, their experience and knowledge can be used in advisory capacities. But in most cases, these are completely lost not only to their own country but also to the African countries in which these valuable assets were acquired. The experience and knowledge they had acquired would have been useful for advisory services, for work on commissions and statutory boards, and for local government and other local services if they had been Africans and had retired to live in their own countries. This is already becoming possible in the older of the African countries like Sierra Leone, Ghana and Nigeria where the few retired African officials are in great demand for temporary high level jobs, for commissions and service on statutory boards. These countries are now in the position to loan experienced staff to serve as experts on commissions, such as salary commissions, in East and Central Africa.

In the ultimate, the real justification for Africanization is the natural and understandable desire of every people to be able to manage its own internal affairs. It is the public service counterpart of the urge for political and economic independence. This independence is, to most people, meaningless unless it is matched by the ability of the people, through its Civil Service, to administer, to run and control it. Moreover, until industry and commerce become large employers, the opportunity for service through state employment is the best means for inculcating qualities of integrity, hard work and *esprit de corps* which are vital ingredients in the character of any nation. It is therefore not an unworthy ambition for any state to wish to accelerate the process of Africanization in its services.

POSSIBLE DANGERS

There are dangers, however, in the acceleration of the Africanization programme beyond the point which may be regarded as wise or prudent. Precipitate or reckless action could result in falls in standards of efficiency which might have a disastrous effect on the whole programme of services and development of the Government. Some reduction in standards is inevitable, and might even be a realistic adjustment to existing situations instead of clinging to the unnecessarily high standards of the past. But they should not be relaxed beyond the point which would jeopardize the policies of the Government and the governmental machinery. All new African states are anxious to demonstrate their ability to run efficient governments as a backing for accelerated plans for economic and social development. Africanization for the sake of Africanization only without relating it to a well-considered plan would undermine this policy.

This is, however, not easy to resist. There are intense political pressures, encouraged very often by African staff unions, and there is the understandable desire of Africans within the service to take over more responsible positions especially as these would also enhance their own personal status. A wise staff development policy should exploit legitimate ambitions to give progressive responsibility to persons who have the capacity for it. But an appeasement policy which gives in too readily to pressures based on unreasonable ambitions might start a process of progressive reductions in standards which would be difficult to arrest and difficult to remedy.

This problem is not eased by the failure of expatriate officers to adjust to the new and changing situations in Africa, people on whose experience governments would wish to rely during the period Africans are being prepared to take over. This encourages precipitate action in Africanization. Fortunately, this problem has not been very important except in one or two of the states. In some cases, however, representatives of foreign states, for motives which are not always honourable, have interfered by putting ideas to Ministers and politicians which have led to precipitate policies being adopted. Very little can be done to frustrate this kind of activity except to ensure that the planned programme of Africanization is realistic and is properly understood by all in positions of responsibility including, especially, Ministers and politicians.

A danger, which presents itself to all new African states in greater or lesser measure according to the stages reached in their staff development programmes, is that they may have inherited such complex standards of administrative and departmental structures and procedures, backed in some cases by statutory provisions, as to invite serious difficulties when they are staffed by local personnel who replace departing expatriate officers. These complex structures were usually imposed by the colonial administrations to ensure effective action without the responsible participation by the indigenous people. They are usually straight importations of structures which had proved workable or effective in the United Kingdom and which could work in Africa so long as there were British officers to man them. Elaborate systems have been set up in some or all of the states to control the use of land, the transport licensing system, immigration, the regulation of internal and external trade, to give only a few examples. In so far as new African Governments have adopted these systems wholesale – because in themselves they are good – and have endeavoured to apply the policy of accelerated Africanization to them, there have been difficulties because of the falling off of standards. Where, however, there had been time to train and give experience to Africans before the expatriates left, the structures inherited have been real assets.

Given a sense of responsibility, all governments would endeavour to regulate the pace of Africanization to ensure that, whilst aiming to achieve an African complexion in the public service as rapidly as possible, the administrative structure would be able to match the Governments' desire for a progressive policy of planning, development and expanding services on all fronts. In the ultimate conclusion, the justification for Africanization rests on the necessity, in the interests of national self-respect, to establish a tradition of integrity and ability which springs from indigenous sources and which is of a standard to command the admiration of the outside world.

PLANNING AND ORGANIZATION FOR AFRICANIZATION

Africanization is essentially a staffing policy of the short-term Once the programme of Africanization is complete, when all top positions are filled by Africans, and there is a flow of suitable candidates to meet all normal requirements of the Civil Service, there is no further need for emergency operations for pushing an Africanization programme. The whole operation then merges into the normal staff development programme outlined in the previous chapter.

Normal bureaucratic institutions for staff development are, however, not adequate in most countries to give emphasis and impetus to the Africanization programme. This is because the institutions are geared to the requirements of a normal stable situation. And yet, Africanization, to be effective, requires an emergency operation to deal with an emergency situation. It requires the adoption of extraordinary measures for the mobilization of the manpower resources available for the Civil Service, and the development of these resources so that they provide efficiency of operations whilst getting the maximum number of African into posts to replace non-local staff. It means a complete review of the structure of staff in departments, and the qualifications required for the grades of posts within the reformed structure so that they are related to what are essential for adequate services and standards, and not necessarily what were suitable for recruitment from former traditional sources in Britain. New instructions, shaped to fit the requirements of an emergency situation, are therefore necessary. Their form and scope would naturally vary, however, according to the situation in each country.

The first essential step in each situation is to formulate an operational policy, that is, to translate Africanization policy of the Government into a plan of operations. If an adequately staffed office responsible for Africanization is available, it can itself prepare this operational plan. In most of the African countries, however, it has been found necessary to set up Commissions on Africanization which have been charged with the responsibility for formulating policy to be followed in preparing a blue print for action and for establishing, to the extent that a forecast of availability of manpower and training facilities can be made, a time-table for implementing the Africanization plan. In very few cases, however, has it been possible to prepare a comprehensive time-table. The manpower availability is too uncertain, and there are a number of other imponderable factors too which make it impracticable to prepare a reliable step-by-step plan. The most that it has been possible to achieve, therefore, is the establishment of a working machinery that has responsibility for preparing and executing programmes of action on the basis of what can be predicted with a reasonable degree of certainty.

For this purpose, some Governments have preferred the setting up of standing Africanization Commissions with executive responsibility for action in the field of Africanization. This body would review the situation in each department of government and determine the training programme necessary for accelerating the pace of Africanization in the department. It would also review the claims of all Africans in the department for advancement to more responsible positions and decide when and at what pace, notices should be given to non-Africans to make room for Africans. The standing Commissions are normally headed by non-officials or even politicians and therefore their actions are likely to be influenced by the day-to-day political situation and pressures.

If a Commission of this nature had the staff which would carry out a proper investigation into the situation in each department and which would present facts upon which a realistic programme of Africanization could be formulated, then it would work. But it is a function of the Africanization situation in all new countries that the right calibre of staff very often does not exist. In any case, it is in the nature of political institutions in African countries to show quick results and the temptation to take short cuts in the acceleration of Africanization is very great and is not often resisted. But the main objection to a standing Commission is that it interferes with the functions of the Public Service Commission. The Public Service Commission is charged normally with the responsibility of executive or advisory responsibilities in all appointments and promotions. In carrying out its responsibilities, it adopts a judicial and impartial approach to the consideration of the claims of all candidates within the framework of the policies, especially the Africanization policy, laid down by the Government. If then, another Commission has already determined who should fill a particular post, then either the Public Service Commission becomes a mere rubber stamp or else situations are created which lead to conflicts between the two Commissions. Such conflicts would not be healthy for an organization and might result in the Public Service Commission being discredited as being too conservative a body, one not working in consonance with the declared policy of government. The consequences of this to the integrity of the Civil Service as a whole are likely to be most unhealthy.

For that reason, it is better to set up an official machinery which is capable of action in consonance with government policy whilst at the same time working in close co-operation with the Public Service Commission without interfering in its functions. In fact, states which have tried the standing Commissions on Africanization have eventually abandoned them for the kind of machinery indicated. In Nigeria, Ghana and Sierra Leone, the machinery is in the form of an office of Recruitment and Training with a Secretary or Director of Recruitment and Training at the head. In East Africa, the tendency is to appoint an Africanization Officer or the head of an office of Africanization (or Ugandanization or Kenyanization). An office of Recruitment and Training, however, more accurately reflects the purpose and functions of the machinery, namely, responsibility for mobilizing resources in the whole of the recrtuiment field for Africanization and promoting training programmes which in the long run so improves the recruitment field that no special machinery is eventually necessary to promote Africanization.

DIRECTOR OF RECRUITMENT AND TRAINING

The Directorate (or Secretariat) of Recruitment and Training should be responsible to the Government for the maintenance of the impetus of Africanization in all departments in accordance with the policy laid down and also for all the steps to be taken in all departments to this end working in close collaboration with all Heads of Departments. In particular, it would have to produce Schemes of Service as well as Schemes of Training for all departments and implement them. It would see to the recruitment of local graduates and other local qualified personnel from educational institutions at home and overseas. It would, within the appropriate departmental machinery, review the manpower resources in each department and ensure that no African of ability is overlooked either for promotion to a more responsible post or for the further training necessary to advance him to a higher post. It would work with the Public Service Commission so as to provide it with the support and knowledge it needs in order to encourage Africanization. It would promote training schemes as a whole but, in particular, schemes for the upgrading of junior officers which would enable the Government to make the most of available talent within its service whilst at the same time satisfying the natural ambitions of the staff. It would phase the programme of retirement of expatriate staff – working in collaboration with the Public Service Commission – with a view to ensuring that no local talent is wasted, and the end-products of training schemes would be synchronized with the availability of vacancies to accommodate them. It would liaise with educational institutions not only to recruit more efficiently from them but also, when possible, to persuade them to tailor courses to meet the priorities and needs of the Civil Service. The Directorate would organize and run central training institutions necessary to provide for the needs of all departments, such as courses for administrative officers, supervisory staff and secretarial staff.

The Director of Recruitment and Training thus has a really formidable task, especially if he is to give impetus to the programme of Africanization which the emergency situation deserves and which in any case the Government and the public expect. To discharge his responsibilities satisfactorily, he needs to have adequate staff. In the West African states, the Director was given very high status so that he could command the authority necessary for the prosecution of the policy entrusted to him. Moreover, the office was so organized that as, with time, the recruitment policy aspects of his functions became less important, the training aspects had so built up as to become the permanent central training organization described in the previous chapter. In Ghana, for instance, as soon as the policy and programme of Africanization had been effectively implemented and the process was virtually complete, the office was transformed into a Directorate of Training as part of the overall machinery for the programme of staff development in the service as a whole. Needless to say, the Director of Recruitment and Training should himself be an African.

In summary, the principal task of the Director of Recruitment and Training is to prepare a bold programme of Africanization with a time-table, if possible, and to provide the machinery for continued review of progress. He is responsible for ensuring that this programme is carried out in consonance, as far as is practicable, with the policy of the Government and the wishes of the public, whilst at the same time ensuring that there is reasonable efficiency in the Civil Service so that the Government can rely on an effective administrative machinery for carrying out the people's other needs for increased well-being under independence. These two objectives – accelerated Africanization and efficient administration machinery – are not easily attainable together. It is only possible to achieve compatibility between them if the Government has a clear and declared policy for achieving the optimum rate of Africanization compatible with the maintenance of reasonable standards in the service. Even where, as in Ghana, Nigeria, and Sierra Leone, the Government's policy was quite clear and definite, there was yet room for differences of interpretation and opinion, and the Director of Recruitment and Training had therefore an exceptionally difficult task. Essentially, the job is an unpopular one since it is difficult to satisfy, on the one hand, the politicians and African Civil Servants that enough progress is being made even in spite of the policy laid down, and, on the other, the heads of departments that their ability to discharge their responsibilities is not being undermined by too rapid a rate of Africanization. The Director of Recruitment and Training and his staff should therefore be the ablest officers that can be obtained and should have integrity – moral and intellectual – above the average as well as the experience to prepare realistic programmes according to the policy laid down. The Director should, of course, be in the position to propose a change in the policy if this becomes necessary.

METHODS OF OPERATION

Whatever the machinery set up to give impetus to Africanization, there are certain methods of operation necessary to meet each local situation. Some of these will be discussed briefly. A programme of Africanization implies preference for African citizens over all others who might be equally or better qualified. Where the policy is one of localization, the programme would give preference to all citizens over non-citizens in the service. If then – to discuss only Africanization in this context – an African citizen has adequate experience and qualifications to do a job, even though there are others better qualified or with greater experience, the policy laid down should be such as to give preference to the African.

The first obvious method for promoting Africanization is to ensure that Africans are recruited or promoted to fill posts as they occur. In the initial stages, there might not be a sufficient number of qualified, or otherwise suitable candidates even for this limited method of approach, but as the process of manpower development gathers momentum, it would be found that,

I

except for highly technical or specialized positions, this method of approach is too slow and would certainly not match the accelerated programme laid down by the Government. Another drawback to this method is that Africans would normally enter at the bottom of the particular classes of posts and would be unable to rise to the top within a reasonable period of time because of lack of vacancies. As a method, therefore, it is unlikely to prove acceptable beyond the first short period of the Africanization programme. If, however, as happened in East Africa, the rate of departure of expatriate officers on compensation is fast, then this method of approach may be forced on the system since there would be far more vacancies than there are local available candidates to fill them, and it would be some time before even further expatriate recruitment becomes unnecessary.

At some stage in the progress of Africanization, however, there would be the need for a more drastic method of approach and one such method is to adopt a policy of displacing non-Africans to make room for suitably qualified Africans. In East Africa, for instance, all the Governments have introduced schemes of limited retirement benefits for the pensionable Asian and other non-African non-expatriate staff so that, whenever Africans are available to fill posts occupied by non-Africans, the latter could be retired with limited compensation. This compensation has taken the form of increased pension terms, as if the posts had been abolished, with the right to commute a part of the pension for a lump sum based on actuarially calculated higher commutation factors. The terms of agreement for payment of compensation to pensionable expatriate officers, who were designated by the British Government on the taking over of the Civil Service by the local Government, contain usually a provision for the compulsory retirement of any designated officers if this is found necessary to provide vacancies for qualified Africans. If, of course, the officers to be displaced are on contract terms, then the usual notice clause can be invoked. This scheme of compulsorily retirement of non-Africans in the interests of Africanization can give cause for hardship and it therefore has to be applied with as much humanity as possible. But, in situations such as exist in East Africa with large blocks of Asian staff intervening between Africans and the senior posts, it is inevitable that this scheme should be applied extensively for a few years.

To a limited extent and in special cases, supernumerary posts could be created to accommodate qualified Africans. This method is necessarily expensive and can only be justified if the supernumerary posts are required for relatively short periods and if there is adequate work to keep the new officers employed. There has been much confusion caused in some countries by supernumerary posts being used as training posts. It has to be made quite clear that when a person is appointed to a post, he should be fully qualified for normal entry to it whether that post is supernumerary to the establishment or not. It is thus wrong in principle to appoint an unqualified person who requires training to a post supernumerary to the establishment and then proceed to treat him as a trainee.

Another technique used is one of job dilution. In Ghana, for instance, when expatriate recruitment to the Administrative Service ceased in 1949, there were not enough graduates available to fill all the vacancies. A number of the posts of Assistant District Commissioners in the field and Assistant Secretaries in the Secretariat were downgraded to those of senior Executive Officers. These were then filled by the promotion of senior clerical staff with ability and experience. They took over the routine, although still responsible, jobs formerly performed by administrative officers in addition to their policy responsibilities, leaving policy decisions and the higher responsibilities to the reduced number of administrative officers. In some other cases, it is possible also to split jobs so that they can be filled by Africans. For instance, where previously a works superintendent was required to supervise staff for a whole building operation, it might be possible to split the job so that Africans with experience in either masonry or carpentry could be appointed as Foremen instead to supervise either section.

Another method that has been applied is promotion on trial. In considering a candidate's suitability for promotion, it is necessary in present African circumstances to pay less attention to educational certificates, diplomas or degrees and more attention to the candidate's experience since leaving school, his general intelligence level and his capacity to learn. The practice of measuring qualifications by reference to educational certificates is administratively a very convenient formula in situations in which there is a ready and abundant supply of suitable candidates. Until this happy situation arrives in a particular State, it is necessary to take calculated risks and make the fullest use of all available talent and experience. In such circumstances, the risk is reduced considerably if the candidates are appointed on trial for short periods so that those who are unsuitable can be weeded out at an early stage. The trial method can also be applied where candidates for appointment or promotion to very senior posts needing considerable experience are being considered. If there is reasonable doubt as to the suitability of such candidates, they can be put on trial for a short period to enable them to prove themselves.

In East Africa, a method of accelerating the progress of Africanization is the creation of posts in special 'Trainee' grades. Candidates are appointed or promoted and then given training, either institutional or by directed experience on the job, to qualify them for advancement to higher posts. This scheme is very widely used especially in the executive and technical classes of posts. For instance, there are posts of Trainee Accountant, Trainee Assessor of Income Tax, Trainee Tax Officer, Trainee Statistician, Trainee Research Officer and Trainee Meteorologist. This scheme is essentially, however, short-term until the staff and salary structure of the service are such as to ensure a flow of ability from the lower grades upwards without the necessity for the creation of special incentive training grade posts. For instance, if the Accounting Service provided a structure which enables an officer to join from secondary school as, say, Junior Accounting Assistant and to progress by stages to the grade of Accountant, there would be no need to select young persons from school and put them straight into Trainee Accountant posts.

In some of the African states, particularly in East and Central Africa, Africanization at the top is impracticable unless there is some dilution of the standards of experience normally expected. For instance, in the past, an officer could not expect to attain the status of Permanent Secretary or Head of Department until he had had experience over many years, perhaps as much as twenty years. Obviously, twenty years would be too long to wait, but the process has been shortened to as little as four to five years in some places. This is taking a risk which would be feasible if there is a strong supporting staff, which is not often, however, available. In these circumstances, it is essential to retain or obtain experienced staff in a consultant capacity to give support to the new African officers during the period they are consolidating their experience. In 1963, the headquarters administration of the East African Common Services

Organization lost most of its expatriate staff. African staff available, although not having wide experience, were able and had a sufficiently high sense of responsibility to risk putting into the key posts which had become vacant. In the circumstances, however, it was considered necessary to seek, under technical aid from the United Kingdom, consultant staff with the necessary experience to do the development thinking and to carry out examination of the facts bearing on issues requiring policy decisions, thus providing the African staff with the material on which to take or recommend wise decisions. This they are fully capable of doing. Consultant staff were sought to reinforce experience in Civil Service administration, recruitment and training and Treasury control. It is essential, if this scheme is to function properly, that the African Officers do take all the decisions and accept full responsibility for them. In this way, they would steadily rely less on the consultant staff and more on their own ability to do their own development thinking and policy examination.

In some cases, senior expatriate staff have been induced to give way to Africans and they are then retained as 'advisers' to these Africans. This is, apart from a few exceptional cases, a psychological mistake and should not be encouraged. It is better to seek the 'advisers' from outside or else delay the promotion of the Africans until they are able to take over full responsibility without having their predecessors in office breathing down their necks. Confidence in their own ability is not likely to flower in these circumstances.

It is comparatively easy to make rapid progress in Africanizing posts which are administrative, executive and non-technical. In technical, professional and scientific departments, however, the standards laid down are usually international and there is no short cut to the training process for qualifying Africans to fill them. This is generally recognized by governments and even by the general public. They know that doctors, engineers, research officers and technical officers of all kinds should be qualified up to certain recognized standards, and they accept with reasonable patience the prospect of having to wait a long time to produce Africans with these qualifications. Public sentiment, however, expects that Africans should, as early as practicable, be in charge of departments employing these types of professional personnel. Here is a situation in which selective Africanization is feasible. Africans with the basic qualifications, and after an approved minimum period of experience, could be considered for accelerated advancement to the top policy and directing posts. They have, however, to be good and command the respect of their very largely expatriate staff since otherwise demoralization might set in and the staff might disintegrate.

BASIC PROPS OF THE AFRICANIZATION PROGRAMME

As pointed out earlier, Africanization is essentially a short-term staff development programme. All the activities for staff development outlined in the previous chapter should therefore be deployed to support the Africanization programme. In particular, the whole apparatus of training should be applied to this programme and should be so fashioned as to become eventually a permanent feature of the administration of the Civil Service. Training is the main prop for any Africanization programme and it requires massive investment of funds. It is not the kind of programme which can be had on the cheap if standards are to be maintained at a resonable level. It is essential, therefore, that governments should be willing to invest heavily in a comprehensive training programme either from their own resources or from technical aid sources. There is no short cut to success in this programme. For that reason, it is essential also that there should be purposeful and realistic planning in order to avoid wasteful uses of resources in personnel and funds.

It is inevitable that an accelerated and progressive programme of Africanization should cream the junior ranks for personnel to fill more senior and responsible posts. An alarming feature of most Africanization programmes is thus the weakening of the intermediate executive and technical grades. It is highly dangerous therefore to attempt to increase the rate of Africanization without at the same time taking steps to institute intensive and systematic training of intermediate supporting staff at all levels throughout the service. To advance existing junior staff to senior positions without, at the same time, taking steps to ensure that they have the necessary support of fully-trained junior staff is unfair to the officers themselves and unjust to the taxpayer. The newly promoted African staff would normally have experience and skills which would be no more than adequate to the responsibilities of their posts. Lack of support from below would certainly make them ineffective and would therefore lead to inefficiency and waste.

As a final and general comment on Africanization, it is appropriate to remark that the transformation of the service from one predominantly expatriate at the higher levels to an indigenous one, even under the most favourable circumstances, is bound to be accompanied by some disruption of services. During the period of taking over, therefore, there would inevitably be a reduction in the standard and extent of services provided for the public. This would occur to a greater or lesser degree irrespective of how highly qualified the incoming staff might be. If the programme has been properly organized and operated, however, this should be purely temporary. But it is important that the governments and the public should have this issue put to them so that they are willing to accept a temporary reduction in standards of service during the period of change over. That this understanding has not been achieved in most countries is evidenced by the disappointment frequently expressed by many persons when Africanization is accompanied by some loss of efficiency and by the impatience demonstrated by the public while this temporary phase persists.

Any person who has had some responsibility for the preparation and operation of the policy and programme of Africanization knows what an exciting experience it is. It has its disappointments, distress, strain under hard work, the pain of unhelpful criticisms and misunderstanding. But in the end, the sense of achievement is a sufficient reward for all the difficulties experienced on the way. This sense of achievement might even lead to elation on looking back some years later to see the emergence of an efficient, strong and indigenous Civil Service which maintains the traditions of high standards, integrity, and loyalty which could compare with some of the best in the world.

CHAPTER 8

The Public Service Commission

No subjects are of greater concern to Civil Servants than those affecting their appointment, promotion and discipline. Although remuneration in the Civil Service has to be high enough to enable an officer to maintain himself and his family in reasonable comfort and save something against contingencies, yet one of the main inducements for seeking entry into the service is the security it offers. An officer can look forward to a long and rewarding career and a pension at the end of it. Anything which affects his security of tenure is therefore of great importance to him. The machinery which is set up by the Government to regulate appointments, promotion and discipline should, therefore, attract and retain the best personnel, as well as maintain the morale of the service.

In the type of Civil Service being considered here and in the former British African States, it is agreed as a principle by all that the Civil Service should be efficient, stable and impartial, and its morale high. Only thus can it serve as an effective machinery for executing the policies of government. It should therefore be able to recruit from the best talents available in the community and assure them the conditions that would induce them to stay in the service. It follows therefore that the procedure for selections for entry into the Civil Service and for promotions within it, must be not only impartial but must be seen manifestly to be impartial. This procedure must be based on the criteria of merit and public interest, and not on political influence and patronage or nepotism. Similar considerations apply to the procedure for handling disciplinary matters.

THE PUBLIC SERVICE COMMISSION

The machinery that has been adopted in all the States is the Public Service Commission – called the Civil Service Commission in some States. The Commission is charged with responsibility for making (or advising on in some States) appointments, promotions and transfers in the service and for handling all matters concerning discipline. For the highest posts, the Commission has usually to act in consultation with the head of Government and usually also delegates action on the lowest posts to heads of Departments. In all its actions, the Commission should act with independence and impartiality. The constitution and membership of the Commission is therefore of some importance to all Civil Servants.

It is interesting to reflect that the institution of Public Service Commission is comparatively new to the Civil Service in African states. It was not heard of before constitutional changes brought about self-government and independence. In the Colonial era, such appointments as were not made by the Colonial Office and the Crown Agents, were made by officials in the country's Colonial Secretariat. Selection boards were no doubt set up for certain purposes, but all selection procedures, whether for appointments or promotions, were regulated by administrative instructions issued in the name of the Governor. The Governor was in effect the appointing authority in all local cases. Disciplinary codes and procedures were laid down in General Orders and Colonial Regulations which were themselves administrative regulations. Appointments, promotions and disciplinary measures affecting the more senior posts came under the supervision of the Governor and his Executive Council, and there was the right of appeal to the Secretary of State for the Colonies open to all in the service. By and large, this system worked with impartiality and justice mainly because, in practice, the whole of it was managed by Civil Servants whether in the country or in Britain.

When self-government emerged on the scene, however, the Civil Service came more and more under local control, and the Public Service Commission system was introduced to insulate appointments, promotions and discipline from politics. As political Ministers took over responsibility for the affairs of government, it was felt that it would not be right to hand over responsibility in those sensitive fields affecting the Civil Servants to the Ministers. The Commission system was introduced, therefore, as part of the self-governing constitutional process. In the initial stages before there was complete internal self-government, the Public Commission was advisory to the Governor, and technically the Civil Service was still under the ultimate control of the Secretary of State for the Colonies. Complete internal self-government, however, transferred control completely from the Colonial Office to the local government, and the Public Service Commission was thereupon given executive powers over appointments, promotions, transfers and disciplinary matters. The one category of appointments that was excepted concerned the posts of Permanent Secretary or posts of equivalent or higher status. For these, the usual arrangement was that the Prime Minister had to be consulted in making appointments.

STATUS OF THE COMMISSION

There has been much argument over the question whether the Public Service Commission should be an advisory body or an executive body. In Ghana and Tanzania appointments, promotions and discipline are vested in the President by the Constitution. The manner in which the President's powers are exercised here is defined by Act of Parliament. The Public Service Commission has delegated powers to act executively over certain classes of posts, in fact over all posts in the establishments except the lowest (which fall within the responsibility of Heads of Departments and Ministries) and the superscale posts. In these latter posts, the Commission is given limited advisory functions. In the other States, however, the Commission has complete executive responsibility over appointments, promotions and discipline in respect of all posts except those of Permanent Secretary and posts of comparable or higher status. The Commission is further empowered to make delegations to heads of Departments and other authorized officers usually in respect of the very junior posts.

The case for an executive Public Service Commission is that, if politicians were given any responsibilities in these sensitive areas, there is a great danger of political patronage and nepotism undermining the integrity and morale of the Civil Service. An independent and impartial Commission which has full executive powers and which is therefore not subject to Ministerial influence, would apply the principles of merit, impartiality and justice in the discharge of its responsibilities. The integrity of the Civil Service would in these circumstances be safeguarded. This is a powerful argument, and certainly in the period of constitutional transition and where Ministers are relatively new to public office, the institution of an executive Commission is perhaps essential to the maintenance of a viable Civil Service which is also kept in good heart. It would also remove temptation from the paths of Ministers who would otherwise yield to the pressure of party agitation for rewarding political zeal with plums of office in the Civil Service.

As Ministers become more settled in public office, however, they begin to question the validity of the argument that the integrity of the Civil Service can be safeguarded only by establishing an executive Public Service Commission. They do not see how it is possible to discharge their management functions in relation to the Departments within their portfolios unless they have some share in the control of the Civil Servants through whom their policies are executed. Ministers cannot be expected to defend, in Parliament and in public, the official actions and conduct of Civil Servants who work in their Departments unless they also have some means of exercising discipline over them. Nor can they be expected to give their complete confidence to senior officials if they have had no part in placing them where they are. In any case, the system enforced in the Constitutions of the newly independent states and which they inherited is not what is practised in the United Kingdom whose philosophy and practice in relation to the Civil Service have been adopted by all these States. In that country, all promotions and discipline are managed by, or in the name of, the Minister responsible for the Department. It is true that selections for entry into different classes of posts in the service are made by the Civil Service Commission. But once the initial appointments are made, the machinery instituted in the Departments for promotions and discipline is subject to the jurisdiction of the Minister. Certain categories of appointments such as Permanent Secretary, Establishment Secretary and Deputy Secretary are made by the Prime Minister with the knowledge of the Minister concerned.

In practice in the United Kingdom, there are conventions that have come to be strictly applied, which ensure that merit, impartiality and justice are the criteria for regulating these sensitive functions and that political patronage and influence and nepotism have very little room to flourish. African Ministers could not be expected, for an indefinite period, to accept a situation in which they are to be regarded as being incapable of exercising proper responsibilities in Civil Service matters and of establishing conventions in the African context which would be as strong as in the United Kingdom in safeguarding the integrity of the service. If the Constitution prevents them from having control, eventually they would be bound to find means of circumventing it in order to achieve control. In the long run, therefore, it is much healthier to introduce a system on similar principles to those in the United Kingdom which would result in a commonsense arrangement for giving Ministers participation in the responsibilities which would otherwise be left entirely in the hands of an executive Public Service Commission.

The system in Ghana is a fair example of how such a system can operate. The whole service is divided into four categories, A to D. Category A posts are those of Permanent Secretary status and above or equivalent, and certain posts of heads of Departments which are regarded as sensitive or particularly important, as for instance Directors of Broadcasting and Information, Chief Medical Officer, and General Manager for the Railway. Category B posts are the other posts of heads and deputy heads of Departments, and also the other superscale posts in the Administrative and Foreign Services. Category C posts are generally all posts below Category B and above Clerical and analogous grades. The rest of the posts are in Category D. The Civil Service Act defines how the President's responsibilities under the Constitution are to be exercised. All category A appointments, promotions and discipline are reserved to the President who has complete discretion over how he seeks advice in the exercise of his responsibilities. In practice, the President relies on his Secretary to the Cabinet who is also Head of the Civil Service to assist him in this matter, and he has on occasions called also on the Chairman of the Civil Service Commission. As regards Category B posts, the Minister in the cases of the Foreign Service, heads and deputy heads of Departments, and the Secretary to the Cabinet in the case of the Administrative Service, make submissions to the President, but the Civil Service Commission's comments are automatically sought before the President takes decisions on the submissions. Action on Category C posts are delegated to the Civil Service Commission and on Category D posts to heads of Departments.

This system in Ghana has been in operation since July 1960, and worked extraordinarily satisfactorily until 1962. The Civil Service Commission and Heads of Departments, under delegated authority, dealt with the greatest volume of business affecting appointments, promotions and discipline since Categories C and D posts constituted the bulk of the service. The President and

Ministers were for a time encouraged by the system to take a healthy interest in staff matters, and the more senior staff also found it exciting to make a real effort to work within the political climate of the policies of the government in power. There was very little sign, in that short period, of political patronage or influence or nepotism affecting the exercise of the responsibilities of the President and his Ministers. In fact, the same care in selecting people for appointments and promotions, with merit and suitability as the principal criteria, was exercised. There was a positive gain in that the two-way loyalty between Ministers and officials flowed more naturally and there was a more relaxed approach to relations between Ministers and their official advisers. For a time, therefore, there was hope and optimism that a pattern was being established which would eventually result in the establishment of conventions governing the stability and integrity of the Civil Service and healthy relations with the political Government.

The experiment failed, however, when the then Ghana Government, after 1962, adopted a policy of integration of the whole public service system in the political party machinery. Party interest permeated all programmes and policies for appointments, promotions, and discipline. The Civil Service Commission was abolished and its functions assumed by the Establishments Secretariat under the executive control of the Presidency. The effect on the Civil Service would have proved disastrous if the regime had continued for too long. The change of government in the country in 1966 enabled this dangerous policy to be reversed and the pre-1962 policy to be restored.

While the experience of Ghana may not be entirely relevant to the situations in other African states, it does provide a warning that there are risks in tampering with the autonomous status of the Public Service Commission. The approach in each state would have to be different depending upon the prevalent political policies, the stage of constitutional progress, and the state of development of the Civil Service itself, particularly in relation to Africanization, and the internal stability of the country. The problem is how to reconcile, on the one hand, the interest of Ministers who, having been charged by the electorate under the constitution for managing the subjects within their portfolios, desire to exercise management control over the staff who are required to execute their policies, with, on the other hand, the need to safeguard the integrity and viability of an impartial Civil Service. Obviously a feeling of frustration should be avoided. Ways should be continually explored therefore to avoid any conflicts of interest and to establish as soon as practicable the conditions under which healthy conventions may develop to safeguard the integrity of the service and true interest of Civil Servants.

STATUTORY BASIS OF THE PUBLIC SERVICE COMMISSION

It is usual for provision to be made in the Constitution granting self-government or independence, for the establishment of the Public Service Commission. This provision defines the powers of the Commission, how its members are appointed, their tenure of office, and the qualifications for appointment as members. It is usual to provide that a Public Service Commission shall be established; that it shall consist of a particular number of members who are to be appointed usually by the head of government or State; that certain classes of persons are disqualified for appointment, such as Ministers, Members of Parliament, office holders of political parties and serving officials; that, apart from certain top posts such as Permanent Secretary where the head of Government has to be consulted, the Commission has power to make appointments and promotions and exercise powers of disciplinary control and dismissal over all officers; and that the Commission has power to delegate some of its functions subject to certain conditions. In a few cases, the constitution lays down the main provisions for setting up the Commission, leaving the detailed provisions to be spelt out in an Act of Parliament.

In some countries, however, notably Ghana and Tanzania, the Public or Civil Service Commission was established completely by Act of Parliament which defines its powers, its membership, how members are appointed, and their terms of appointment. The question whether the Commission should be enshrined in the Constitution or set up under an Act of Parliament will depend on the role and status of the Commission in preserving the integrity of the Civil Service. Undoubtedly a Commission established with its powers defined under the Constitution is in a stronger position than that created by an Act of Parliament since, in the former case, a change in Constitution is necessary if its powers are to be reviewed, a process which is more difficult to contemplate or carry out than the amending of an Act. For that reason, most people would prefer the Constitutional Public Service Commission. Certainly, in a period of transition and until politicians have been in power long enough to appreciate the essential role of an impartial and efficient administration, the staff of which are selected, appointed and advanced purely on merit, it is safer to have a Commission whose status and powers are enshrined in the Constitution. In the long term, however, the integrity of the Civil Service depends on the willingness of the Government to preserve it as such and the acceptance by the general public that this is essential for a healthy administration. When that stage is reached, then the Act of Parliament approach would seem to be a more flexible one than the rigidities of the Constitution.

REGULATIONS

Provisions in the Constitution or Act of Parliament, which establish the Public Service Commission, are designed to state the general principles affecting its powers and functions. The detailed definition of the functions and procedures are laid down in Regulations. These regulations are made, in some cases, by the Commission itself, in others, by the Government on the advice of or after consultation with the Commission and, in others still, by the Government with no obligation to consult with the Commission. During the period of development of the Civil Service through which all African states are passing, it is essential that the preparation of these regulations should be by a process of co-operation and consultation between the Government and the Commission. Since the terms of the regulations are bound to have some impact on policy in that they serve to translate into practical procedures and actions the policy laid down in the statutory instrument and in other ways, the Government should be concerned about what is contained in them. On the other hand, the Commission has to operate these regulations, and in practice has considerable experience in the functions assigned to it. It is a wise policy therefore to involve it in the regulation making process.

The regulations make provision for defining the status of members of the Commission and the legal protection and privileges of members when acting as such; for the staffing of the Commission, and procedures for the conduct of meetings and for arriving at decisions; for the exercise of the powers of the

Commission over training in the Civil Service, procedures for appointments, promotions, notification of vacancies, advertisements, examinations and selections; for termination of appointments, disciplinary procedures, punishments and appeals; for the delegation of certain responsibilities to authorized officers; and for other miscellaneous matters necessary for the efficient functioning of the Commission. The method of amending the regulations should be flexible enough to enable changes to be made in the light of experience and changing circumstances.

ROLE OF THE COMMISSION

Essentially the role of the Public Service Commission is a quasi-judicial one. It should not be responsible for laying down recruitment policies, such as Africanization and terms of service, policies on qualifications and standards, and the disciplinary code. These are matters for the policy-making heads of the Government to formulate, such as the Establishments Division and the Director of Recruitment and Training, who would provide the machinery through which the Government would act. These and other matters of policy are political in the sense that the Government must arrive at its decisions within the context of its political policies and, where appropriate, after consultation or negotiation with the staff associations and unions. Once the policies for appointments, promotions and discipline have been determined and published, however, it is the responsibility of the Public Service Commission to administer and interpret them in practice or where it delegates any of its functions, to lay down the procedures for action.

The reason for not involving the Commission in the policy decisions on these matters is that it is important, in order to retain its impartiality, to prevent it being drawn into political controversy. At all costs, the Commission should not be placed in the position in which it can be criticized in legislatures or on political platforms over such matters as the policy for Africanization, the terms of service and the policies for promotions and discipline. There is wisdom in consulting its members over some of these matters, but the Government must accept full responsibility for decisions on them since these are subject to political criticisms sometimes of a searching nature. Like the Judiciary, the Public Service Commission should adjudicate on the law and interpret it; it should not be involved in the 'law-making' process, which is a political matter.

If, however, as it is suggested in Chapter 4, a state adopts the policy of merging the functions of the Commission and those of Establishments into one central authority for the complete management, control and development of the Civil Service, then the role of the combined organization would be completely different from that of a quasi-judicial Commission. In these altered circumstances, it would become inevitable that the central authority should be made answerable politically for, at any rate, those parts of its responsibilities outside the processes of recruitment, selection, appointments, promotions and application of the disciplinary code to individual cases. The actual machinery, including that of Ministerial responsibility, adopted would have to be formulated in each case according to local circumstances.

MEMBERSHIP OF THE PUBLIC SERVICE COMMISSION

It is normally the case that the Chairman of the Commission is appointed on a full-time basis as also the Deputy Chairman where one exists. In some countries, the other members are also full-time appointees while in others they are part-time, the nature of the appointments being based on the volume of business that falls to the Commission. There is general agreement, however, that it is on the whole preferable to have all the members appointed on a full-time basis. It makes for expeditious dispatch of business and removes them from an unhealthy influence arising out of day-to-day outside business contacts. The size of the Commission varies from one State to another but is usually not less than three. Where full-time appointments are made, the smaller number is preferred.

The members of the Commision are appointed by or on the advice of the head of Government and for a fixed term of years. A member cannot be removed during this period unless he resigns voluntarily or becomes disqualified by law except for proved inability to discharge his functions whether arising from infirmity of body or mind or from any other cause. A person is usually disqualified for appointment if he is a public officer, a Minister, a Member of Parliament, an official of a political party or an officer of a staff association or union. The salaries and

K

remuneration of Members of the Commission are laid down by Parliament and once laid down, cannot be altered disadvantageously after appointment. Such salaries and remuneration are a statutory charge on the revenues of the State. Furthermore a member of the Commission is not eligible for appointment to any public office for a minimum period, usually three years, after he ceases to be a member. The object of these provisions is to provde security of tenure, and remuneration for the members so that they are able to act with complete impartiality and justice without fear of favour or influence, whilst at the same time ensuring that members' actions are not influenced by hopes or expectations of future public office appointments.

RECRUITMENT PROCEDURES

It may be appropriate here to discuss some of the procedures and techniques applied by the Commission and the officers to whom some of its powers are delegated, in relation to appointments, promotions and discipline. The first stage in all these is the recruitment for appointments into posts, usually on first entry.

It should be the normal policy that all posts which are vacant and which are required to be filled by direct appointments, should be advertised. The advertisements should receive the widest possible publicity so that any candidates who are qualified within the terms of the advertisements and are interested may have every opportunity of submitting applications on time. The advertisements should state clearly the qualifications and experience required of candidates to be considered for appointment, including educational and age qualifications, the salary scales and grades, future prospects where these might be relevant, the closing dates, and where and how applications should be submitted. The Commission advertises only, however, where the vacancies are notified by an authorized officer, for instance, a head of Department or Ministry. Advertisements are not necessary where they are not likely to yield response from eligible and suitable candidates other than those who are already known. For instance, at certain stages in the development of African States, the only Africans with specialized qualifications in the sciences and technologies are well known, usually those being trained under the governments' own training programme. No useful purpose is served by advertising in these cases nor in cases where the vacancies should be filled by promotions, transfer and re-engagement of serving officers.

EXAMINATIONS

The selection of candidates for actual appointments, whether after or without an advertisement, is by examination and interview. Examinations may be used either to test aptitude or achievement in relation to standards of skills or knowledge which are laid down, or even merely to reduce the field of selection to manageable proportions. Thus, where the field is very wide, as for instance in the case of Clerical Officer posts, examinations are most useful in reducing the numbers to be finally considered for appointment. In a number of cases, where regular professional qualifications are necessary, for instance, in engineering, law, medicine and certain graduate scientific disciplines, there is no need for any further examinations to test achievement of the appropriate standards other than the possession of the recognized professional or scientific qualification.

Aptitude tests are necessary where it is proposed to select candidates for training in the acquisition of specialized skills and where it is necessary for them to demonstrate their aptitude for these jobs. Thus, aptitude test are applied to candidates for training as technicians, machine operators, technical officers of the different kinds, and even for engineers, architects and pilots. The former British States are very backward in the use of aptitude testing facilities for the selection of candidates for training for, or entry into, classes of posts where misfits cause inefficiency and wastage of human and training resources. Backwardness is apparent by the lamentable lack of research and investigation into the objectivity and relevance of testing techniques in use or of new ones that might be applied with profit. Progress has been made only in the limited areas of tests for entry into the engineering and industrial trades. Obviously the greater the correlation between the tests applied and the success subsequently achieved on the job, the more economical it is for the system to be applied. In Kenya, however, an Aptitude Testing Unit has been in existence for some time and is extensively used by government Departments in all the East African States and by industrial concerns.

Achievement tests are applied to select candidates who have already acquired the knowledge and skills up to the levels of proficiency required for the posts to be filled. Such tests should produce candidates who, on appointment, are able, subject to the usual local orientation, to provide efficient service without any further training. Thus, proficiency tests are applied to select typists and stenographers, artisans and technicians, machine operators and accountants. Certain examinations designed for promotions or confirmations are also of this type, as for instance examinations for draughtsmen and assistants in agriculture, forestry and survey. Here again, examinations to test proficiency is used to only a very limited extent in the African States, and very little work has been done in research into techniques and relevancy.

The type of examination which is more generally applied is the one which tests general education or intellect. This is used extensively in the general service classes, that is, in the Clerical, Executive and Administrative Classes and classes analogous to them in various Departments. This type of examination has already been described in Chapter 6. Where there are large numbers of candidates and it is desired to reduce them to manageable proportions, or where it is desired to test candidates' intellectual capacity for the responsibility of higher class posts, this examination is a useful instrument. It should not, however, be applied indiscriminately as has sometimes been the case.

As pointed out earlier, a great weakness in all the examinations systems used is that they are not scientifically applied and very little work has been done either in research into new techniques or in correlating tests with subsequent performance with a view to improving existing techniques. This is a field in which the Public Service Commission should be given the resources for studying the best methods to be applied in examinations, or else be encouraged to commission such studies to be carried out on its behalf by public administration consultants or institutions. For the present, no great harm appears to have been done since the main task is to fit available qualified candidates into vacancies in a situation in which there is a chronic shortage of trained personnel.

The time will soon come, however, when real competitive selection will be the order of the day and that is when economy in the use of manpower and training resources will be important and therefore the system of selection should as far as humanly possible have a high degree of relevance to the vacancies required to be filled.

INTERVIEWS

Interviews, which are another selection procedure, are really another form of examination. In some countries, interviews are called 'oral examinations' as opposed to 'written examinations' described in the previous few paragraphs. The same degree of skill and care in the use of the technique of interviews is therefore necessary as for examinations.

Interviews are used by themselves for the selection of candidates for such classes of appointment as scientist, professional engineer, doctor, lawyer and architect, and for technical and sub-professional appointments where recognized qualifications are laid down. The purpose of the interviews in such cases is to test the suitability of such candidates, on grounds of personal qualities or relative experience, for the posts required to be filled. Interviews can be used for the same purpose also where the field of candidates is small and written examinations are therefore superfluous. For instance, where, as in most States, there are only a handful of graduates each year available for consideration for senior posts, the interview method is used to place the graduates in the job each is best fitted for. Interviews have also been used to supplement written examinations. This is widely used either for appointments or promotions. The usual approach is to rate the results of the interview in marks which are aggregated with the marks in the written examinations for preparing an order of merit for selection. In some cases, however, passes in the examination are regarded as qualifying for consideration, the final selection being then based entirely on the results of the interviews.

The technique of interviews is a most difficult one in which to achieve objectivity in criteria for selection. It is very easy for interviewers to become subjective in their judgement of the worth of candidates. It is most important, therefore, that special attention is paid to the training of those who are used for regular interviews of candidates and that the criteria for each element in the qualities to be measured are as closely defined as humanly possible in order to reduce the area of subjectivity. For that reason also, it is wise to use at least three persons on each panel of interviewers so that the averaging out of the results may achieve a reasonably high degree of objectivity.

PROMOTIONS

Promotion is the transfer of an officer from one post to another involving an increase in salary. The techniques and procedures discussed above for appointments apply in greater or lesser measure, according to the circumstances, to promotions as well. Advertisements are used less in promotions because usually the field of selection is well defined. Examinations and interviews are frequently applied also.

The criteria to be applied in considering officers for promotion are merit, official qualifications, seniority and experience. Of these, merit is the most important and, indeed, the over-riding consideration in making all promotions. All the other criteria are relevant mainly in so far as they assist in determining the most meritorious candidates for promotion. A Civil Service that does not strictly adhere to these criteria in its promotions policy becomes reduced gradually to mediocrity in quality and performance. Where merit is recognized as paramount, however, it has a tonic effect on the whole quality and morale of the service. It is easy enough to say this, however, but difficult to enforce it since there is in every service strong pressure to use seniority as the main principle of promotion.

DISCIPLINARY PROCEDURE

Procedure laid down for handling disciplinary matters should satisfy the following conditions, among others:

(i) Any person who is under disciplinary inquiry must be made fully aware of the charges against him, be given access to relevant documents, and given full facilities for confronting witnesses giving evidence against him.

(ii) He must be given every opportunity of defending himself. This includes the right to appeal in certain cases.

(iii) The procedure laid down should be such as to ensure expedition in handling disciplinary cases. This implies simplification as far as possible without endangering the first two conditions laid down above.

The main considerations are that the public interest should be served and also that justice and equity should be accorded to the accused officer. If the procedure does not ensure prompt and effective handling of disciplinary cases, and if there are protracted proceedings and technicalities to be followed, not only do heads of Departments tend to feel that they would rather turn a blind eye to inefficiency or, if the case is prosecuted, the accused officer is kept in suspense over an unduly long period. If heads of Departments are unwilling to do their duty in disciplinary cases because they cannot be bothered, inefficiency results.

The regulations establishing the procedure should make a distinction between senior, as opposed to junior, grades of officer and also between major, as opposed to minor, offences or misconduct. A more elaborate procedure is necessary for the more senior officer and where the offence is a major one. For minor offences and for the very junior officer, summary procedure should be adequate. The other principles to be observed in laydown the procedure should be that the appointing authority should have the power to terminate an appointment, that the inquiry should be conducted by a senior officer with a knowledge of the circumstances and conditions under which the alleged offence is committed, and that the proceedings should move as far as practicable by continuous stages to the officer who has power of final decision without reference back or interim reports. For the very junior officer such as the non-pensionable and daily-rated employee, discipline and justice are best meted out by summary procedure, promptly. Delays and difficulties resulting from the application of an elaborate procedure are not understood by him as being necessary for justice and are frequently taken advantage of to flout authority. So long as the right of appeal to higher authority is preserved, summary justice in these cases should result in fairness whilst serving the public interest.

It is the responsibility of the Public Service Commission to administer any regulations laid down, after advice or consultation as to the procedure in handling disciplinary matters. These regulations should clearly state all the steps to be taken when offences of different categories, and in relation to different classes of staff, come to notice, culminating in final determination of any inquiry necessary and the processing of appeals where applicable. The regulations should also define the penalties liable to be imposed and for what circumstances each type of penalty is appropriate. The delegation of responsibility for disciplinary inquiries should also be stated. If the Disciplinary Code can be compared with the Criminal Code then the regulations on discipline in the Public Service Commission Regulations can be compared with the Criminal Procedure Code.

CONCLUSIONS

The role of the Public Service Commission described above makes it a quasi-judicial body which has executive responsibility in making appointments, transfers and promotions and in exercising discipline over the Civil Service. It has no policy responsibilities in establishments, recruitment and Africanization and training matters, nor does it lay down the policy for the disciplinary code. It is like a court which administers the law but has no function in laying down the policy for legislation. This is the type of Commission that has been established in all the former British States. Any modification of this role has been in the direction of making the Commission advisory to the head of Government rather than giving it more executive powers.

There are some countries, however, in which the Commission, or a Public Service Board, has much wider responsibilities. The Commission in these States combines the functions of establishments control, personnel policy, recruitment and training policy, with executive responsibilities for appointments, transfers, promotions and discipline. The Public Service Board of Australia has functions of this broad nature. It is a matter for argument which is the better system. There is no doubt that the comprehensive role of Public Service Board enables all matters concerning the administration of the Civil Service to be, so to speak, under one roof. This, if properly organized, should lead to efficiency and to a much clearer definition of where the responsibility for the Civil Service lies.

There are good grounds for stating, however, that in newly developing States such as in Africa, where officials as well as Ministers have not fully appreciated the proper role of the Civil Service as a State apparatus and the need to maintain its integrity whilst making it responsive to the policies of the Government, it is wiser to continue to adopt the present division of responsibilities between the Public Service Commission, the Establishments Division and the Directorate of Recruitment and Training. As explained earlier, this removes the Commission from the political areas of conflict and it ensures that it is able to handle the sensitive responsibilities assigned to it away from the limelight and with complete impartiality and fairness. An assurance of this is essential for maintaining morale in the service and safeguarding its integrity. It may well be, however, that future developments and a greater degree of sophistication may compel re-examination of the present position, and result in a combination of functions under one organization without any harmful results either to the government or to the Civil Service.

CHAPTER 9

Staff Relations, Efficiency and Discipline

THE morale, the efficiency, and the discipline of the Civil Service go together. Efficiency is materially affected by morale in the service, and in a similar manner, morale and efficiency have an effect on the attitude of officers towards the disciplinary code. The machinery established for regulating the working relations of the staff with the administration of the service is therefore of some importance. The general arrangements for administering the Civil Service have been discussed in Chapter 5. It is intended here to focus attention specifically on staff relations and some of the factors that contribute to the maintenance of efficiency, discipline and morale in the service.

STAFF RELATIONS

Whereas a disciplinary code has always formed a part of Colonial Regulations, General Orders, or Staff Regulations, only comparatively recently in the services we are discussing has the machinery for handling the development of discipline (as opposed to its administration) been given enough attention. It is possible that the practice by business houses of paying a great deal of attention to staff consultations, and there being negotiating machinery for handling disputes, have had their impact on the thinking of governments. All governments have consequently in recent years paid a great deal of attention to the problem of ensuring that there is adequate machinery for consultation and negotiation with the staff, and seeing that those matters which could affect the morale and efficiency, such as counselling and housing, are covered by proper and systematic arrangements. Thus in all countries now provision is made in the Civil Service and its major departments for Staff Relations Officers and Industrial Relations Officers who are responsible for administering the machinery for the regulation of all matters concerning staff consultations, negotiations and staff welfare.

The importance of an adequate consultation system cannot be over emphasized. It is the duty of every head of Department and supervisor to make arrangements for keeping in close touch with his staff so that the staff understand, in general or specifically as necessary, the programme of work of their section of the Department, and where their own work fits into the general whole. This is a steady continuing process which should go on in the day-to-day contacts between an officer and his superior. But regular informal meetings between the supervisor and his staff at which the department's programme and problems are discussed and at which the staff are given some appreciation of the contribution they are making to the efficiency of their department, cannot fail to have a tonic and healthy effect on the staff's morale and discipline. The experience of many who have taken this matter seriously and brought even the lowliest staff into the confidence of their head, has been that it is a very good investment which yields returns in local *esprit de corps* and a high sense of duty.

On a more personnel scale, it is important also that arrangements should provide for the handling of individual problems. Personnel counselling is a matter to which very little systematic attention is paid in the Civil Service administration arrangements of African States. Where the supervisor is worthy and interested, it is adequately handled. But in other situations, no attention is paid to it. In the United States and many business houses, however, personnel counselling is regarded as a most important factor affecting morale and efficiency in any organization. If an individual has a personal problem which he has been unable to resolve himself, whether that problem has arisen from his official responsibilities or outside of them, he cannot be expected to maintain a high output of work nor can he remain a healthy team-mate. There should therefore be a systematic arrangement for ensuring that such cases are promptly and efficiently dealt with. In some places, professional personnel counsellors are appointed, who are available for confidential consultation by members of the staff on their personal problems. This is, however, too sophisticated an arrangement for most African Civil Services. What is important is that all training schemes for supervisors, personnel officers and staff relations officers should sensitize these men to the personal problems of their staff so that personnel counselling becomes part of their responsibilities. The systematic introduction of this in all training arrangements should ensure that this matter is given attention by supervisors down the line to the most junior.

NEGOTIATION MACHINERY

While regular staff consultations in general terms and personnel counselling are important for the maintenance of efficiency and morale the bulk of the time of the staff relations machinery is taken up with the arrangements for handling disputes. Any large organization, such as a Civil Service, has disputes as a constant and recurring problem. Their efficient handling and, of equal or greater significance, the measures taken to prevent disputes arising are important factors in ensuring the maintenance of good relations between government and its staff which undoubtedly have a direct bearing on efficiency.

The arrangements made in regard to the establishment of negotiation machinery in the African States have derived from the British experience of the Whitley Council and the trade union systems. These arrangements started in West Africa after recommendations made by a Commission on Civil Service Salaries under the Chairmanship of Sir Walter Harragin in 1946, and in East Africa after a similar Commission under the Chairmanship of Sir Maurice Holmes in 1947/8. The system of Whitley Councils and industrial relations machinery has been adopted with various adaptations in practically all the States. Some have the full Whitley Council arrangement whilst others have a consultative body only, without the full negotiating powers. In other fields, there exists for industrial staff an elaborate industrial relations machinery while others fall in line with the general system laid down by the industrial disputes legislation of the States. It is a matter for serious consideration whether the sophisticated systems evolved in Britain in fact do suit African conditions.

The objects and functions of the Whitley Council system[1] have been described as 'determination of the general principles governing conditions of service, e.g. recruitment, hours, promotion, discipline, tenure, remuneration and superannuation' and 'proposed legislation so far as it has a bearing on the position of the civil servants in relation to their employment'

[1] Report of the Lidbury Commission, Gold Coast, 1951.

and 'means for securing to the staff a greater share in and responsibility for the determination and observance of the conditions under which their duties are carried out'. Under this system, the Civil Servants' representatives on the Council are termed the 'Staff Side' and the Government is represented by the 'Official Side'. The principle applied in the United Kingdon in negotiations is that the 'decisions of the Council shall be arrived at by agreement between the two sides, shall be reported to the Cabinet and shall thereupon become effective'. Even in Britain, this principle has been regarded by some of the authorities as going too far. In any case, agreement is only possible if the official side is authorized in that sense by Ministers. The spirit of this principle was nevertheless adopted in these former British colonies where the Whitley Council system was established, but it was modified specifically by the provision for the over-riding authority of the Governor and the approval of the legislature where this was necessary.

Similarly, in many of the former colonies, an industrial relations machinery was established by law, or by agreement, in industrial departments, to provide for negotiations at different levels from the shop floor level to the national level, and for machinery for dealing with failure to agree including conciliation, boards of inquiry and arbitration.

The question arises whether, for African States and especially at this stage of their development, the Whitley Council system originally adopted by nearly all of them is suitable. These States are all in various stages of transition and the constitutional positions are materially different from that of the United Kingdom. In the first place, the system is too cumbersome and sophisticated. All the Governments have embarked on major and accelerated development programmes, and expeditious decisions are required to be taken on matters such as the policies of recruitment, hours of work and remuneration as well as the legislation which would stabilize the conditions of service over such an important executive machinery as the Civil Service. The procedures of the negotiating machinery adopted are too slow to prevent impatience resulting in hasty action on the part of the government and sometimes also of the men.

Secondly, Ministers of the African States were, and still are, never really in the position to understand and appreciate the worth of the system. It is frequently the case therefore that decisions have been taken at Cabinet level on such matters as hours of work and legislation affecting terms of service, before the need for consultation with the staff associations and unions had been considered. African Ministers are not schooled into accepting those traditions in this matter which have applied in Britain. The sense of frustration that can result can easily be imagined when the negotiation machinery is frequently by-passed, decisions taken without negotiation or even consultation, and impatience is shown at complaints of the staff representatives.

Moreover, the official side is placed in the position in which it does not enjoy the confidence nor command the authority of the government. It does not know what is going on in the mind of the Ministers concerned and frequently has to negotiate with the other side knowing that the government has already taken a decision and is unlikely to vary it no matter what the outcome of the negotiations might be. Very often the staff side is also aware of the situation and the whole exercise therefore becomes futile, even farcical.

The machinery for negotiation for the industrial Departments, on the other hand, has worked better than the Whitley Council system. This is principally because the staff side is constituted by trade unions which are normally dynamic and aggressive and which therefore have to be taken seriously. Trade unionism has provided the path for many an African politician to high office and in the colonial era was frequently the spearhead of nationalism. Since in this era also the official side was normally all expatriate and represented the colonial Government, a fight in the industrial council was regarded as merely a phase in the general effort to prevent the 'exploitation of the masses'. In nearly all the African States, therefore, the industrial negotiation machinery has been more effective and, indeed, most of the time of the Staff and Industrial Relations Officers is devoted to paying attention to this side of their responsibilities. Here again, however, one is entitled to question the need for a rigid and sophisticated system such as has now been established. In a developing country which requires stability, industrial peace and steady wage conditions to prosecute its development plans, it seems a luxury to permit conditions which have frequently resulted in wage increases without attendant improvement in productivity, or irresponsible strikes which lose many man-hours of work to the nation.

In the face of frustrations and difficulties, some governments have dismantled the elaborate system for conducting negotiations. In a few cases they were not installed at all, and *ad hoc* arrangements were resorted to. Obviously, a balance has to be struck. On the one hand, there should be the machinery which would ensure that no major policy decisions affecting the conditions of service and employment of staff are taken without the staff being given an adequate opportunity to make representations; that the staff is consulted as often as necessary on all matters of organization and welfare which affect their working conditions and on all other matters where their views would assist in the shaping of policy; that grievances are promptly dealt with and disputes negotiated; and that ideas of the Government are tested on the staff with the possibility that they might have to be modified to meet the wishes of the staff without necessarily infringing the principle. On the other hand the machinery should not be so cumbersome as to impede the decision-making process of the Government, undermine confidence in its efficacy, and frustrate in any substantial degree the programme of the Government during the period of accelerated development.

What is needed is a method which functions in the interests of staff as well as government, and which leads to the preservation and improvement of morale and efficiency and creates the atmosphere in which healthy discipline is the order of the day. The Government would have to realize that it could not act arbitrarily and without consulting the interests of the staff without undermining morale and the health of the service as a whole. It is in its interests therefore to take the initiative for establishing the means by which there could be regular communication between its representatives and the staff. Staff which is contented and has confidence in the government is able to give effective executive backing to the government's programmes, but, better than that, is able to contribute constructive ideas which could make a material improvement to policy and development.

Such a machinery of consultation and negotiation should reach all the way down to the smallest unit. In the industrial Departments, this is well understood and shop-floor arrangements for consultation and negotiation are made so that managements and workers are in constant touch. There is a line of communication from this level upwards to the departmental and national body. This is, however, not always the case in the non-industrial Departments. Much trouble is saved where arrangements are made for consultation and negotiation of local disputes in offices between the local supervisor and the staff association representatives. There should then be provision for reference upwards of any matters not capable of local solution or having wider repercussions so that they are promptly and expeditiously settled even at the highest level where this becomes necessary. This is not a matter which should be left to look after itself. The staff relations arrangements should have a built-in scheme for superintending the working of the system from the bottom upwards to ensure that line supervisors and divisional heads are paying attention to this essential morale and efficiency promoting machinery. It is important, therefore, that this matter is included in the training programme of all supervisory staff, and that conferences or discussions of heads of divisions constantly draw attention to its importance and so assist participants in finding solutions to any problems they might have in operating the system.

TRADE UNIONS

Reference has been made to the activities of trade unions in relation to the industrial relations councils. Where trade unionism functions in industrial departments, that is, in those departments of government which operate on a similar basis to private industrial concerns, it is normally healthy and useful. In a number of the African States, however, no sharp line has been drawn between industrial undertakings in government departments and the others, and trade unions have embraced a wide section of the staff, mostly the junior staff, regardless of whether they are industrial or not. The labour legislation in nearly all the States permits the registration as trade unions of Civil Service Staff associations and unions even where these are non-industrial in membership. An obvious tidy distinction would be to exclude all industrial staff from the regular established Civil Service so that their unions are registrable as trade unions and are able to negotiate with complete freedom all terms and conditions of service for their members on the same basis as other trade unions. They should be able also to belong to the national trade union body such as the Trade Union Congress or Federation of Labour and be able to participate in its political activities without embarrassment. Established staff would then comprise only those who are non-industrial and who, since they might be required to handle policy papers, do not become involved in the kind of political action in which trade unions regard themselves free to indulge.

This tidy distinction has not, however, been possible to arrange. The reasons for this include the fact, as stated earlier, that in the African States, a trade union was often the most convenient organization for nationalist expression. It was well organized and aggressive and got results for its members. It was natural therefore for African Civil Servants who were, as again explained earlier, in the lower segments of the service during the colonial era, to organize themselves as trade unions and use the trade union movement as an intrument for fighting for the raising of their status in the service. This course was the more readily adopted because Africanization and the raising of the African's salary were hot political issues and, in some States, still are. In these circumstances, when all Africans felt they were in the same boat, horizontal distinctions between industrial and non-industrial staff were irrelevant. Moreover, in all States, industrial staff have been established for a long time and are permanent members of the Civil Service with terms of service similar to other pensionable staff. They are therefore subject to the same staff regulations as the others. In these circumstances, vertical unions embracing all classes of staff in a department were the more easily established. Another reason too has been that since the junior service was all African and the senior branches of the service were until comparatively recently non-African, the African service tended to be organized under the trade union system while the rest of the service had its Staff Association outside the trade union system. There has consequently resulted a rough and ready distinction between the senior service and junior service with the latter only being organized as trade unions.

In Ghana, the 1960 Civil Service Act automatically embodied all Civil Servants in the Trade Union Congress, the exceptions being those holding superscale appointments, legal officers, industrial relations and labour officers and a few other officers holding sensitive posts. Relations between the staff and the Government were therefore subject to regulation by the Trade Union Congress. This system led to a number of difficulties, the principal one being that office supervisors and local heads of departments were subjected to conflicts of loyalty. If they

L

were zealous in representing the interests of the Government as an employer, this frequently led to clashes with the local staff union officials who did not hesitate to remind them that they were subject also to union discipline. Furthermore, there was considerable apathy in the handling of staff relations especially as a large section of the staff were neither interested nor used to the methods of operation of the trade union system. The risk of indiscipline in the service has led to a review of the system so that under present arrangements, the trade unions embrace only the junior segment of the service. In Tanzania, the Civil Service Act excludes all categories of staff in the senior service (that is, those with basic salaries of £702 per annum and above) from membership of trade unions. Staff relations between the junior segments and the Government are regulated by the general labour disputes legislation with the Federation of Labour representing the interests of the staff. For the senior staff, a special negotiation machinery has been established.

In principle, the objective should be to so organize the system of staff relations that a clear distinction could be drawn between non-industrial established staff and industrial staff. Conditions and terms of service should then be so organized as to take into account the fact that the established non-industrial staff, comprising administrative, executive, clerical, secretarial, managerial, professional and supervisory staff, are the principal instruments for carrying out government policy and, in the higher echelons, have responsibility for policy formulation and advice. They should not therefore be part of any organization that could participate in political parties or political action. For that reason, they should be insulated from the trade union system. The employees who are truly industrial could then belong to the trade union system and participate, together with their counterparts in other industries, in political action without in any way embarrassing the Government. This is an ideal arrangement, however, which might take a long time to realize, if ever.

Whatever the system or arrangement that exists in any particular country, it is important that there should be rules for according recognition to staff associations and unions with which the Government would negotiate and consult on staff matters. These rules should provide for recognition of associations and unions being based on their acceptance as representing the majority of staff in the particular category and on the organization being non-racial, non-sectarian and non-party. If there are rival unions, the Government should make up its mind which commands the most support among the staff and recognize it.

STAFF RELATIONS OFFICERS AND INDUSTRIAL RELATIONS OFFICERS

The importance of Staff Relations Officers and Industrial Relations Officers cannot be over-rated. If they are properly trained and are effective in the discharge of their responsibilities, they can make a great contribution to the establishment of harmonious relations between staff and government and ensure that no disputes arise due to neglect of rules for management-staff relations. Their responsibility is to ensure that the machinery installed for consultation and negotiation at all levels is effectively used, that the legitimate requirements of staff are met promptly, and that grievances are dealt with quickly to avoid any build-up of frustration and resentment. Their task is difficult since it is not easy to enjoy the confidence of the staff whilst also having the trust of the head of the Department. Nevertheless, this must be aimed for if reasonable and stable relations are to be established between departmental heads and their staff.

DISCIPLINE

Even when all the conditions necessary for ensuring contentment and stability are established, there are still occasions when Civil Servants will commit offences or acts of misconduct. The private morals of officers are, generally speaking, not the business of the administration. So long as an officer does his work efficiently and conducts himself with reasonable respect as well as keeping within the regulations laid down for official conduct, he has done all that is necessary for the maintenance of his position as an official for this particular purpose. His private life outside his official duties can only be called into question if his conduct is such as to bring discredit on the service to which he belongs. Thus, an official who is convicted for a felony or serious misdemeanour and whose drinking habits and private morals are so excessive as to become notorious is not fit to remain in the service. The rule therefore that an officer's private life is his own and should have little or no bearing on his official standing should be regarded as a relative one only.

Since it cannot be assumed that all officials will, on their own, act on general principles of good official conduct, it is necessary to lay down a disciplinary code which sets out the minimum rules of conduct expected of an official. These were formerly laid down in Colonial Regulations and all disciplinary codes for the Civil Services of the African States derive from this source. General Orders and Staff Regulations have adopted from the Colonial Regulations rules of official conduct to suit them to local conditions. The disciplinary code normally lays down rules of conduct in respect of the following matters: obligation to discharge duties assigned, absence from duty or from the country, insubordination, engagement in trade, private business and private employment, financial interest in local business, pecuniary embarrassment, private agency, publications, relations with newspapers and other organs of public opinion, receipt of valuable presents, official secrets, receipt, custody and disbursement of public funds, custody of government stores, and political activity. This list is not exhaustive but includes the most important matters embodied in the disciplinary code.

It is necessary to comment on some of the items on the list at this stage. An officer is, of course, required to discharge the usual duties of his appointment but he may also be assigned to any other duties, in which case he must carry them out without question. Obviously, no insubordination can be tolerated. An officer cannot leave the country without express permission and if he vacates his post without permission for more than a specified period, usually ten days, he is automatically dismissed. A Civil Servant who is employed on a full-time basis is not permitted to engage in trade or any other form of private business. This rule has come to be so generally accepted in the African States which are subject to this treatise that it may cause surprise of many to realize that it is not a universally accepted principle of official conduct. In Liberia, for instance, it is permissible for a lawyer in certain classes of the public service to engage in private practice. In some States, it was and still is part of the terms of service for doctors that they should be entitled to private practice within prescribed limits. The rule also that officers shall not without permission acquire or possess investments or shares in a company carrying on business in the country or have any direct or indirect interest in any local business has not been applied rigidly. It is only in cases where such interests are likely to conflict with an officer's public duties, or influence him in the discharge of his duties, that it is obviously improper for him to retain them. Also, an officer is not permitted to undertake any private agency in any matter connected with his public duties. This is obviously a common-sense and necessary provision.

An officer who is in serious financial embarrassment is assumed to have his efficiency impaired and he renders himself liable to disciplinary proceedings. This is a matter so much within the experience of all who have supervision over staff that it needs no comment. An officer who is heavily in debt may even not be trusted with public funds as this may place him under intolerable temptation. There are also very rigid rules and procedures laid down for the custody and management of government funds and stores. This is the area in which there are the most causes for imposing disciplinary measures since the possibilities for dishonesty are great. Some of the rules may appear irksome, but where officials are dealing with public funds or property they cannot be allowed to do what they like even when their personal integrity is not in question. In formulating rules of management, therefore, the conduct of the average person is what must be borne in mind. There is, in fact, very searching and close supervision exercised in this area through the investigations of the Audit service and Boards of Survey. This ensures not only that frauds and other forms of dishonesty are checked, but also that there is efficient management of public funds and property.

An officer's relations with organs of public opinion are also closely defined. Obviously, he should not be allowed to publish anything of a political nature or anything which comments on public policy even if it is administrative policy. It is improper for him to be associated in any capacity with the publication and management of a newspaper or similar periodical nor should he allow himself to be interviewed on questions of public policy. There is no objection, however, to an officer publishing anything, including a book, on subjects of general interest. Any information which comes into the possession of an officer in the course of discharging his official duties, or which he knows in any case to be confidential, must not be disclosed either to the press or to any other person who is not officially entitled to have that information. The Government must have complete confidence in its officers so that its secrets and other matters of a confidential nature will be absolutely respected. This is where the principle that the Civil Servant is the custodian of his government's reputation is particularly true. The sanctity of official secrets is so important that every officer who is likely to have access to them has to sign a special undertaking to respect them which is prescribed by law. Failure to comply with the undertaking leads to prosecution. An officer is liable to lend himself to influence in the discharge of his duties if he accepts valuable presents from members of the public. This is therefore expressly forbidden not only for the officer but also for members of his family. This rule is only relaxed, with permission, when an officer is about to retire from the public service.

One of the most important provisions in the disciplinary code is participation in politics. The Civil Service can be regarded as politically impartial by the public only if its members are not publicly or actively engaged in politics. In some States, it is forbidden for a Civil Servant to belong to a political party or any association of a political nature. This was the case in East Africa until 1964 when Tanzania decided to permit Civil Servants to join TANU. In other places, however, such as in Nigeria and Ghana, an officer is not permitted to hold office in a political party or association and to take an active part in such a party or association. He may, however, belong to a political party so long as this is not allowed to influence or be apparent in the discharge of his official responsibilities. This is a difficult matter to regulate. Obviously, if an officer is known to be a member of a party opposed to the ruling party, it is not going to be easy for him to function under a Minister. But it is equally improper for an officer to make it quite open that he belongs to the ruling party. He may be tempted to do so to demonstrate his zeal for the government of the day, and this may be of apparent advantage to his career. In many cases, this is temporary only and, in fact, may adversely affect his prospects when he least expects it. In any case, however, the spirit of disharmony and distrust that is generated around him is not conducive to healthy co-operation with his colleagues, nor does it create the right spirit for dealing with members of the public who would expect him to be biased in their favour or against them according to their political affiliations. Obviously, too, a Civil Servant should not be a candidate for election to parliament or political office. The normal rule is that he must resign before he can stand for election.

In the previous chapter it has been stated that generally the administration of this disciplinary code, when it is infringed, is handled by the Public Service Commission or by other officers by delegation under regulations laid down by the Commission. The areas of responsibility, if any, of the head of Government and Ministers have also been discussed. The application of this code of conduct does not, however, absolve Civil Servants from observing the laws of the land. In fact the code regarding such matters as dishonesty and fraud are those embodied in the Criminal Code and any offences in this regard are liable to be prosecuted in the state courts. The disciplinary procedure for the Civil Service in fact provides that, where criminal prosecution intervenes, any disciplinary proceedings being conducted officially against an officer should be suspended. If conviction is secured, then consideration has to be given to what further disciplinary action is appropriate. Normally, except in minor offences like certain classes of traffic offences, conviction for felony or misdemeanour results in dismissal from the service and forfeiture of any right of pensionable appointment in the future unless a formal pardon is secured.

Although action has to be taken against an officer who has offended against the disciplinary code, it is obviously in the interests of the public service that its affairs should be so organized as to minimize the incidence of breaches of code. This does not mean relaxing the code, although there is the need to keep it under review to ensure that its provisions are realistic in terms of new situations that may develop. It does mean, however, that every effort should be made to create a healthy atmosphere in the service as a whole and in the offices of government departments; that special care should be taken to raise and maintain staff morale at a high level, and that attention is paid to the promotion of healthy staff and human relations in all departments. Any instrument or machinery that can contribute to this end should be exploited, such as the inclusion of instruction in disciplinary matters in training schemes, the training of supervisors, the adoption of personnel counselling techniques, machinery for regular consultation with staff or their representatives, and the infusion of a sense of high purpose in all the staff by example and by precept. Indiscipline may not be entirely eliminated but it flourishes less readily in a healthy atmosphere.

CONFIDENTIAL REPORTS

One of the essentials of a sound Civil Service administration and the promotion of service efficiency is the establishment of a complete and accurate record of the staff, including records of service and confidential reports. It is the aspect dealing with confidential reports which will be discussed here, although the maintenance of records of other service particulars of officers is of some importance. Regular reporting covering the full period of service, from the time of first appointment to the end of an officer's career, provides an efficient machinery for administering policies on promotions and discipline. The fact that an officer knows that there will be a confidential report on his work and conduct each year should stimulate him to maintain a high standard and therefore help in maintaining efficiency. It also helps in the more effective and healthy approach to promotion programmes since a complete set of reports on officers should make it less difficult to rate officers on the basis of merit. The absence of such regular reports implies that *ad hoc* assessments are made by the recommending officers when promotions come along, and this is likely to breed discontent and inefficiency and suspicion among officers that promotions have not been based on merit. This is most important since, unless promotions policies are based entirely on the need to maintain and improve efficiency which implies that the best fitted for a job or the most meritorious should be promoted to it, inefficiency would soon become an endemic state for the department or service. Merit cannot be recognized easily, however, unless it is based on a proper assessment of an officer's work and conduct recorded over a reasonable period. For one thing, it implies that the system does not easily fall into the trap of promoting an able officer merely because he happens to be immediately within sight of higher authority whereas there might be an abler officer who is doing a far better job out of sight.

Confidential reporting, to be any good as a reliable guide to the relative merits of individuals, has to be as objective as possible. This is difficult to achieve since standards of human judgement vary so widely between individuals. Much thought has been given to the designing of report forms so as to eliminate human error as far as possible. For the bulk of Civil Servants, it has been possible to classify the factors under which character, personality and ability can be judged reasonably objectively under such headings as reliability, output, judgement, initiative, alertness, zeal, ability to organize, address and tact, and grading for promotion with reports under each heading under the classifications: outstanding, very good, satisfactory, indifferent, poor or no opportunity for assessment. Where such classifications and heading are used, care is taken to give a full explanation in guiding notes on the purpose and significance of the terms used. This should form the basis of training sessions for reporting officers to make assessments as uniform as is humanly posible.

For more senior officers whose work cannot be assessed by the more simple procedure outlined above, it is normal to prepare reports in a comprehensive and fully informative note. This obviously lends itself to wide variations in reporting standards which can be minimized only to some extent by 'training' discussions and conferences. It is important therefore that in this, as well as also in the cases of the more junior officers, there should be arrangements for a reviewing panel of officers, senior to the reporting officers, to review the reports on all officers in a particular division or department with a view to attempting to moderate the differing standards of reporting officers so as to make it possible to compare the merits of individuals within the same field of promotion. In a small unit the reviewing exercise need involve only one very senior officer. Even with such reviewing arrangements it is found necessary, in cases where large numbers of officers are eligible for promotion, to resort to written examinations or interviews for the selection of the most meritorious for promotion. In that event, the report records at least enable the recommending authorities to eliminate from consideration those whose records are unsatisfactory.

It has been suggested in some quarters that confidential reporting is not a very satisfactory way of dealing with this important matter. The danger of subjective assessment is always present and, in any case, except where an officer is adversely reported upon, he does not know what his superior officer thinks of his work and conduct. In certain organizations, especially in America, an employee is entitled to see his annual report and, if he is dissatisfied, he is permitted to make representations. This system suffers, however, from the danger of the normal human failing of unwillingness to present an unfavourable but fair judgement on the work or character of an individual which is likely to be challenged and be the subject of interminable arguments and appeals. Many reporting officers would be inclined to play for safety and be less than frank. On the whole, therefore, and subject to the proviso that an officer is entitled to be told when his work is regarded as unsatisfactory, the confidential reporting system is the better from the point of view of efficiency.

ORGANIZATION AND METHODS

Efficiency depends, among other things, on the organization of the departmental machinery and procedures as well as on the effort of the individuals to maintain high levels of output and discipline. Some of the factors bearing on efficiency have been discussed. In an earlier chapter the contribution of training and staff development and an effective system of supervision, to the raising of standards of efficiency has also been mentioned. There are a number of other factors such as hours of work and manuals of procedure which also have an effect on efficiency. The importance of an Organization and Methods programme is now fully recognized as having a major role in creating the conditions for efficiency and economy of operations in departments and in the government machine as a whole.

Organization and Methods is a technique concerned with the definition of the objectives of government, or in a limited field, of the assignment allotted to a department, in clear terms which are readily understood, and devising the machinery and procedures designed to carry through these objectives with efficiency, avoiding waste, duplications, gaps, overlapping responsibilities and delays. Organization and Methods is a tool of management. It is not a luxury. It is as vital to the government or any organization as lubricating oil is to an engine. Organization and Methods is a 'staff' function and has therefore no administrative and operational responsibilities except, of course, administering its own set-up, but is concerned principally with investigating a situation, preparing a scheme for improvement and increased efficiency, discussing it with the responsible head of Department and presenting the final scheme to him. Once accepted, the scheme is left to be implemented by the department. If Organization and Methods becomes executive, its ability to 'sell' its programme would be impaired since departments would cease to regard it as a consultant system willing and prepared to co-operate in bringing about efficiency and economy but rather as an executive body sent from above to detect and find faults and push people around.

Generally speaking an Organization and Methods team would have as their objective the improvement of the organization and administration in a department. It would make proposals for the best administrative organization for handling the programme of the department, co-ordination of planning, supplies, the work methods, preparation of procedure manuals, editing, forms design, office equipment and methods, and the use of modern computer aids for producing economy in the use of resources, and the training effort required for installing any improved methods and procedures agreed upon. This is a continuous process since developments in administrative and other techniques are accelerating and the Government itself is taking decisions on policy all the time, all of which require the reformation of the machinery and organization to match these developments and changes. The Organization and Methods programme should therefore be a permanent feature of all government administrations. Properly managed, it would introduce economies which should more than justify its existence in financial and personnel savings alone.

Needless to say, the Organization and Methods staff should be specialists trained to be efficient in the application of their techniques. They should also be experienced officers not only in these techniques but as operational officers as well. Obviously, they cannot devise realistic schemes for organization and efficient methods of operation unless they themselves have proved themselves to be good operational officers. A man who has been responsible for running an office efficiently would command confidence in those he advises on schemes for improving their own. Because the Organization and Methods Division is concerned mainly with matters of efficiency and economy, it is the usual policy to attach it to the Treasury or Ministry of Finance. There is, however, the need to have close co-operation between the Organization and Methods staff and the staff in the Establishments Division concerned with staff inspection and grading and recruitment and training. Unless the work of these two units is closely co-ordinated, there is the danger of overlapping responsibilities introducing causes for inefficiency. Where it is possible, therefore, to bring both under the same direction it is an obvious advantage to do so. This is in fact the position in the United Kingdom Civil Service.

Although Organization and Methods techniques are now accepted as a tool of efficiency and economy, some of the governments have been slow in establishing programmes for them. There is still a certain amount of resistance from old-established staff who do not feel able to give the programme high priority among so many other competing claims for the use of resources. And yet, the role it can play in advising on all the factors of efficiency is incalculable. Failure to take advantage of this is being penny wise and pound foolish. On the other hand, bold action in installing an Organization and Methods Unit, which is well staffed with experienced officers and which is given high level backing, is bound to result in the division justifying its existence and more.

CONCLUSIONS

The subjects dealt with in this chapter – Staff Relations, the Disciplinary Code, Confidential Reports, and Organization and Methods – may appear at first sight not to have very much in common. All of them, however, are tools for the creation of efficiency of operation in the Civil Service machinery and for the maintenance of a healthy spirit and morale which are necessary for the normal growth of an efficient approach to responsibilities by Civil Servants. They are not the only tools of efficiency and morale. Others such as the administration of the Civil Service, staff development and training and proper supervision all down the line have been described in earlier chapters. Civil Servants would also work better if they had confidence in the political direction of the affairs of the State and if their loyalties to their Ministers and the Government of the day were not brought under any unhealthy strain. There are obviously a number of other contributory factors in the bid for improved efficiency and morale, but proper attention to the factors discussed in this and previous chapters will go a long way towards achieving these objectives.

CHAPTER 10

Structure and Functions of Ministries and Departments

STRUCTURE UNDER THE COLONIAL ERA

THE structure of the government machinery during the colonial period, that is, prior to self-government constitutions, was virtually the same in all the colonies. There was, in each case, the Governor at the head of the structure. He was the direct representative of the Crown as well as of the United Kingdom Secretary of State for the Colonies. His commission placed in his hands complete and ultimate responsibility for the administration of the territory, and the whole machinery erected for this purpose was subordinate to him and, in effect, advisory to him. Subject therefore to general or specific instructions which he had received from the Secretary of State through the United Kingdom Colonial Office, he had complete authority, fettered only by such statutory institutions as the Executive Council, the Judiciary and the Legislative Council. The Executive Council initially was composed of local high officers of state, usually the Chief or Colonial Secretary, the Attorney General, the Financial Secretary, the Director of Medical Services and one or two others. Later, unofficial appointments were made to bring local views on to the Council. Constitutionally, however, the Executive Council was advisory to the Governor, although a wise Governor would normally accept advice given after due consideration. The Executive Council, over which the Governor presided, had all matters of high policy relating to executive acts of the Government referred to it. It also considered draft legislation to be sponsored by the Government and even advised the Governor in the exercise of his prerogative of mercy in judicial cases.

In accordance with the normal constitutional position in Britain, however, the Governor had no power of intervening over the Judiciary and over the administration of justice, although at the lower levels where field administrative officers were also Magistrates, it was often questioned whether the opportunity for interference was not often used in order to prosecute the policy of the administration. It can be said, however, that the principle that there should be no intervention by the administration in judicial matters was always officially observed. The Legislative Council was, however, in a different position. Where it existed, it started by having an official majority and such unofficial members as existed were nominated by the Governor. Later, the unofficial members were made broadly representative of the people through the grant of the right to elect members by municipalities and councils of traditional rulers. It was not until the post-World War II period that unofficial majorities elected through a more liberal franchise were possible. Thereafter, as is now well known, there was rapid constitutional development starting from West Africa and spreading to the East and more recently to Central Africa. For the purpose of this exercise, it is the administration under the Governor that is of interest. It is interesting to reflect here, however, that until after 1946, democracy as practised in the United Kingdom did not exist in any of her colonies. The people were not given the opportunity in any of the colonial constitutional arrangements to play an effective democratic part in government. When, therefore, after independence, African governments are expected to be modelled on the Westminster pattern, it is legitimate to ask whether Britain had in fact used her opportunities wisely, during the period she was responsible for administering her overseas territories, to bring the people up in democratic ways. What is really the difference between the authoritarian regimes of colonial Governors and the authoritarian governments of some of the African States? It can be argued therefore that British Colonial policy has a lot to answer for over the political developments in her former overseas territories.

The administration under the Governor had at the apex of its structure the Chief Secretary, also known as the Colonial Secretary in many of the territories. The Chief Secretary was at the head of the Secretariat which was composed of a relatively small band of administrative officers who were responsible under the Chief Secretary for the formulation of administrative policy and advice on all other major matters of policy. The Attorney General was physically part of the Secretariat but his staff consisted of legal officers and he enjoyed a large measure of autonomy although subordinate to the Chief Secretary in all matters of administration. The Financial Secretary was, however, virtually part of the Chief Secretary's staff and his advice to the Governor was always given through the Chief Secretary. The Secretariat was a key institution in all the colonial administrations. It was effectively the standing machinery for translating the Governor's policies into action, for co-ordinating the functions of all the Departments of Government, and for maintaining the effectiveness of the administrative grid all over the territory. The Secretariat was the super-Ministry for all Departments of Government which were subordinate to it. It conveyed decisions on behalf of the Governor, and the introduction sentence in all official formal letters from the Secretariat began with 'I am directed by the Governor . . .', a phrase which became very familiar to all.

As stated earlier, the Secretariat was usually a relatively small body of senior officers drawn from the Administrative Service. In 1949, for instance, the Secretariat in Accra had no more than eighteen administrative officers. In the capital, there were also the headquarters offices of the Departments of Government such as the Medical, Public Works, Police, Education, Survey, Agriculture, Forestry, Lands and Veterinary Departments. Each Department maintained a headquarters staff of specialists and supporting executive/clerical staff for the administration of the affairs of the Department and for formulating policies for inclusion in the general policy programme of the Governor. The head of Department enjoyed considerable autonomy in the functioning and administration of his Department, subject always to the over-riding authority of the Governor as exercised through the Secretariat. Such intervention as was exercised by the Secretariat was, however, usually much resented by heads of Departments particularly as decisions were conveyed to them by comparatively junior Secretariat officers. But the solidarity of the Secretariat and the Governor was always such that heads of Departments were never able to carry any complaints they had too far. This feeling of resentment against Secretariat Administrative Officers was to have its important impact on the structure of Ministry staff in later years.

The main administrative framework of the whole country was based on the Regional Administrations. The country was divided into a number of regions at the head of each of which was a Lieutenant-Governor or Chief Commissioner. Within each region were provinces under Residents or Provincial Commissioners, and then each district had District Commissioners or Officers in charge. These officers were all members of the Colonial Administrative Service and they formed a chain of command starting from the districts at the base and moving up through provinces and regions to the capital. Lieutenant-Governors and Chief Commissioners were directly responsible to the Governor for the political administration of their regions, for the maintenance of law and order, for relations with natural rulers where these existed, for the administration of local authorities including native authorities and native courts, and for the co-ordination of all departmental activities within their regions. Administratively, however, the regional administrations were subordinate to the Secretariat. The most important level of the hierarchy was the District Commissioner or Officer and his assistants. They were in direct touch with the people and their natural rulers. They exercised directly the main responsibilities of the political administration given in outline above. In a period of very little development money, they did the best they could to mobilize local resources for social development projects, such as schools and health facilities, and even for such economic development projects as roads and agricultural improvement. They and such departmental officers as had responsibilities for their departmental activities in their districts, constituted the district teams concerned with promoting in association with the local authorities, social and economic well-being and progress for the people of the areas. The District Commissioner also had responsibility for collecting political intelligence and passing it on to headquarters. He kept the people, through their chiefs or leaders, informed of policies and political development which the government wished them to know. He also exercised magisterial responsibilities in the absence of resident magistrates.

The political administrative structure was a most important instrument for governing the country and the one through which the Governor effectively exercised control. It maintained a channel of communication, upwards and downwards, from the Governor to the people and achieved the co-ordination of all the field activities of all departments through an administration whose members were in the same service as the Governor. The cohesion and solidarity of the political administrative service were really impressive and these gave them in most colonial territories a prestige among the people which was more effective in exercising authority than any statutory powers they had – which were few. Normally the officers in this service were few in number, especially in countries in which the policy was that of indirect rule. It is true to say that the officers of the political administration were treated as an *élite* corps of the colonial service. Even at the district level the authority they exercised was enormous. Local politicians called them 'bush governors' in resentment of this authority, and this was echoed in the attitude sometimes displayed by departmental officers. Its role as the instrument of colonial rule was, one supposes, the reason why there was great reluctance to admit Africans into its ranks. Indeed, it was argued that it constituted the framework of colonial rule which would have to be dismantled after independence and there was no purpose therefore in appointing Africans to it since they should not be identified with the colonial and imperialist regime. It was not until 1942 that the first Africans were admitted into this service, but the really effective penetration did not take place until long after the war.

The service also was the first immediate target of attack by nationalist parties when they emerged, with the object of undermining the control of the colonial power at the local level. Many a national figure in politics in many States had started their political careers pitting themselves against the Provincial and District Commissioners. There was one lesson, however, which impressed itself on the politicians and that was the effectiveness of this framework of control. After independence, therefore, the first policy reaction was either to abolish the field administrative service or, at any rate, so to curb its powers as to reduce its significance. In Ghana and Tanzania, the Governments took a leaf from the colonial administration's book and established a hierarchy of Regional Commissioners and District (Area) Commissioners which provided the control and channel of communication with the people which was the role of the colonial administration structure. The new Regional and other Commissioners were political appointees, and in fact the Regional Commissioners were Ministers or had ministerial status. In parts of Nigeria and Sierra Leone, the regional heads also had ministerial status and were political appointees.

M

STRUCTURE UNDER INDEPENDENCE

The incidence of self-government and independence had its greatest impact on the Secretariat structure. The Governor ceased to have executive authority under the self-government constitutions and was replaced after independence by a completely new arrangement. The executive authority passed on to a Prime Minister and his Cabinet, and later – in a number of states – to a President assisted by a Cabinet. In effect, the Secretariat became transformed into a number of Ministries each with a Minister at the head. The Departments were then grouped under Ministries according to the responsibilities they discharged. Initially, this was all that happened on the ground to reflect the very fundamental constitutional changes that had taken place.

The grafting of a Ministerial system – in place of the old Secretariat – over an administrative structure that had proved satisfactory under the colonial regime was not the best way of re-organizing the structure to meet the demands of a new and complex situation. The Departments were inclined to carry on as before and to regard the Ministry as merely replacing the former Secretariat. Although there could not be physical integration between Ministries and departments for practical reasons of the short term, there should have been an attempt to bring about organizational changes to make the departments feel themselves to be integral parts of their Ministries, able to respond effectively to the changed constitutional circumstances and the new policies. Instead of this, however, for some time at any rate, one got the impression that the departments were carrying on as before under the momentum of the old regime, and even took pride in enjoying a measure of insulation from politics. This situation obviously could not last since Ministers would sooner or later wish to have effective control over all matters that came within their portfolios. When the realization came, the adjustment brought about was not as logical as it might have been if there had been proper planning for the future.

The new system has followed broadly the United Kingdom pattern. There is, in most cases, the system of Prime Minister supported by a Cabinet. All Ministers in the Cabinet are, by the Constitution, collectively responsible to Parliament and the people for the policies of the Government. Each Minister is, however, assigned certain subjects by the Prime Minister to constitute his portfolio, and he is responsible for the proper management of these subjects to the Prime Minister and his colleagues, but he is also answerable specifically to Parliament for the administration of these subjects. This is not the place to discuss the constitutional relationships between Ministers, the Cabinet and Parliament, nor the changes in this United Kingdom system brought about by the creation of the position of President (in several states) who is also head of Government with wide powers vested in him under the Constitution. It is sufficient to say only that the conventions for these relationships are bound to be different from those established in the United Kingdom, and indeed as between the African States also, since the peoples and their traditions are different.

The position in each State, however, is that each Minister has responsibility for a group of subjects that come within his portfolio. He is the political head of his Ministry and he is normally assisted in his political and parliamentary functions by a Deputy Minister or Parliamentary Secretary. The Administrative head of the Ministry is, however, the Permanent Secretary (also called Principal Secretary). The Permanent Secretary is responsible for advising the Minister on policy matters, for ensuring that the Minister's policies are translated into administrative action, and for administering the services of the Ministry and the Departments under the Ministry on behalf of the Minister. The Permanent Secretary is normally also the Accounting Officer for the Votes of the Ministry within the country's budget, and is thus answerable to the Public Accounts Committee of Parliament for ensuring that expenditure under the Votes is incurred in accordance with standing instructions and with the Appropriations Act.

The staff of each Ministry consists of the Permanent Secretary and a team of Deputy Permanent Secretaries, other senior and junior administrative officers – with ranks of Under Secretary, Principal Assistant Secretary, Senior Assistant Secretary and Assistant Secretary according to the convention adopted in each State. There are also supporting executive, clerical, secretarial and subordinate staff. The numbers of each rank of staff depends on the volume and level of responsibilities that fall to the Ministry. For instance, it is unusual to have more than one officer of Deputy Permanent Secretary rank, and a small Ministry may not have even an officer of this rank. It is normal to organize each Ministry into functional divisions and sections to handle subjects covering the Departments under the Ministry as well as for such subjects as finance and personnel within the Ministry. The form of this organization and the assignment of responsibilities between divisions and sections would naturally depend very much on the numbers of Departments and the range of subjects assigned to the Ministry. The organization should, however, be such as to handle all the subjects reasonably efficiently, to respond to the requirements of the Departments and, where necessary, to the needs of the public, and to provide an efficient machinery for the degree of co-operation with other Ministries which is frequently necessary. The object of this is to provide for the Minister, through his Permanent Secretary, an effective administration of the subjects assigned to him and the means by which his policies can be made effective.

As stated earlier, the Ministry system was grafted on to the previous structure and, in particular, Departments were not affected to any significant extent. Integration of the Departments within the Ministries was not therefore an initial feature in the early days of independence. Complete physical integration may not be a practicable proposition in all cases but, on the other hand, to continue to have complete autonomy of Departments outside their Ministries is not the most effective way of running the services of the Ministries. There is therefore in all the States a move steadily to integrate Departments in Ministries physically if possible, but at any rate organizational integration is usually possible. Under a policy of integration, the Departments cease to be autonomous and instead become Divisions of the Ministry. The head of Department becomes head of Division and is responsible within the Ministry for the administration of the services of the Division.

Integration makes it possible for the specialized Divisions to be more closely identified with the administration of the Ministry and reduces considerably, if not avoiding completely, the friction that arises when separate autonomous Departments work to a headquarters Ministry. Professional, Technical and Service heads of Divisions become part of the policy formulation process and their expert and policy advice is given in the normal course in close association with all those other officers whose contributions are necessary for a co-ordinated policy to be formulated. In this way, the resentment caused by the advice of heads of Departments being screened and modified by administrative officers in the Ministry before reaching the Minister is very largely eliminated. The process of consultations within the Ministry should ensure that the advice given by each officer, whether head of Division or Administrative Officer, is regarded as a contribution towards the making of an integrated policy in a form ready for the consideration of the Minister. What is important also is that the heads of Divisions are available in the Ministry, organizationally or in person, to give direct advice to the Minister. Direct access to the Minister becomes a matter of routine rather than of formality, and no resentment need be caused because the head of a Division sees the Minister without the permission or knowledge of the Permanent Secretary, or alternatively because the Permanent Secretary insists on knowing what the head of Department wishes to discuss with the Minister before he is allowed to do so. Where senior officers are operating as a team in a Ministry and, if the spirit of the Ministry is as healthy as it should be, informality in relations between the Minister and his senior staff should not undermine discipline; rather it should create a sense of *esprit de corps* which is a vital ingredient of discipline. The Minister, in this spirit receives advice on policy matters which had been digested within all professional, technical, political, financial and administrative considerations and which may even expose conflicts of opinion on an objective and honest basis. He should then be able to take his decisions on the basis of the best advice available to him.

There is one other advantage of integration and that is that it should be possible to effect economies on administrative overheads. This is an Organization and Methods exercise and it is essential that the whole programme and process of integration should be organized so that this economy is achieved. Experience in some countries in this matter has often been that integration has increased administrative cost rather than reduced it. This obviously should be avoided. Such services as establishments and personnel, and finance and accounting can be made central services. Integration should therefore not take place without a well-considered plan being prepared for it based upon the advice of organizational experts. It is important to avoid the disillusionment that might result if ill-considered intregration arrangements bring about confusion instead of proper coordination and efficiency.

Relations between the Permanent Secretary and heads of Divisions (or heads of Departments) are most important. This subject has been the cause of much trouble in all the African States in the period immediately following independence when the administration of Ministries is still in the process of settling down. Professional and Technical heads feel that nothing should stand between them and the Minister. They claim that their advice to the Minister is based on their professional and specialized knowledge and experience which no administrator is competent to comment on or criticize. For this reason, there is frequently pressure to carry the integration of the Ministries and Departments to the extent of eliminating the Administrative Officer from the position of Permanent Secretary and, in fact, combining the posts of Permanent Secretary and head of Department in one office. Thus, the Permanent Secretary to the Ministry of Education would at the same time be the Chief Education Officer. In Africa, this problem is aggravated by the revival of old resentments. The Administrative Officer is normally drawn from the old Colonial Administration whose status in the field as Provincial and District Commissioner very often offended heads of Departments. Also, the creation of a number of Ministries provided phenomenal promotion opportunities which usually went to comparatively junior administrative officers, although there were officers in the professional, technical and service Departments with greater seniority and equal or better competence who should also have been considered for these senior Ministry posts.

Fundamentally, however, this is an old quarrel which has been ventilated quite often in the United Kingdom where also the principal professional officers have claimed the right to 'be in direct line of responsibility to the Minister and there should not be any interpolation of another officer purporting to give advice when in fact he can become only a transmitter of the advice of others'. The real complaint, however, is that, by denying him direct responsibility to the Minister for the affairs of his department, his status has been lowered and his profession is not valued in relation to the Administrative Service. The permanent head of a Ministry, however, is in the position of being general manager of the Ministry, with a duty to run the Ministry, to canalize all its activities, and to have prepared for his Minister at any time recommendations on policy matters from whatever source they may originate. The final decision is, of course, the Minister's. The feeling of resentment of professional heads of Departments can be met if they are always given direct access to the Minister when either they or the Permanent Secretaries wish it and if in fact the high responsibilities of the professional class are recognized in giving them parity of treatment in salary status with the administrative class. This is the case in East and Central Africa where, in addition to having the same salary structure, heads of major Departments are rated at the same salary status as Permanent Secretaries. In West Africa, this only applies to a few heads of Departments such as the Chief Medical Officer and Chief Engineer of the Public Works, who in fact have higher salaries.

But the real solution to the problem is to open the door to professional and specialist staff to the highest administrative position of Permanent Secretary. Administrative officers make the mistake of regarding themselves as the only persons qualified, by training and experience, to become heads of Ministries. There is not one sole road to administrative competence, and in Africa, where there is a general shortage of talent, all branches of the service should be surveyed when material for high level administrative positions is being sought. The field of selection for the post of Permanent Secretary should cover the senior ranks of the administrative service as well as the ranks of heads of Departments. The test is that the persons selected should be capable of acting as general managers of their Ministries and be able to formulate policies and advice to the Minister against the background of political, financial and administrative considerations, and other factors that have a bearing on national policy. If they meet this test and if they also are versatile enough to be posted, when the exigencies of the service demand, to other Ministries where their specialist knowledge may not be directly relevant, the professional and specialist staff should be as good as any for heading Ministries. It should never be conceded, however, that merely because an officer is an excellent head of his professional or specialist department, he qualifies also to be a good head of Ministry. This is a fallacy which must be combated whenever it is seriously presented.

If the organizational structure for a Ministry which is integrated with its departments is arranged on a systematic basis, professional and specialist heads would be able to concern themselves mainly with the policy and routine matters which relate to their special knowledge and experience, leaving purely administrative matters, establishments and personnel and finance operations to heads of other divisions of the Ministry experienced in these fields. As an example, a Ministry of Agriculture and Natural Resources might have the following Divisions operating under the Minister and his Permanent Secretary: Agricultural Extension, Forestry; Veterinary; Research; Game; Fisheries; Development; Administration including Personnel Management and Accounts; and Training. The head of each of these Divisions would be responsible for initiating policies on the responsibilities falling within the Division as well as run its services He would normally function under the co-ordinating authority of the Permanent Secretary, but, where necessary, would have direct access to the Minister. The organizational structure is illustrated in tabular form in Appendix III.

DISTRIBUTION OF PORTFOLIOS

The President or Prime Minister is responsible not only for assigning to Ministers particular Portfolios but also for determining what the subjects in each Portfolio should be. The President or Prime Minister usually holds himself responsible for certain subjects himself as, for instance, Foreign Affairs, the Civil Service, and Defence. This is a matter entirely in his discretion. The subjects assigned to each Portfolio do not necessarily follow any particular pattern, but there are obvious advantages in grouping them together in related subjects. The usual groupings would be something like this:

(a) *Political*
   Foreign or External Affairs
   Justice and Legal Affairs
(b) *Security*
   Defence
   Interior or Home Affairs
(c) *Economic and Financial*
   Finance
   Economic Planning
   Agriculture and Natural Resources
   Commerce, Industry and International Trade
   Communications, Power, Works and Transport
   Water Development
   Co-operative Development

Science and Research
(d) *Social Services*
   Education
   Health
   *Community Development and Welfare
   *Local Government
   *Labour Relations
   Culture and Youth
      * Local Government sometimes goes with Home
        Affairs, and Labour Relations overlaps Economic
        Affairs as also Community Development.
(e) *Miscellaneous*
   Cabinet Business
   Civil Service including Establishments, Personnel and
      Training
   Public Relations and Information

The arrangements of these subjects within Portfolios is a matter for local consideration. It is sometimes difficult to understand why in some countries certain subjects are linked together in certain Portfolios or why there are so many Ministers. A lot depends on the number of interests the Prime Minister has to reconcile in constituting his Cabinet and the personalities involved.

As far as the Civil Service is concerned, its role is to fit into whatever pattern is decided on by the President or Prime Minister and to endeavour to give the best service it can. Obviously, however, the service is used at its optimum efficiency if its different branches are grouped together in Portfolios which make for easier co-ordination and co-operation between them. It is important therefore that those who are suitably placed for advising the head of Government, such as the Secretaries to the Cabinet or the Permanent Secretaries in the President's or Prime Minister's Offices, should address themselves to this problem and provide the Presidents or Prime Ministers with the facts and information on which they would base their decisions. It is in the interests of all – as much for the Civil Servants as for the general public – that the arrangements of the Portfolios make sense and contribute to the efficient management of the Government's business.

REFORM OF THE MACHINERY OF GOVERNMENT

The concluding paragraphs of Chapter 4 have discussed policies for the reform of the structure of the Civil Service and it is stated that no programme of structural reform can be complete unless considered in relation to reforms in the machinery of governments as a whole. The structure of Ministries and Departments which has been described so far in this Chapter has, in a number of African states, had the unhealthy effect of over-centralization accompanied by unrealistic planning; has provided fertile ground for abuses which spring from excessive power; has resulted in serious reduction of popular participation in government; and has concentrated the major part of government high level personnel in headquarters Ministries and Departments.

In many states, therefore, the need for taking a hard look at the machinery of government as a whole is urgent, and reforms designed to make the machinery more responsive to the priority tasks of government should be introduced as soon as possible. The policy should be to provide a machinery that efficiently carries out the present priority objective of providing accelerated economic and social development and that can provide an effective communication channel between the government and the governed. Over-centralization has resulted in a congestion along the communication lines and this has bred inefficiency in government operations. The system has not only retarded the progress of agrarian reform but has positively encouraged concentration of development in the cities and other urban centres.

It is now accepted in most African states that the type of development activity, at the present stage of their development, that would yield the quickest returns in terms of economic growth is one which provides for development at the grass roots levels, namely development of the rural sector of the economy. If this objective is to be achieved, then there must be a tilt in the balance of government presence in favour of the rural sector. This implies that the Government should be taken to the people in the rural areas, and government activity should be greatly increased at regional, provincial and district levels and within local government. There should be considerable delegation of authority and responsibility downwards from the central Ministries to the provinces and districts so that the people may be made to feel a real sense of participation in decisions on priorities and programmes affecting their own well-being.

Obviously, no blue-print can be formulated which would apply to all African states since conditions differ from one country to another. In Tanzania it is now government policy to give priority to economic and social growth at the level of the rural sector so that the 80–90% of the population of the country should benefit from the results of modern progress in science and technology. The machinery of government is consequently being re-examined so as to provide that it is able to deal with, and make an impact on, agrarian reform problems.

In Ghana, a Commission on Public Services Structure and Salaries which reported in late 1967, has proposed the strengthening of the machinery of government at the district and regional levels which would give them considerable autonomy in all those matters affecting the provision of services and the economic and social development of these areas. The Ministries would concentrate on providing highly professional agency services 'concerned with determining objectives, priorities and strategies for the nation as a whole and for assessing, marshalling and allocating resources. (They should be divorced as far as possible from responsibilities for the management of programmes.)' The Ministries would have a more compact staff and the surplus would be devolved on the regional and district authorities. The district authorities would be the effective local government units although smaller local councils would still deal with 'parish' type responsibilities. These district authorities would combine traditional local government functions and those functions of the central government which apply in the districts, such as roads and buildings, health (not large hospitals) land administration, social services and community development, agricultural extension services, primary and middle schools and general amenities. The regional authorities would handle other functions such as planning and co-ordination – and services which can more effectively be performed at the regional level, as for instance, larger hospitals, secondary schools and teacher training colleges. Where functions could not conveniently be decentralized to regions and districts, they would be devolved on functional organizations at the national level which would also be given real autonomy in management and control. In cases like the Police, the Armed Forces. Revenue

Departments, etc., the Ministries would continue their operation as at present.

In other states, the machinery of local government and of provincial and district administrations could be strengthened and authority for the management and accountabiliy of regional and local responsibilities given at these levels. The purpose of any policy of reform that may be adopted in any particular state is to bring government to the people; to improve management so that whoever is accountable for a particular function or responsibility should be known; to produce machinery to avoid abuses of power which arise more easily with centralization of authority, and to achieve a better and more equitable distribution of the resources of the nation.

The staffing of the regional, provincial, district and local agencies should also receive proper attention. This has been considered elsewhere in this book. Provided, however, that a decentralization policy in the government machinery is made effective, it should not be too difficult to attract personnel of real ability, competence and experience to work in the field. Indeed with the new forces for development and growth, field work would offer opportunities and responsibilities for senior officers which should be both prestigeous and attractive.

CHAPTER 11

The Policy-making Process

SOMEONE has described the United Kingdom system of government as 'government by amateurs advised by experts'. This may be an exaggeration even for United Kingdom circumstances but the principles on which relations between a Minister and his staff are based assume that the Permanent Secretary and the professional and service heads of Divisions are experts in their own fields, although they may be working very much in the background. Their experience and knowledge in administrative, professional and technical matters puts them on a basis of equality in relation to their Ministers' political knowledge and experience. In African circumstances, local senior officers did not start holding high-level policy advising and directing positions until self-government brought in African Ministers. In some States, the accession of Africans to high-level positions followed sometime after Ministers were already in position so that they lacked the confidence derived from having experience, in their own fields, to match the political experience of the Ministers. Consequently the expert knowledge and experience that existed among local Civil Servants could not be said to be as rich as in the older countries. It is possible for knowledge in professional, technical and specialist fields to be borrowed under technical assistance arrangements or to be purchased by contracting with individuals. But most countries regard administrative and executive positions as sensitive positions which should be filled by citizens. It is for these posts that experience is usually not up to the level which would provide Ministers with satisfactory support in the short term. Experience in West Africa has, however, demonstrated that provided the officers have the right basic training in practice and theory, and provided also that they are the right potential material for high responsibility, they quickly build up the knowledge, expertise and experience necessary for their assignments.

The situation described above, however, makes it far more difficult to establish the convention, which exists in Britain, that Ministers will seek the advice of their staff on all policy matters. Where Ministers feel that their experience of public affairs is equal to, or greater than, the experience of their principal official advisers, they make their own decisions; they do not automatically turn to them on every major issue that arises. Nevertheless, if the Civil Service is to carry out its functions and role satisfactorily, this convention must be established as soon as possible. The Minister is the political head of his Ministry and expounds the policy and manifesto of his political party. The Permanent Secretary and his team, however, should know which policy or programme would work and which would not. They should know also how to translate the broad policy objectives of the Minister into practical policy programmes so as to make them effective on the ground. They should be in the position also to make policy proposals, in tune with the Minister's broad politics, for consideration by him. The discussions between the Minister and his Permanent Secretary should therefore be on equal terms and on the basis of an understanding of each other's role. The final decisions taken by the Minister, even if it is against the Permanent Secretary's advice, would be implemented to achieve the best possible results in the circumstances.

This is the ideal situation. As explained earlier, however, this can hardly apply yet in nearly all the African States. Even where the Government has retained some expatriate officers as heads of Ministries until Africans are available, there is always a lingering feeling that they might be tainted by their colonial past. Their experience is welcomed and exploited but the degree of confidence that exists between them and their Ministers is not all that might be expected. When they are replaced by Africans, on the other hand, their experience, at any rate in the initial stages, does not match up to their responsibilities. But the most important factor in the situation is that the political traditions in African States tend to evolve along different lines from those of the British from which many of them originally got their inspirations. This is understandable since these new political party systems are grafted on to African political trees which have grown out of different types of soil. It could not be expected, therefore, that African Ministers would accept completely the British conventions on the role of the Permanent Secretary in relation to themselves. Nor could it be expected that the Civil Service itself would have any long-standing local experience which would enable it to make its positive contribution towards the establishment of this convention.

Although, therefore, the British pattern is accepted in principle, the practice is bound to be different. Generally speaking, the pattern that is evolving is that the division of responsibilities between the Minister and his Permanent Secretary would be a matter of personal adjustment in each case. There would be cases where relations would be such that the Permanent Secretary is able to commit his Minister to policy decisions which would be fully accepted and backed. In other cases, however, the Permanent Secretary should endeavour to understand precisely the Minister's objectives and to appreciate his motives within the context of the policy of the Government as a whole. In this way, he should be able to fashion the strategy of his work so as to avoid disharmony and so also as to make the optimum contribution to the discharge of his Minister's responsibilities. In effect, therefore, the Permanent Secretary must work in the context and atmosphere of his Minister's politics. He does not necessarily have to accept these politics as his own. Indeed, if he is a well trained and experienced administrator, his personal political convictions would be detached from the politics of his responsibilities in relation to his Minister. This is not to say that the Permanent Secretary has no mind of his own, but he is a professional man who has to prepare the plans for his 'client' according to his instructions. It is similar to the position of an architect who would respond to the instruction of a client even though he is in the position to make or initiate suggestions which the client may or may not accept.

Similarly, professional and service heads of Divisions who are responsible for blocks of functions within the Ministry, should endeavour to work in harmony with the Ministers' policies. It is not enough to give advice on professional, technical and specialist grounds only, leaving others to fit this into a political policy. Their task is to endeavour to relate their specialist knowledge and experience to the Minister's policies and advise in what ways they could best serve these policies. Where the policies are nonsense in terms of the practical possibilities, they should be prepared to say so, politely but firmly, whilst being prepared to make alternative suggestions which might achieve the same or similar objectives as the Minister wishes.

It is worth repeating here that the Minister's responsibility is to lay down political policy, and it is the duty of the Permanent Secretary and the heads of divisions in the Ministry and their staffs to execute this policy and translate it into action. The officials have the responsibility for advising on policy, on modifications of existing policy instructions and, moreover, on the formulation of new policies; but once the Minister has taken his final decisions, there should be no further arguments in the normal way. What should follow is action to implement the decisions. There could, of course, be cases where, on grounds of conscience or personal conviction, a Permanent Secretary or head of Division might feel unable to carry out a decision pronounced by his Minister. If such an occasion should arise, then the officer should be honest with himself and consider his position in his Ministry. He might request a transfer and, in extreme cases, he might even consider resignation. Happily, such situations very seldom occur, but they could occur and put the integrity of an official to the severest test.

Most of the work in a Ministry and its Divisions, however, does not reach the Minister and, indeed, may not even reach the Permanent Secretary or heads of Divisions. A properly organized Ministry would provide for delegations of responsibilities all down the line so that even clerical officers have areas in which they take their own decisions even though these are on minor routine matters. Again, in a well organized Ministry which has senior staff who are trained, experienced and disciplined, officers get to know the general framework of policy of their Minister and the Government within which detailed policy matters could be handled on behalf of the Minister. Thus, once a Minister of Education has decided on, or approved, a general programme of technical training, the detailed planning and decisions on day-to-day matters arising under the programme should rest with the Chief Technical Education Officer. The Minister should, however, accept full responsibility for everything that is done in his name or on his behalf. This is a most important principle. Unless the Minister is prepared to stand by his staff who act in good faith in carrying out his policies, he cannot expect initiative and efficient work from them. Loyalty is a two-way matter; the staff would be loyal to the Minister in the same measure as he is loyal to them. The Minister should, and does, accept full responsibility in Parliament and in public for everything that is done on his behalf or in his name. If he does not, the Speaker usually reminds him of his

duty if the matter arises in Parliament. Incidentally, this underlines the importance of associating Ministers with the responsibility for appointing the key men in his Ministry.

There are two ways in which policy questions arise and are
processed. In the first place, the Minister may propose a particular policy. This may be policy that may arise from political
party considerations, such as policy forming part of the election
manifesto, or it may be some idea for a new development that
the Minister has evolved himself. However the Minister arrives
at the policy he proposes, it is the duty of the Permanent Secretary and head of Division to examine the implications of the
policy, its practicability, and feasibility, any possible political
and practical snags, the financial implications and the best
method of presentation or execution, including possible alternative plans of operation. Should the Permanent Secretary and
the other officials, after thorough examination, agree that the
policy is bad, they would so advise the Minister and give their
reasons. If the Minister decides that he should accept this advice,
that is the end of the matter unless he is also advised about an
alternative policy which might satisfy the same or similar objectives. Where, however, the Minister decides, nevertheless,
that his policy must be carried out, he would receive advice on
the best programme for executing it having regard to the
national interest.

In 1951, for instance, the Minister of Education of the newly
elected Government of Ghana (then Gold Coast) informed his
staff that the Government had decided on a policy of universal
primary education in the shortest possible time, and he wished
this policy to be implemented with immediate effect. After
thorough examination, the Minister was advised that although
the policy was sound as a long-term objective, there were a
number of major obstacles that might make it impracticable in
terms of immediate implementation. These obstacles included
the financial burden of an accelerated programme, the shortage
of qualified teachers and the dangers of dilution, the shortage
of classrooms, the inability of some parents to meet the cost of
educating their children, and the danger of lowering standards.
Nevertheless, the Minister confirmed that it was the Government's firm determination to go ahead with the policy. Thereupon, the Chief Education Officer and his team got down to
preparing an accelerated education plan on a national basis
which, whilst taking advantage of every possible improvization

N

– such as planned dilution of teachers, temporary classrooms, emergency teacher training colleges, week-end classes for untrained teachers, modifications and streamlining of curricula, a national grid system of supervision of schools and teachers – provided built-in safeguards for preventing dangerous falls in standards. A most progressive and imaginative programme was evolved which has laid the foundation for primary and higher education for Ghana and which, after the initial period of adjustments, is now providing standards of education which compare favourably with the pre-1951 standards and with standards in neighbouring countries.

The second way of promoting policy, of course, is for it to be proposed by the Permanent Secretary, a head of Division or any of the officials in the Ministry. This is a regular and continuing responsibility of all officials and is a fruitful source of a substantial body of policy proposals. The fact is that these officials are constantly living with the problems that fall within their individual assignments, they are discussing with other people new ideas or are picking up new ideas from reading about the experience of other countries and people, and they are addressing their minds all the time to methods of improvement or innovations. When therefore new ideas or improvement on old ideas are evolved by them, they are in the position to translate these into policy proposals which they put to their Minister for his consideration. Naturally, they, and especially the Permanent Secretary, do their best to test these proposals against the Minister's known general policy. If the Minister accepts the policy proposals, then they become his policies just as if he had initiated them himself, and he accepts full responsibility for them. If he does not approve the proposals, then that is the end of the matter.

CABINET POLICY

Whether a particular policy proposal has arisen through the Minister's initiative or on the suggestion of his staff, it may be the subject of a Cabinet Memorandum to obtain the full backing of the Government as a whole. If it is a relatively minor matter or merely the implementation of a policy arising out of a major decision already taken by the Cabinet, then the Minister may be in the position to go ahead without reference to the Cabinet. In some instances, he may seek the support of the President or

Prime Minister, as the case may be, to go ahead without reference to the Cabinet. On all really major issues, however, the normal procedure is to clear the policy with the Cabinet. For instance, in the earlier example given, the policy on the Accelerated Education Plan was so important that it must have been approved by the Cabinet. There were a number of stages in its implementation, however, which the Minister could approve except in cases where they involved fundamental changes in the conception of the whole programme as approved in the Cabinet. On such major policies which have, or could have, far-reaching repercussions and results, the spirit of collective responsibility of the Cabinet makes it necessary for Ministers to seek the support and approval of their colleagues.

The responsibility for drafting Cabinet Memoranda naturally falls to the Permanent Secretary and his staff. They may be prepared on the specific instructions from the Minister or may be presented to the Minister for consideration as part of the process of making policy recommendations to him. However a Cabinet Memorandum may originate, it is important that it be specifically approved by the Minister before it goes forward. This is important as the Minister has to speak to the Memorandum in the meeting of the Cabinet at which it is considered, and unless he knows all the points made in it and is able to explain and defend them, he is not likely to get his policy accepted. For this reason also, it is essential that the Permanent Secretary makes sure that his Minister is fully briefed on all the issues that might arise in the consideration of his Memorandum in the Cabinet so that he is able to ensure that the right decision is taken. This is important also because a Cabinet Memorandum should be as concise as possible, setting out succinctly what is proposed, what the objectives are, as much background as is necessary to present a fair picture of the factors necessary for proper consideration including references to snags, advantages and disadvantages arising out of alternative courses of action, and finishing with a clear statement of the propositions to be approved. A Cabinet Memorandum that is too lengthy or rambling usually causes irritation and might seriously reduce the chances of the issues it seeks to resolve receiving proper consideration. It is of assistance to the staff of Ministries, therefore, if a model Memorandum could be made available to them upon which to base their own drafting. Other matters that need to be considered when preparing a Cabinet Memorandum are the cost of any proposals in it and the effect of any likely decisions on the proposals on the interests of other Ministries. If there are any financial implications, then the Ministry of Finance should be consulted and its views embodied in the Memorandum. Where there are legal implications, the Legal Department's comments should also be in the Memorandum. It is necessary further that if other Ministries' interests are involved, the proposals be agreed with them if possible and, in any case, that their views are clearly indicated in the Memorandum.

When the Minister has approved a Cabinet Memorandum, the next step is to forward it to the Cabinet Secretariat for placing on the Agenda of the first convenient meeting. The Cabinet Secretariat is part of the Office of the President or Prime Minister and is headed by the Secretary to the Cabinet. The other important official in the Cabinet Secretariat is the Clerk to the Cabinet. In some countries, the Secretary to the Cabinet is also the Secretary to the President or Prime Minister. In these circumstances, the Clerk to the Cabinet has a really key role to play in the management of the business of the Cabinet. In any case, the primary responsibility for managing the Cabinet Secretariat and controlling the work of the other staff would fall to him.

The functions of the Cabinet Secretariat include :

(a) accepting Memoranda from Ministries and examining their readiness or suitability for placing on the Agenda of the Cabinet meeting;

(b) referring back, on the specific or general instructions of the President or Prime Minister, and under his authority, any Memoranda which are not ready or suitable for presentation to the Cabinet, as for instance because the necessary consultations with other Ministries had not taken place;

(c) preparing Agenda papers after approval of the Agenda by the President/Prime Minister and transmitting them to Ministers in good time for the meeting at which they are to be considered;

(d) recording decisions of the Cabinet in the form of Minutes and clearing the Minutes with the President/Prime Minister;

(e) transmitting to Ministers and Ministries decisions taken at the Cabinet meetings so that action may be taken on them;

(f) following up later to ensure that action is taken on all the decisions;

(g) keeping in safe custody all Cabinet papers that are on the classified list other than those which have been sent to Ministers; and

(h) ensuring that those Ministers and officials who are entrusted with Cabinet papers respect the secrecy of these papers.

The responsibility of the Secretary to the Cabinet and the Clerk for managing the business of the Cabinet is a most important one, and it is therefore essential that not only they are knowledgeable and efficient, but also that they have an efficient supporting staff. The two of them are present at all Cabinet meetings and are responsible for recording the proceedings. They do not, however, participate in the deliberations of the Cabinet, and only speak if they are asked to elucidate points of information and facts. They also have a responsibility for briefing the President/Prime Minister on all issues on which his guidance may be required at the meetings.

Very nearly all the matters which are under consideration in the Cabinet are on the classified list and only decisions which are released for action or publication may be taken off it. The officials who handle these papers must therefore be completely trustworthy and, in some countries, the Secretary and Clerk to the Cabinet have to take special Cabinet secrecy oaths. Special arrangements have to be made for the custody and security of Cabinet papers, not only in the Cabinet office but also in the offices of the Ministers. Periodically, all Cabinet papers in the possession of Ministers have to be called in for storage in the Cabinet office or for destruction if they are no more required.

It is important also that the Cabinet secretariat follows up decisions and ensures that they are acted upon. This may appear to be an elementary consideration but quite often it is discovered that Ministries have not taken action on important Cabinet decisions through neglect or, sometimes, by a deliberate attempt to bury awkward decisions instead of seeking a review.

CONCLUSIONS

The policy-making process is thus seen as one in which at the base in the Departments and Divisions of Ministries, officials are able to act in the name of their Ministers on a very wide range of subjects, taking decisions on comparatively minor issues and putting forward ideas for policy formulation on major issues. This is where, in practice, the bulk of government business is done and where government touches most intimately the man in the street or the man upcountry. The Agricultural Assistant or Extension Officer who decides on the service to be given to the farmer on what crops and where to grow them; the Forestry Officer who takes decisions on encroachments on forest reserves for fuel or building-timber by local people; the Tax Officer who uses his discretion on marginal tax allowance issues; the District Officer who takes decisions on local issues and problems of law and order; the Lands Officer who determines who should have leases of parcels of state land and on what terms; the Customs Officer and the Immigration Officer who exercise their discretion daily on the application of rules and regulations; the Treasury Officer who takes decisions on the limits and amounts of expenditure permissible: all these and others like them are daily conducting Government business, taking decisions affecting the life, well-being and pockets of ordinary citizens and keeping the wheels of the Government administration moving. On their integrity and efficiency depends whether the Government enjoys good standing with the public. To a great extent, therefore, these can be said to be the custodians of the Government's reputation. They constitute the broad base of the pyramid of government policy making.

Further up the pyramid are the heads of Administrations, Ministries, Departments and Divisions who are responsible for large blocks of government business. They carry very heavy responsibilities in determining almost completely all administrative, professional, technical and service policies; and these constitute a very large chunk of the mass of policy decisions taken on behalf of the Government as well as being of very high importance. They are also responsible for most of the policy formulation which finally is considered by their Ministers. On their sense of responsibility and initiative, their integrity and competence, their experience and knowledge, and their efficiency and loyalty depend most of the major actions of policy that enable the Government to meet its commitments to the people. They must of course discharge their policy responsibilities within the context of, and in consonance with, the general political policy of their Ministers and the Government generally.

Near the top are the Ministers who exercise full policy responsibility for all matters in their portfolios subject only to the over-riding authority of the President/Prime Minister and the Cabinet who are at the apex of the whole process of policy making. They, of course, have to test their actions against the sovereign legislative authority of Parliament which stands for the electorate as the final arbiter in all matters of policy. In all this process, the Civil Service has a major role to play and is vital to the management of the whole programme of the Government.

CHAPTER 12

Financial Control

In carrying out its functions of servicing policy decisions of the Government, the Civil Service is inevitably involved in the expenditure of public funds. The total amount of expenditure to which the Government is committed is very large indeed. In most African States, Government is the biggest business in the State and employs the largest number of persons. The arrangements made for running the financial aspects of the Government's business are therefore of the greatest importance, and it is essential that Civil Servants who have the responsibility for the custody of public funds and their disbursement should be made to do this wisely and in accordance with certain clearly defined rules and regulations. These rules and regulations as well as the machinery established to develop and safeguard them are necessary if the public interest is to be protected. Obviously, at the higher levels in the Civil Service, a certain amount of discretion has to be permitted. This is the level at which policies are being formulated and the Government's policies are being given practical form and interpretation. These processes themselves determine to a great extent how public funds are to be dispensed. Even at this level, however, there must be checks and balances since the public must be assured that no arbitrary decisions are being taken by individuals (no matter how highly placed) which are likely to involve ultimately additional tax burdens.

Parliament, in terms of the Constitution, has the final say in the control of government expenditure. Parliament gives the authority for expenditure through the Appropriations Act. Each year the Government has to present to Parliament its budget in the form of Estimates of revenue and expenditure as well as the policies, economic and political, that relate to the priorities for expenditure proposed. Nor only does Parliament, during the debates on the Budget, bring the policies of the Government under searching criticism, but it also considers in detail a number of the heads of expenditure within the proposed

Budget. There may not be time to scrutinize all the heads, but then the decision as to which will be discussed rests with Parliament itself and not with the Government. Where the Government enjoys an overwhelming majority of support in Parliament, it can usually get its proposals approved without much difficulty. In most Parliaments, however, there is always vigorous debate and great interest in the philosophy as well as the details of the Budget, and there are some sharp criticisms from the backbenchers even of the Government party in Parliament. In a number of cases, either in Parliament or in the Parliamentary Party meetings, backbenchers are able to influence the policies of the Government, and even on occasion cause the withdrawal of measures which are unwise, ill-conceived or unpopular. A vigilant Parliament is hence a great check on improper policies and therefore of the expenditures that go with them. In any case, the fact that Parliament may ventilate in debate the implications of any particular heads of expenditure does provide some assurance that those who advise Ministers in preparing their Estimates would take care in ensuring that their provisions can be justified.

Parliament follows up the authority for expenditure given under the Appropriations Act by assuring itself that the disbursements by the Government and its officials are in accordance with this law and its intentions in the Act. This it does through its Public Accounts Committee. This Committee is, by tradition, chaired by a member of the minority party where there is any. It receives all the reports of the Auditor-General on Ministries and Departments, and examinates all irregularities which are exposed in these reports. It has the right to summon any Accounting Officers before it to explain these irregularities or the justification for certain items of expenditure. The Public Accounts Committee reports to Parliament, and any serious breaches of the law or misuse of public funds would normally be debated. In any case, the reports (being public property once they are presented to Parliament) could be the subject of public comment in the Press and elsewhere. This whole process, therefore, is a strong deterrent against the abuse of their responsibilities by public officers, the wrongful appropriations of public funds, and frauds and dishonest expenditure. Another weapon in the hands of Parliament to ensure vigilance is the right of any Member who is not in the Government to ask questions on any matters of public policy. This right could be, and is frequently, used to expose what might turn out to be abuse of power or fraud and dishonesty in the expenditure of public funds. Since Civil Servants are the Accounting Officers, they share with Ministers the responsibility for being answerable to Parliament for the proper use of public funds which are committed to their care.

Two main stages involved in the process of financial control are: (a) the Budget and Treasury Control and (b) the Audit and Public Accounts Committee. The first stage is really part of the normal machinery within the Government for ensuring that public funds are applied to purposes approved by the public through their elected representatives and that, once approved, their disbursement is in accordance with the purposes for which they were approved, and such rules and regulations as are laid down to safeguard public expenditure. The second stage is the means by which Parliament satisfies itself that public funds have been properly spent and that there has been no extravagance or dishonesty on the part of those entrusted with the custody and disposal of these funds.

THE BUDGET

The Ministry of Finance, in most countries, has the responsibility for initiating action on the budget and for approving measures for any variations of, or addition to, the provisions of the budget. In one country at least, an experiment was tried of having a Budget Bureau which was independent of the Ministry of Finance, but this was given up after a little over a year's experience. The Ministry of Finance, commonly referred to as the Treasury in this context, has the responsibility therefore for finally presenting the layout of Government revenue and expenditure for approval, and exercising control when approved.

The budgeting procedure involves a number of steps. Not less than six months before the beginning of the next financial year, the Treasury should have made a forecast of revenue expectations for the following financial year. This implies that the Treasury Division concerned with the Budget should have officers trained and experienced in the study of economic trends and their likely impact on revenue. On the basis of this estimate of likely revenue yields of the following financial year, the Treasury decides on the provisional allocation of funds for each Ministry – and each extra-Ministerial Department – within which its estimates of expenditure for the following financial year should be contained. This provisional allocation is necessarily related to the previous Ministerial Estimates as approved in the budget of the current year, taking into consideration expanding or contracting programmes and normal salary increments. But the over-riding consideration is the total amount of expected revenue that would be available for sharing between Ministries and Departments. It is naturally not often that Ministries are satisfied with their allocations and there are always attempts to obtain increases to enable them to cover new programmes which have been promised or which for policy reasons it is necessary to carry out. Since usually the revenue position is inelastic, increases for certain Ministries cannot be approved without cutting back allocations to other Ministries. In other words, at some stage some authority has to take the final decision on priorities. The Treasury does its best to clarify these priorities, but if it is unable to reach agreement on compromise decisions, then the matter has to be settled elsewhere.

Simultaneously with informing Ministries of their allocations, the Treasury also issues Estimates Instructions which lay down in detail the procedure to be followed in presenting Ministerial and Departmental Estimates. The instructions would include the format for the estimates so that all the Budget estimates have a uniform pattern as far as practicable. The rules on what types of expenditure will be allowed or disallowed are also clearly laid down as well as scales of allowances, extraordinary expenditure and miscellaneous expenditure. Development expenditure, although included in the annual Budget, is governed by different considerations. There is normally already formulated a Development Plan which embodies within it the annual targets. It is a matter for consideration each year, having regard to expected revenue from existing or increased tax impositions, as well as the size of other resources such as revenue reserves and credits, whether the targets for the next financial year would be attainable. Whatever decision is taken on this is included in the Budget for the following year. Where, as is usually the case, the Development Planning authority is not part of the Ministry of Finance, very close liaison and co-ordination must be maintained between them, and the necessary machinery has to be established to ensure this.

The next step is for Ministries to prepare their estimates, which should come within the allocations made to them, and which should consequently be related to priorities in each case determined by considerations of policy. There are certain commitments which must be provided for unless a policy of retrenchment is envisaged, and these include salaries and wages of permanent or full-time staff, the financing of programmes which have not been completed, and the maintenance of established institutions. Usually, by the time these standing commitments are provided for, there is not much left in the allocation of a particular Ministry to apply to all the desirable new programmes. The tendency therefore is for Ministries to exceed their allocations and hope that they can persuade the Treasury to agree to increases, expecting that there is always an undisclosed reserve allocation at the disposal of the Treasury.

When, therefore, the estimates from the Ministries are submitted to the Treasury the next stage is for a thorough and detailed examination of the estimates proposals of each Ministry to be carried out. It is usual so to organize the Estimates Division of the Treasury that its officers specialize in the affairs of particular groups of Ministries. They are then in the position to provide a critical examination of the budget proposals of the Ministries of which they have special knowledge. It is also normal for the proposals of Ministries to increase the establishments of posts to be critically examined by the Establishments Division both as regards the justification for having additional posts at all and also in regard to the grading of the posts proposed to be created. In some countries, the examination of the budget proposals finally takes the form of budget hearings at which the head of the Estimate Division of the Treasury and his team, sometimes supported by the Establishments Division personnel, go through the Estimates head by head with the representatives of the Ministries and Departments concerned with a view to reaching agreement, at the official level, on the scope and scale of the Estimates. If agreement can be reached at this level, then this generally forms the basis of the proposals to be incorporated in the national budget. If agreement cannot be reached, then a further effort has to be made to do so by further discussion at Ministerial level between the Minister concerned and the Minister of Finance.

It is unusual, however, for complete agreement to be reached at this level in respect of all Ministries. It is necessary then for the issue to be settled finally in the Cabinet. Only the Cabinet is in the position to determine finally what the overall priority programme of the Government should be and, if there is not enough money to match all the desired programmes, which should have priority. In most cases, the final say rests with the President or Prime Minister, since he is the effective head of Government, and is in any case in the position to take decisions where there is a conflict of interests between Ministers. Once a final decision is taken on the estimates, the draft Estimates of Expenditure for the whole Government is published and circulated to Members of Parliament, and made available to members of the public.

The Estimates of Expenditure are formally presented to Parliament when the whole Budget is introduced. The Finance Minister, in introducing the Budget, normally reviews the State's entire economic position and outlines the measures taken to improve it. He puts forward the Government's development and industrialization programme for the coming financial year, and the financial measures required to raise the revenue for meeting the expenditure estimated and published. The traditional pattern in all the States is that the tax and tariff proposals to be announced by the Minister of Finance are kept a close secret and, although the President or Prime Minister is taken into the confidence of the Minister of Finance and his approval obtained, the other Cabinet colleagues are informed only a few hours before they are announced. Any leakage could have very serious consequences to the prospects of achieving full results or impact for the measures proposed, and no temptation should be placed in the way of individuals who might take profitable advantage of prior knowledge of what is to come. The measures proposed usually take effect from the moment they are announced for the same reasons.

The next stages in passing the Budget are a general debate on the Budget and consideration of the detailed expenditure estimates in the Committee of Supply of the Legislature. During this stage, not only Treasury officials but also Ministry officials should be available in the officials' box in the legislature to provide their Ministers with the facts and information on which they could base their replies to queries raised by Members of Parliament in considering the estimates of their Departments. The Committee of Supply stage is followed by the passing of the Appropriations Act which gives authority for the expenditure as approved in the Estimates. The passing of the Appropriations Act completes the whole process of budgeting for a

season. In most countries, however, this is followed almost immediately by preparation in the Ministry of Finance for the
start of the whole process once again for the following year's
Budget.

TREASURY CONTROL

Although the Budget lays down the Votes of Expenditure for
Ministries and Departments, Parliamentary approval is, in effect,
approval of the services for which the expenditure is required.
In other words, all that Parliament has done is to give policy
approval to the programmes and services embodied in the
various items in the estimates of expenditure, the expenditure
not to exceed the amounts stated in the Votes. There is still a
need, however, for a measure of control over the disbursements
of the funds under the Votes, and Treasury control is exercised
for this purpose. Treasury control implies approval for every
new item of expenditure, every new service, any change of
policy involving increases in expenditure, and any variations in
the conditions on which expenditure was originally authorized.

Another aspect of Treasury control is the release of funds.
This is regulated by the issuing of Expenditure Warrants to the
Ministries and Departments authorizing warrant holders to
incur expenditure under the heads and items specified and to
the extent of the amounts stated and, at the same time,
authorizing the Accountant-General and his officers to honour
payment vouchers issued within the terms of the warrants.
Where the Treasury is not satisfied that it is opportune or necessary to incur expenditure under any particular vote it will not
issue a warrant to cover it even though the vote is approved in
the Budget. It will only do so if the necessity for the expenditure
is self-evident or is justified.

The Treasury should also be consulted, as stated earlier, when
Memoranda to be put to the Cabinet have financial implications, and in particular when there is likely to be increased
expenditure. The chances of the Cabinet approving proposals
in a Cabinet Memorandum are materially improved if the
Treasury were to say that it had no objections on financial
grounds. Treasury approval is also required for *Virements*, that
is, transfers of funds between sub-heads or items, which do not
involve increases in expenditure or change of policy. Transfer
of funds from one head to another, or additional expenditure

without compensating savings under sub-heads, requires legislative approval through a Supplementary Appropriations Bill. It is usually approved by the Treasury as a Supplementary Provision, or for payment out of the Contingencies Fund, and this is then covered subsequently by the approval of the Legislature.

The Treasury is responsible for the promulgation of Financial Orders or Regulations which lay down rules for the management of Votes of Expenditure, for procedures for contracts and tenders, for the purchase and custody of stores, and for the appointments of Boards of Survey. The object of these Orders and Regulations is to ensure that little room is left for fraudulent and dishonest transactions and other improper actions without their being detected. These rules should maintain a balance between the need to place confidence in the integrity of officers, so that they have some flexibility in the management of the affairs entrusted to them, on the one hand, and the need to ensure that those who are inclined or tempted to be dishonest are deterred, on the other. The Treasury or its Accountant-General's Department, does scrutinize all transactions, as stated on payment vouchers and stores purchasing and transfer documents as well as reports of Boards of Survey. Any apparent irregularities are followed up by queries to the officers responsible for the transactions. If the arrangements for exercising control over expenditure work efficiently, therefore, there should be very little scope for unjustified expenditure of public funds, for unauthorized disbursements, for uneconomic measures and policies, and for fraud and dishonesty in the custody of public funds and property. Civil Servants who function in the Treasury therefore have very heavy responsibilities and they should consist, therefore, of some of the best men in the service. They should not only be well-trained and educated but should also be experienced. This is important since those responsible for exercising responsibility for Treasury control and budgeting, and who are therefore the principal advisers to their Minister on policy matters in these fields, should not just be persons who keep strictly to the rules, but should be administrators who could view every situation presented to them in terms of the broad political and economic policies of the Government and the best use of the resources available in the country.

Rigid Treasury control which does not relate its actions to accepted principles of policy, could lead to much frustration and resentment in Ministries and Departments, and in the end defeat its purpose. The Treasury usually has a bad name with other Ministries because of its role in controlling expenditure. Where its actions are justified, any resentments caused are merely the result of the deflation of individual ambitions and can therefore be combated. The principles behind financial control, however, derive from, firstly, the need to guard against Ministerial and Departmental subjective thinking. Treasury scrutiny of Ministerial proposals ensures a more detached and objective approach to expenditure policy. Secondly, there is a need to arrange priorities in the use of resources and to avoid overlap. This is most important in African States which embark on accelerated development programmes. Resources are limited in these States, and even where the Ministry of Finance is not responsible for development planning, it has a duty to ensure that the most economic use of resources is reflected in the Ministries' expenditure policy; and this it is in a good position to do because it sees all departmental plans and proposals. Thirdly, there is the need to keep a watch on the total use of national resources for the purposes of Government as against their use for other purposes. Governments cannot function in isolation from the private sector, and a comprehensive development plan takes into account the needs of all aspects of the national economy. Government should, therefore, keep its own expenditure within the limits sanctioned by national considerations. Finally, there is the need to see that resources devoted to government go to the most worthwhile purposes. This is commonsense but it does not always appear to be understood.

The close control exercised by the Treasury could be irksome and troublesome and also could hinder the proper exercise of initiative in policy matters in the Ministries. It is essential, therefore, that it is exercised in a spirit of mutual trust and confidence, and the onus is on the Treasury officials to convince the others that this is the spirit in which they work. They should exercise their responsibilities in a desire to help rather than hinder the legitimate programmes of Ministries. If Ministries are persuaded that the Treasury is helpful and not obstructive, their officials would not hesitate in bringing their problems to the Treasury for advice on how to proceed. Admittedly, this spirit of constructive co-operation is not a feature of relations with African Treasuries at the moment, but it is nevertheless an objective which is worth pursuing since the Treasuries must discharge their obligations to the electorate whilst at the same time the Ministries have a duty to carry out programmes of development and services essential for the progress and well-being of the people.

AUDIT

The second stage in the process of financial control is the Audit system. This control is exercised by the Auditor-General and his staff. The Auditor-General, although a public officer, is responsible only to Parliament in the exercise of his responsibilities. His appointment is governed by special rules which vary from one State to another. Usually, however, he is appointed by the head of Government on the advice of the Public Service Commission. Once appointed, however, the Auditor-General cannot be removed before the end of his period of contract by the authority that appointed him unless, and until, special resolution to that effect is passed by the Legislature, usually by a majority of two-thirds of all Members, on the grounds of stated misconduct or infirmity of mind and body. In the exercise of his functions, the Auditor-General is not subject to the direction or control of any person or authority. This, together with the provision against his easy removal, gives him the freedom to exercise his functions with courage, impartiality and integrity, without fear of loss of position or influence from any quarter.

The Auditor-General and his staff are charged with the duty of auditing all the accounts of the Ministries and Departments and of officers and authorities of the Government. For this purpose, they have access to all books, records, returns and other documents relating to these accounts. They have the right to call for explanations in any case where they are not satisfied that the expenditure is covered by proper authority or where standing instructions and regulations have not been observed. The Auditor-General must present reports periodically to Parliament on the state of the accounts of the Government. This report would indicate where there has been proper management of the affairs of Ministries, in so far as expenditure is concerned, while at the same time bringing to notice any irregularities, frauds, losses of funds and unsatisfactory regulations or arrangements which have resulted, or might result, in inefficiency or losses to the Government. The reports of the Auditor-General are examined by the Public Accounts Committee of Parliament

o

which could call on Accounting Officers to explain any short-comings exposed therein. The Public Accounts Committee reports to Parliament and these reports might attract debates if any matters of public interest are disclosed in them.

ACCOUNTING OFFICER

The Accounting Officer is the person held directly responsible to the Public Accounts Committee – and therefore to Parliament – for the proper control of the expenditure on the Votes of his Ministry and the departments under it. In most States, the Accounting Officer is the Permanent Secretary of the Ministry although, in some, the heads of the separate Departments are the Accounting Officers. The Accounting Officer may not have direct and day-to-day control of the Votes under his Ministry, but it is up to him to institute the machinery within his Ministry or Department which would ensure that the accounts are properly managed, that there is no expenditure without proper authority, and that, where there is irregularity or any expenditure above what is authorized, remedial action is promptly set in motion.

The relations between the Accounting Officer and his Minister require some understanding. The Minister is responsible for policy decisions which lie behind the authority for the expenditure, but this does not relieve the Accounting Officer of personal responsibility for advising his Minister if any policy instruction received from him does not conform to the proper principles of control of finance or, in his view, is wasteful and extravagant. If the Minister insists, then the Accounting Officer should make a formal submission in writing and the Minister should register his decision also in writing. In the United Kingdom, the Accounting Officer is then obliged to report the matter immediately to the Controller and Auditor-General. This latter requirement, however, has not been followed in all the African States. Normally in these States, once the Minister has conveyed his decision in writing, the Accounting Officer would regard himself as fully covered, and any criticisms, blame or charge of irresponsibility that might arise would automatically be attached to the Minister. This sort of situation, however, very seldom arises where there are relations of trust and confidence existing between Ministers and their top officials. Ministers in these circumstances would not wish to act in defiance of policies and regulations laid down or approved by their own Government. They would rely on their senior officials to advise them on steps to be taken to obtain authority for carrying out any policy decisions that do not conform to the rules; and they would in any case accept advise given on grounds of extravagance or waste.

Any gross negligence, or irresponsibility, or acts of officers which result in losses to the Government may be subject to penalties varying from censure to a part or the whole of the amount of the loss being surcharged to the officer responsible. If, of course, there has been fraud or dishonesty, this may lead to prosecution. The Accounting Officer cannot escape responsibility even where it is proved that some other officer is guilty of a breach of the regulations, or of negligence or of a criminal offence. He may find himself being liable also to a surcharge.

CONCLUSIONS

The whole process of financial control, from the stage of ensuring in the Estimates that the Government is not committed to unnecessary, wasteful or extravagant expenditure, to the control of the final accounts by the Auditor-General, may be rather elaborate. Government nowadays, however, is a large body disposing of relatively vast sums of public money and determining the priorities for the use of the nation's resources. The members of the public, one way or the other, are paying for all the recurrent and development expenditure of the Government. The Government therefore has a duty to ensure that its expenditure is incurred with due regard to the public interest, in accordance with defensible priorities, and with proper regard also for economy and proper husbanding of the nation's resources. It is the complexity of government activities that determines the elaborate nature of the system instituted to control public expenditure. Provided there is understanding and trust, however, no Minister or official who is doing his duty by the country need feel harassed or hindered. The system exists mainly to ensure that little room is left for irresponsibility, negligence, or dishonesty. It operates reasonably well. It could be improved but it certainly has a sound basis for its existence.

CHAPTER 13

Other Public Services

THE Civil Service is the best known of the public services and in fact, in the colonial period, it embraced all the others – the Judiciary, the Armed Forces and the teaching service (in so far as teachers in government institutions were concerned). It is now accepted that the Armed Forces and the Judiciary cannot properly be included in the Civil Service as defined. In fact, the definition of the Civil Service stated in Chapter 3 specifically excluded the Judiciary and also the Armed Forces because employment in them is not in a civil capacity. The teaching service by that definition, could be within the Civil Service but it is usually excluded since most teaching institutions in the African states have developed outside the government's direct administrative responsibility. There are three other services which, being para-military in nature, are usually modelled in some respects on the Armed Forces, and these are the Police, the Prisons and Preventive services. Indeed, they are usually classified with the Armed Forces as the Disciplined Service. They are, however, regarded as part of the Civil Service in most of the States, although in some the Police at least is now classified as another Public Service outside the Civil Service proper.

The one common characteristic applying to all these public services is that all those employed in them are paid directly and wholly out of monies voted by Parliament. For that reason, it is the normal policy to harmonize the levels of remuneration among them so that those in them who have comparable levels of experience, training and responsibility enjoy comparable rates of remuneration. There are differences, sometimes significant, but these reflect the different types of staff and organizational structure relating to the functions of each service. The highest levels of posts in the Judiciary usually enjoy much higher rates of remuneration than comparable levels in the other services. This is partly traditional but is partly based on the consideration that members of this service must have the highest degree of integrity of any of the public services. All the services should of course be completely loyal to the State although in different ways. For instance, the Disciplined Services should, like the Civil Service, have as the focal point of their loyalty the head of State and the head of Government whereas the loyalty of the Judiciary is to the State as an entity since its responsibilities must be exercised impartially and according to the law and the constitution regardless of what the political and administrative policies of the Government might be for the moment. The Disciplined Services should, ideally, be completely insulated from politics. Their responsibilities are quite clearly defined and they should be exercised in relation to any legitimate demands of the Government of the day. Intervention by the Disciplined Services in the political affairs of the State has usually resulted in military insurrections and military take-overs of governments. In certain circumstances, military intervention may be justified as the only way of safeguarding the people's liberties where constitutional governments have taken powers to become autocratic, corrupt and oppressive. Most people would however regard it as a national disaster for the situation to have so degenerated as to make a military revolution, temporarily at any rate, a welcome development.

THE ARMED FORCES

The role of the Armed Forces is to be responsible for the defence of the nation against any external threats and to reinforce the ability of the Government to exert its influence, and act with confidence, in the exercise of its foreign policy. None of the African States can afford to maintain large Armed Forces since they are in peacetime non-productive in their normal responsibilities. Unless, therefore, there is a real threat to the security of the nation, the size of the Armed Forces should be relatively small. The policy regarding their size should be one which is termed by some people the 'hedgehog' policy, that is, that the Armed Forces should not be large enough to be a threat to neighbouring States but should be such that, although not large, would be prickly to handle by any other nation which attempts to deal with them. Most African States, however, do not expect to be attacked by anybody, but they maintain small Armed Forces partly for prestige reasons – since all – or nearly all – independent states have them – but mainly for the purposes of assisting the civil power in restoring law and order wherever and whenever they break down. This role of the Armed Forces is in fact the one to which greater importance is attached in most of the States even where, as in Ghana, it is not regarded in principle as other than a minor role.

Because of the roles assigned to the Armed Forces, their organization, structure and discipline are distinctive and very different from the Civil Service. The command structure is more clearly defined and the code of discipline is not only different but more strict. The Armed Forces are governed by their own Act of Parliament which defines their role and status, their relations with the civil power, their structure, their disciplinary code, their service regulations and all the other matters appropriate to the organization and functions of the forces. The main differences between the Armed Forces and the Civil Service could be described as follows:

(a) Their functions, organization and operational control are reflected in their peculiar command structure which defines very closely the chain of command from the top to the lowest ranks. Within this structure, the minimum initiative in matters of policy is exercised except in the officer ranks.

(b) Recruitment, promotion and disciplinary control are provided for by special legislation and regulations. They are not subject at any stage below the top-most command positions to political or civil intervention, although in certain classes of disciplinary cases, there is provided the means of appeal to the highest Judiciary courts. Certainly, the Public Service Commission has no part to play in any matters relating to appointments, promotions and discipline.

(c) For disciplinary reasons members of the Armed Forces are not permitted to belong to any trade unions or staff associations. The Service Regulations would provide specifically for the means by which grievances among members of all ranks could be identified and dealt with. Special care has to be taken to ensure that service and pay conditions are such as to ensure contentment, especially as strike action in the Armed Forces is completely out of the question and in any case forbidden.

(d) The importance of morale in the Armed Forces is, therefore, a major factor in the determination of such conditions of service as remuneration, housing, leave, hours of work, miscellaneous allowances and retiring benefits. These should normally be more generous than in the Civil Service since the Armed

Forces operate under sterner disciplinary conditions and under conditions of greater hardship, whilst also having a significant element of risk to life and limb in the discharge of their responsibilities.

THE POLICE, PRISONS AND PREVENTIVE SERVICES

These are para-military in organization and functions. The Police is the closest to the Armed Forces in functions although its responsibilities are purely concerned with the maintenance of law and order and internal security. The Prisons are connected with internal security since they keep in safe custody those who have been proved by the law to be a danger to law and order. The Preventive Service is an arm of the Customs and Excise Department responsible for preventing smuggling and contraband activities.

The Police Service is best organized as a completely separate public service outside the Civil Service and with its own Service Commission. More and more of the States are in fact providing for this in their Constitutions. It should in any case, like the Armed Forces, have its own Regulations. The Prisons and Preventive Services, on the other hand, are usually closely tied up with the Civil Service in their functions and responsibilities. For instance, the Preventive Service is closely tied up with Customs and Excise. They should, however, have special Regulations under separate Acts of Parliament concerning such matters as function, organization and structure which are peculiar to them. Certainly, the Public Service Commission Regulations should provide separately for their appointments, promotions and discipline, giving greater responsibility to institutions established within the services themselves and, in particular, recognizing the special position of the heads of the services.

The Police, Prisons, and Preventive Services share with the Armed Forces similarities of operational control and command structure: the fact that their members must, for disciplinary reasons, be excluded from trade unions and staff associations, and that strike action is prohibited; and the importance of morale and discipline in determining terms and conditions of service. Similar considerations apply to these services in regulating such matters as have been discussed earlier for the Armed Forces.

THE JUDICIARY

The Judiciary is one of the three most important wings of any State's constitution and, in the opinion of many people, it is at least of equal importance to the other wings, namely, the Legislature and the Executive or Government. Without a well-established, independent and impartial Judiciary, personal liberties, individual rights and property, and even the Constitution itself cannot be safeguarded. For that reason, it is usual to define the status of the Judiciary in the Constitution and provide for its independence and protection.

The Judiciary consists of Judges of the Supreme Court, the Court of Appeal, the High Court, and the Magistrates and other minor Judicial Officers. The Chief Justice is the head of the Judiciary. He is normally appointed by the head of State for life, that is, until he retires in the normal course. The mode of appointment of the other Members of the Judiciary varies from State to State. In some there is a Judicial Service Commission, established by the Constitution or by Act of Parliament, which is composed of the Chief Justice as Chairman with members drawn from the Supreme Court and the Public Service Commission. The Judicial Service Commission would then be responsible for making recommendations to the head of State – through the Prime Minister where this is appropriate – for the appointment of all Judges other than the Chief Justice. The Commission would normally also make all appointments of Magistrates, and other Judicial Officers including the professional staff of the Courts. In other States, however, all the appointments are made by the head of State on the advice of, or after consultation with, the Chief Justice. This latter practice is in line with the United Kingdom procedure under which Judges are appointed on the advice of the Lord Chancellor.

It needs to be pointed out, however, that the United Kingdom procedure is based on well-established conventions which ensure that there is no political influence or patronage in judicial appointments and which protects the Judiciary from improper interference in the exercise of its responsibilities. In African States, however, it is necessary to have a constituted impartial machinery for ensuring that appointments to the Judiciary are made having regard to the intentions enshrined in the Constitution and the need to safeguard the public interest. The Judicial Service Commission system provides this essential safeguard especially when it is entrenched in the Constitution, but it has the great disability, like the Public Service Commission system, of being rigid and not permitting the establishment of healthy conventions. Constitutions and Acts of Parliament can usually be revoked, but conventions, although they may have no statutory backing, are very difficult to overcome or ignore. Here again, there is no need to be dogmatic on the issue of which system is better. Much depends on the situation in each State and the stage of constitutional development.

The terms and conditions of service of the Judiciary are similar to those applicable to the Civil Service. This is partly because of the general principle that all public services have to be in general agreement in regard to the broad levels of conditions of service, and also because, historically, all of them were administered by one authority, the Colonial Office, in their initial stages and only comparatively recently, with the acceleration of constitutional development, were they separated. The Judiciary is, however, in a special position in that, by the very nature of its responsibilities, its members have to be somewhat detached from the public and other public services. It is customary, therefore, to permit more generous treatment to be accorded them over such matters as remuneration, housing, leave and travel. It is now becoming increasingly accepted that the Judiciary should be completely divorced, in regard to its terms of service, from other public services.

THE TEACHING SERVICE

As explained earlier, the practice varies in the various States as regards the treatment of the Teaching Service in relation to the Civil Service. In some countries the Teaching Service is completely outside the Civil Service, whilst in others, there are some teachers in the Civil Service, where the Government has direct responsibility for some schools, and other teachers are outside the Service. This situation is related to the historical development of the educational system in the States. In all of them the major impetus to educational development rested with voluntary agencies, almost all of whom were missionary bodies and churches. The governments came in later to regulate the establishment of educational institutions, to lay down standards for the various levels, including standard curricula, to provide inspection services, and to give grants for meeting part of the teachers' salaries and other recurrent expenditures. In some cases, the Governments established a few schools and ran them under the direct control of their Education Departments. The teachers in these schools were automatically classified as Civil Servants. Governments in all the States now accept full responsibility for all schools and colleges which are designated as within the public education system, and provide for the full cost of maintaining these institutions either from their own funds or from provisions made by local authorities or from both. But the distinction still remains in some countries that teachers in government institutions are Civil Servants and the others are not. There is in all cases, however, development towards establishing Unified Teaching Services – outside the Civil Services – which include all teachers in whatever institutions they are employed. This is already the position in a majority of the States.

The establishment of Unified Teaching Services recognizes the principle that they are, and must be, regarded as members of the family of public services worthy of treatment of not less importance than the Civil Service. Every one recognizes this, but its application has been slow in developing. There is a strong case, which fortunately has been accepted in principle by all, that the Teaching Service should be treated, in terms and condition of service, as favourably as the Civil Service and, where possible, should be more generously treated. This is particularly important in developing countries where education is not a mere social service, but one of the major factors of economic development through the training it gives to their manpower resources. Such terms and conditions of service as remuneration, housing, leave, pensions and gratuities, allowances and passages should, as far as possible, be as generous as in the Civil Service. There would need to be variations to suit the peculiar conditions under which teachers have to work. For instance, leaves would have to be taken during school vacations and, where teachers have extra-curricular responsibilities such as housemasterships in boarding institutions, housing might have to be free. There would be the need also to pay responsibility allowances to teachers holding certain duty posts, such as special subject tutors and games masters, which would have no counterparts in the Civil Service. Apart from any such necessary variations, however, it is important that teachers should see that they are not worse off, and may even be better off, than persons similarly situated to themselves in the Civil Service.

In particular, on the issue of remuneration, the principle should be observed that teachers should enjoy the same pay rates as Civil Servants with comparable qualifications, responsibilities and experience. All governments have conceded this principle now in practice. For instance, graduate teachers enjoy the same salary scales as professional officers in the Civil Service; and at lower levels, the salary scales of teachers are parallel to those in the Civil Service. The problem, however, is that the mere application of equivalent salary scales to grades of comparable levels of qualifications and responsibility does not equalize the opportunities for personal betterment and careers. The trouble is that, in the new African States where there has been phenomenal expansion of government services and accelerated Africanization, the career prospects of African Civil Servants have been exceptionally bright. There have, since the end of the last war when constitutional development began to accelerate, been many more top level posts open to Africans of ability and experience and many more posts at the entry levels to provide the opportunities for advancement in the Civil Service. Expansion in education has not provided career opportunities to anything like the same extent or value. The structure of the educational system conditions the structure of the Teaching Service. Consequently, the career pyramid in the Teaching Service has a very broad base and the top is not very high. Most teachers can look forward to headmasterships at the top of their careers, but the responsibilities attached to such posts are not as great or as high as the main top-level positions in the Civil Service, and are therefore rated much lower from the salary point of view. The advantage, therefore, lies with the Civil Service which provides a career pyramid not so broad at the bottom but reaching much higher.

This is a serious problem since it is important for the development of any nation that some of its best brains should be attracted into the Teaching Service, having regard to their importance in laying the foundations for the training of its manpower not only in the acquisition of knowledge and skills but in quality of character. In the long run, a part of the problem relating to the present abnormal conditions would be resolved. But, it must be recognized that, so long as career prospects in other public services remain much better than in the Teaching

Service, the various countries will not be able to attract as many persons of quality as are necessary to run their educational institutions. In addition, therefore, to the present accepted principle of equalizing terms of service, the policy should be examined whether other incentives can be provided for making the Teaching Service attractive. It should be investigated for instance, whether having regard to the nature of the career pyramid in this Service, it would serve the purpose by paying more to teachers in the earlier stages of their careers so that, even if they did not reach the heights provided by the Civil Service, they might in the aggregate over a number of years have earned comparable remuneration. This approach may be ruled out on grounds of expense but it is worth investigating.

It may be considered also whether above a certain level in the Civil Service, the door should not be thrown open to persons in the Teaching Service so that they are able to compete with Civil Servants for the more senior positions. The greatest disincentive to entering the Teaching Service for the able and bright young man is that he may find himself a prisoner of his career and that the longer he stays in it the more he becomes the 'forgotten man'. This feeling can be largely removed if a scheme of service is devised which enables him after a reasonable period of teaching to seek entry into the Civil Service at a level which recognizes the value of his previous service. This approach may be regarded as unorthodox, but something has to be done, and quickly, to ensure that a viable, strong and healthy Teaching Service is established which is able to attract and hold its fair share of available talent for the good of essential and balanced development within the State.

Alternatively, the Teaching Service may be incorporated in the Civil Service structure. This is reversing the trend in previous policy but it may be the only way at present for ensuring that teachers receive the recognition and are accorded the prestige they deserve.

LOCAL GOVERNMENT SERVICE

The Local Government Service in African states has not so far been able to attract able and competent staff. Even in large municipal authorities, there has been a struggle to recruit and retain properly qualified and suitably experienced personnel. There are several reasons for this situation. Local government institutions have so far not generally acquired the political and financial stability necessary for the execution of their functions. In some cases, their functions and the statutory basis for their role in the total machinery of government have not been properly defined. The growth sectors of national development have generally passed them by and their financial resources have not enabled them to participate in the general programme of economic and social development.

As stated in Chapter 10 there has also been a tendency to over-centralize responsibility for government and public services in headquarters of Ministries and Departments in the capital. In this situation, local authorities have suffered the same slow decline in importance and prestige as regional, provincial and district authorities. In consequence, the Local Government Service has stood no chance of attracting its fair share of available trained manpower, particularly since all states experience grave shortages of talent in all fields.

If in any policy for the reform of the machinery of Government, as discussed in the concluding paragraphs of Chapter 10, decentralization results in the local institutions of government – regional, provincial, district, municipal and local – being given real and substantial responsibility, then steps should also be taken to strengthen the Local Government Service. A proposal which is worth serious consideration is the incorporation of the Service in the Civil Service. If this could be done it would make it possible for staff to be assigned to the municipal and local or district authorities who are of the same quality as those in the Ministries and Departments of government. It would also provide for transferability within the enlarged Civil Service so that those in the service of local authorities do not feel they are prisoners of that service. It implies also that specialist staff in the development disciplines, such as agriculture, engineering, health, education, planning and management, could be more readily made available to municipal and local authorities. The Local Government Service would then cease to be the Cinderella of the public services and would join the mainstream of the Civil Service.

There would, of course, be the need to consider such questions as management, control, recruitment, appointment and discipline – and the extent of participation of the municipal and district authorities and councils in these matters. If Local Government Servants become Civil Servants, then appointments, promotions and discipline would transfer to the Public (or Civil) Service Commission which should reorganize its machinery to handle these added responsibilities. The other functions of management and control would rest with the local authorities. The responsibilities of the Public Service Commission would, however, have to be exercised in a manner that consults the interests of local authorities. For instance, Civil Servants would, generally speaking, be appointed to the service of local authorities and not just posted. Also, the chief executives of local authorities would be appointed after full consultation with them.

This proposed scheme might not suit all countries. It is essential, however, that, like the Teaching Service, the Local Government Service should somehow be accorded the prestige which would enable it to attract and hold its fair share of suitable and trained personnel. The means for achieving this would depend in each case on local circumstances.

SERVICE IN THE STATUTORY BOARDS AND CORPORATIONS

There is a tendency in a number of the African States to transfer certain central Government responsibilities previously operated by the Civil Service to statutory boards and corporations. Some of these responsibilities were carried out direct by the Civil Service because in the States' early stages of development the Governments found it necessary to accept direct responsibility in the absence of the conditions for intervention by private enterprise. Thus electricity and power industries, railways undertakings, agricultural and co-operative enterprises, housing, film production, water supplies and others were all run by Governments, and all those employed in them were classified as Civil Servants. It is becoming increasingly recognized, however, that these enterprises, because of their industrial and commercial nature, are not suited to the methods and standards applied in the Civil Service.

In the first place, commercial and industrial undertakings are best run on commercial and business lines with administration and management freed from the 'red-tape' regulations and instructions applicable to the Civil Service. Secondly, greater impact could be made on development in particular directions, for instance in housing development, if the undertakings were freed from the detailed control of the Ministries. Moreover, by being able to draw on African managerial manpower existing outside the Civil Service, these business enterprises are able sooner than would otherwise be the case to Africanize their control and management. It should be added, however, that one of the reasons why African Governments sometimes turn over these responsibilities to boards and corporations is to widen the scope for political patronage. The directorates of these bodies have been a most useful means of rewarding political service for those who have supported the party in power and have also relevant experience. This is possible since service on the boards and corporations is outside the scope of the Civil Service. There is a further consideration. Governments could have handed over some of these undertakings to private enterprise, as for instance, electricity and power, housing and film production. Most African Governments, however, prefer to retain within the public sector the control of public utilities, enterprises which have sensitivity to the social interests of the people and also all undertakings which are related to the economic infrastructure of the countries. This policy is sometimes justified by such political principles as African or democratic socialism. It is, however, defensible also on the ground that the control of these enterprises by the Governments, through public bodies set up by statutory instruments, is essential for development planning and the expansion of services, so that the need to make profits is not a paramount consideration.

Employment under the statutory boards and corporations is not in the Civil Service by definition, but since the Governments have interest, direct and indirect, in them and, in some cases, have to provide funds for their operation from public revenues, there are good reasons why the terms of service in these bodies should have some relation to those applying to the Civil Service. Moreover it is a function of the State to train and develop manpower. When trained manpower is scarce, all bodies in the public sector should keep in step in order to ensure that there is a fair distribution of the persons available for appointments. Either, therefore, there should be some provision in the statutory instruments creating the boards and corporations or else informal consultation arrangements should be established to ensure that there are no great disparities in the employment policies of these bodies as between themselves, and also as between them and the public services.

The main problem here concerns the principles on which service under these public bodies should be remunerated and the conditions of service which should be applied, for instance, in respect of housing and leave conditions. There are two conflicting principles. The statutory boards and corporations are established to free them from the regulatory arrangements in the public services and the usual consideration of detailed Cabinet and Treasury control. Where they are concerned with industrial and commercial transactions, the conditions under which they operate more nearly approach those of business and industrial enterprises than government departments. The terms under which its employees are remunerated and given fringe benefits should, it is therefore claimed, be based on those applicable to commercial and industrial firms. On the other hand, all these boards and corporations are established to carry out responsibilities in the public sector and they normally draw on the same source and types of trained personnel as do government departments. Having regard, therefore, to the chronic shortage of trained manpower in all African States, the terms of service in these bodies should not be too much out of alignment with those applicable to the public services. Where the jobs are really comparable with those in commerce and industry, this principle may be hard to defend. It has to be borne in mind, however, that there is a tendency to adopt the principle of permanent and superannuable service in these public bodies similar to, if not quite the same as, that in the public services. Moreover, in most States commercial and industrial terms of service are themselves geared to those offered in the government service since the Government is the largest employer in each State. It should therefore not be too difficult to reach a compromise over the problem of fixing the terms of employment in the statutory boards and corporations. They cannot be the same as in the Civil Service, since the employees of these bodies do not enjoy the same terms of security of tenure, non-contributory pensions, working conditions, organizational structure and disciplinary requirements. It should be expected therefore that pay rates would be somewhat higher than in the Civil Service. Taking into consideration all factors applying to the different terms of service, the object should be to equalize as nearly as possible the attractions of employment under the two services. It would then be left to individuals to choose which type of employment they prefer having regard to their training and experience and the openings that are offered at any particular time.

Statutory boards and corporations, although not directly controlled in the same way as government departments, are nevertheless subject to the general policy direction of the Ministries within whose portfolios their responsibilities lie. Generally speaking the statutory instrument establishing a board or corporation sets out its functions, and the powers of the governing council or Board of Directors. In most cases, certain functions can only be exercised under covering approval by the appropriate Minister. For instance, Produce Marketing Boards require the specific agreement of the Minister to the fixing of prices payable to the producer. The Civil Servants who staff the Ministry would therefore have certain responsibilities in relation to the board or corporation mostly of a regulatory, advisory, supervisory and inspecting nature, but these should be clearly defined in the statutory instruments. Subject to these, however, the board or corporation would be free to govern its affairs without further interference from the Minister and his staff.

There would be no purpose in bringing in the affairs of boards and corporations in a discussion of the Civil Service had it not been for the fact that they are public bodies and therefore are in competition with the Civil Service for such manpower as is available. Since trained manpower is scarce, there has to be a certain amount of rationing between the various bodies in the public sector of those whose training has been sponsored by the Government. In the absence of compulsory direction of manpower, the only way such rationing could take place is to ensure that no one of the Government employing agencies – the public services and the statutory boards and corporations – is out of alignment, taking all factors into consideration, with the others. Variations in terms of service there have to be, but these variations should be purely marginal and not substantial.

P

CHAPTER 14

Service Standards and Traditions

SERVICE standards and traditions, in some of their aspects, have been discussed in earlier chapters, but it is convenient at this stage to bring together the main threads under a separate chapter. Their importance in any Civil Service cannot be over-rated since the creation and maintenance of healthy traditions of high standards in matters such as loyalty, integrity, political impartiality, and personal conduct constitute the atmosphere in which a Civil Servant works and lives. Members' attitudes are shaped by these traditions or by their absence. There were traditions and values in the old Colonial Service which made it one of the finest services in the world. These are, however, not appropriate to the requirements of the new dispensation in all respects, although there are many of the traditions which are applicable to all public services and therefore are universal in character. The rapid change-over in structure and personnel brought about by constitutional changes and accelerated Africanization and localization has made, in any case, the main-tenance of the old traditions and values difficult. In some cases, they have been seriously undermined. It is worth, therefore, examining some of them and their importance to the mainten-ance of a viable and healthy Civil Service. Morale, efficiency and discipline have been described as being essential elements in the administration of any Civil Service, but they are best sustained in a healthy state where the spirit of the service is influenced by worthy traditions and values.

LOYALTY

It has been stated earlier that in an independent State, the Civil Service is the executive arm of the Government and its effective-ness in exercising this responsibility could have a material in-fluence on the image which the Government presents to the public and the attitude of the public to the Government. This intimacy in the relationship between Government and the Civil

Service requires the existence of a special spirit of loyalty between the two – the Civil Servants to the Government and the Government to the Civil Servants. The tradition of loyalty to the State is one which must persist if the Civil Service is to exercise its special role in the affairs of the Government. In a sense, this loyalty is basic to all the traditions of the Civil Service which must in the true sense be a servant unit of the State. It determines the permanency of the Service – and it implies that loyalty to the State transcends any temporary allegiance to the Government of the day. The stability, the impartiality and the integrity of the Service depends on this concept of the loyalty of the Civil Service to the State as an entity transcending any other loyalty. Normally, this is not in conflict with the other, and immediately more important, loyalty to the Government of the day. But, it is possible that a corrupt and power-seeking Government might try to use the Service for purposes inimical to the interests of State, in which circumstances, the higher loyalty of the service might come in conflict with its immediate loyalty to the Government. Under the Colonial regime, the loyalty of the Civil Service to the State expressed itself as loyalty and allegiance to the Sovereign. Where the constitution of the new independent African State provides for a constitutional head of State – a Governor-General or President – then, it is possible for this higher loyalty to be transferred to him. In cases, however, where the President is also the executive head of Government, then it becomes difficult to identify him as representing in all respects the State as an entity to which the higher loyalty of the Service should be directed. In normal circumstances, as explained earlier, there should be no conflict, but where the loyalty of the Service is strained unduly, there could be serious conflict.

Nevertheless, the Government of the day is charged under the Constitution, and authorized by Parliament (which represents the people) to administer the affairs of the State. In practice, therefore, it is entitled to receive the loyalty of all Civil Servants as a matter of course. If there is a change of Government, naturally the Civil Servants' loyalty to the new Government should be equally strong. This is of course something which it is difficult for the uninitiated to understand and it may well be asked how it is possible for people to switch their loyalties so readily. It can only be understood if it is realized that this sense of loyalty is not one based on personal relationships between officials and their Ministers. It is, in a sense, a professional relationship. The Civil Servant is trained to perform certain functions of a professional or technical nature and he acquires the experience to carry through these responsibilities. He receives his instructions, specific or general, from the Government through his Minister, and so long as he is able to carry out his instructions faithfully without being required to offend his professional or technical integrity, there is no question that he can give his complete loyalty to the Government through his Minister. It may go too far to call the Civil Servant a mercenary, but some of the qualities of a mercenary are evident in his attitude to the Government. He does not necessarily have to believe, or have complete faith in, what the Government stands for. He should, however, believe that the Government is acting constitutionally and that its policies are compatible with the highest interests of the State. He should also believe that he is not being made to act against his professional integrity. He also has to be assured that his Minister's own loyalty to him is equally strong and reciprocates his own loyalty to his Minister. The two-way channel of loyalty presupposes that both sides are acting in good faith. It is possible then for the Minister to accept full responsibility for the acts of his officials and defend them as his own in public and in Parliament even though he might not have prior knowledge of these acts.

Thus a Civil Servant has to work within two frameworks of loyalties. His first loyalty is to the State, in practice the head of State. His conduct and actions must be shaped to fit into this loyalty so that all his official actions are brought into consonance with the highest interests of State. Compatible with this, normally, is the Civil Servant's loyalty to the Government of the day as expressed through his relations with his Minister. In this, he is acting in accordance with his professional conscience and is willing and able to give to the Government the utmost of his professional and technical ability provided that he is never required to act contrary to the integrity of his profession or technical vocation. In return, he is entitled to receive from the Government through his Minister full public support and responsibility for actions taken on behalf of the Minister in good faith where the actions are within the broad terms of the policy directions of the Minister. It does happen occasionally, but fortunately very rarely, that a Civil Servant is required to act in a manner which he could not reconcile with his conception of his duty to the State or with his conscience in relation to his professional or technical integrity. In these circumstances, the Civil Servant is faced with the difficult problem of considering his personal position and a choice between compromising his standards and remaining in the service or else resigning his appointment. Happily, this situation does not often arise.

POLITICS AND THE CIVIL SERVANT

The special relationships between Civil Servants and Ministers which have been discussed above do not imply that Civil Servants should be involved in the politics of the party in power. A Civil Service that is riddled with politics loses its integrity and impartiality and its permanency of status is seriously undermined. Obviously, if there is a change of power, or even a shift in power within the same party, then a purge would have to be carried out in the service to eliminate all those who were supporters of the party or faction which has lost power. Moreover, the public is bound to lose confidence in the integrity and impartiality of the service since it would be assumed that the service would always pursue party political interests and disregard the interests of those who might be known to be politically opposed to the ruling party. Merit and qualifications would cease to be the criteria for appointments and promotions and political zeal would open the doors to high office. Such a state of affairs is inefficient, too, since trained manpower is not used effectively for what the people could best do but rather because they are zealous members of the party in power. Thus officers would tend to look to political action for advancing their careers rather than to their own ability and the proper evaluation of their experience.

The view has been expressed that, where there is a one-party State whether by law or in practice, there is no need to draw a sharp line between the party and the Civil Service. One should merge into the other and there should be the possibility of movement of officials between party organizations and Government Ministries and Departments. The argument in favour of this view is that in new countries where the best talent rests in the Civil Service it is a loss to sound political judgement in public affairs if Civil Servants are denied influence in party political affairs. Obviously, where there are two or more political parties, this view is dangerous. Even in one-party States, this argument is of doubtful validity for the reasons stated in the previous paragraph. It is in the best interests of all States, old or new, to maintain Civil Services which are kept distinct from party political bodies and which therefore are in the position to provide the stable element in the Governments of the States.

This should not imply that the Civil Servant should have no politics at all. He is, like any other citizen, entitled to his own political views. These views should, however, express themselves via the ballot box and not in active and open participation in politics to the extent of prejudicing the officer's ability to act with impartiality. Some Governments permit memberships of political parties for Civil Servants so long as there is no active participation in the affairs of the parties such as holding party office or speaking on political platforms. Other Governments do not permit memberships in political parties at all and even bar office messengers from belonging to political parties. An appropriate approach would appear to be to bar from active participation in politics all those officials who are responsible for policy processing or who handle confidential and controversial policy papers. These would include administrative, executive, clerical, professional and all supervisory staff. Others who are technicians or industrial workers do not normally touch policy papers, and there is no reason why they should not participate fully in politics by holding office in political parties and standing for local or national elections. Where an officer in the first category wishes to stand for elections, he must resign before he is nominated, and even if he loses, he should forfeit all rights to be reinstated. In the case of the second category, however, there is no reason why the officer should not be reinstated if he loses although his resignation should stand if he is elected to Parliament. He should, however, be permitted to remain in service if he is elected to the council of a local authority.

INTEGRITY

One of the most important – if not the most important – traditions of any Civil Service is integrity. It has been stated in an earlier chapter that the standard that must be created and maintained is one of absolute integrity. Rules and regulations exist to prevent fraud and dishonesty, and penalties are imposed on defaulters which act also as a deterrent for others who might be tempted. Ultimately, however, a healthy convention establishing codes of conduct for officers would be the best guarantee of the maintenance of a high standard of integrity in the service. The distinctive quality which the public expects of the Civil Service is honesty in the private and official conduct of its officers. This together with complete impartiality, which is really an aspect of integrity, is what retains the confidence of the public in its Civil Service.

Equally important in this respect is intellectual integrity. The Civil Servant should strive to stand for the highest principles in public life and this should be reflected in the advice he gives to his Minister and the manner in which he carries out his appointed tasks. His advice to his political masters must be based on an honest appreciation of the facts of the situation and what he conceives to be the best to be done in the circumstances. If he is willing, or is persuaded, to trim his advice to what he thinks his political masters would like to have or hear, then he has compromised his intellectual integrity. He cannot expect to retain the confidence and respect of his Ministers for long if he is compromised in this way. They may sometimes use him because he is a convenient and pliant tool, but as soon as he has finished serving their purposes, they will drop him. If on the other hand he always gives honest and unbiased advice the Ministers should discover in time that they are able to rely on him and he may thus win their confidence. Even if in certain circumstances intellectual integrity irritates and becomes irksome to politicians, the officer has the satisfaction of knowing that he has never compromised his standards and has never lost respect either in the eyes of his peers or in his own eyes.

THE CIVIL SERVANT IN THE COMMUNITY

In a sense, Civil Servants are a class apart. In their official activities they are required to shun publicity and to seek anonymity. This is even more necessary in private life. When an official leaves his office, he leaves behind him his official titles and position and assumes his place in the family and traditional society. He has a private life and personal place in society and should accept the normal obligations of an ordinary citizen. He should not attempt to seek special privileges for himself merely because he is a Civil Servant. In this sense, the Civil Servant is not part of a special and privileged class but an integrated member of his own traditional society. He must seek, however, to retain his integrity within that society and it would be improper for him to attempt to set himself apart from his neighbours and his family because of any official position which he might hold. Incidentally, this is one of the strongest arguments against setting Civil Servants apart in special residential areas.

The attitude of the Civil Servant to the public should be normal and co-operative. This may appear obvious, but how often have officials been charged with behaving as 'civil masters' instead of 'civil servants'? Regrettably, the conduct of many officials in relation to the public leaves much to be desired. And yet, unless actions taken which affect the interests of members of the public are related to what they seek, even though they may not always get what they want, such actions are valueless. The main test here is whether the official shows normal courtesy to members of the public. It costs nothing to be courteous to people and yet there is nothing that irritates people more than to be shown discourtesy. Discourteous conduct brings the whole service into disrepute. It is useful to remember Aggrey's advice in this connection: 'you can kill more flies with molasses than with vinegar'.

It is important also that the public should see that the Civil Service displays an attitude of responsibility to public property. If officials are seen to be careless with the use of property committed to their care, such as vehicles, if they are seen also to be misusing such properties and if they divert official materials to their own use whether these be pencils, or cars, or houses, then they bring the whole service into disrepute even where they are not caught out or their actions are not liable to prosecution. Infringement of regulations over the custody and misuse of government property can be dealt with by the appropriate disciplinary procedure. Obviously if the Civil Service has too many incidents of such infringements, there is bound to be loss of confidence in its ability to safeguard the interests of the Government. There are many cases, however, which do not infringe regulations but which are plainly improper or immoral. This attitude to public property is unhealthy and wherever it prevails does great discredit to the Civil Service.

Another unfortunate reputation which attaches to the Civil Service is the one of being riddled with bureaucratic 'red tapeism'. This charge is very often unfounded but there are a few examples of actions which are unnecessarily formal or deliberate to make this charge stick to the Civil Service. Obviously the Civil Service should exercise proper caution in every action it undertakes and should give a thorough examination to every policy proposal. This very necessary precaution observed by officials leads to impatience and irritation sometimes but often this irritation is induced by the frustration of selfish or improper proposals by the persons complaining. Nevertheless, it is most important that the Civil Service should do everything possible to combat this unfortunate reputation and to get rid of it wherever it exists. Only then could false accusations be properly exposed. For this to be possible, the Civil Service should become aware of the urgency of spirit of their new Government in its anxiety to accelerate its economic and social development programmes. If the Civil Service can work within this new political rhythm then the effort to bring about proper examination of policies and programmes would be regarded as being helpful rather than obstructive.

CONCLUSION

The following paragraphs quoted from *A New Charter for the Civil Service* – a Ghana Government White Paper published in 1960 – provides a fitting conclusion to the matters discussed in the preceding paragraphs:

'He (the Civil Servant) is a member of a corps dedicated to the service of the community and he should maintain a code of conduct and morals which should not only avoid bringing that Service into disrepute but should positively enhance its reputation in the eyes of all with whom he comes into contact. If at any time, a Civil Servant becomes identified in the eyes of the public with a particular political ideology or party his impartiality in the performance of his official duties becomes thereby prejudiced. To that extent he has brought the Service into disrepute.

'Though it is necessary to make written rules and regulations governing the conduct of Civil Servants, in a healthy Civil Service, tradition and convention, to a large extent, transcend the written codes and provide an unwritten code of ethics and conduct for which the most effective sanction is the public opinion inside the Service itself. It is upon the maintenance of a sound and healthy faculty of self-criticism within the Service that its value and efficiency will in the long run depend.

'Tradition, conventions, self-criticism, self-improvement, all depend on technical competence, professional knowledge, confidence in objectives and sympathy with ideals. These are the virtues which should be cultivated by the Civil Servant. All possible facilities will be provided by the Government for the development of a healthy, competent, self-confident Civil Service but that Civil Service must cultivate its own traditions, the greatest of which should be the conception of a section of the community bound together by acceptance of the common purpose that their talents are dedicated for the service of the community and that they seek their satisfaction in the knowledge of a job well done . . .'

A Civil Service in which this tradition is widely accepted and understood is secure in its future.

CHAPTER 15

The Civil Service in Contemporary Africa

Much has been said in earlier chapters about the role of the Civil Service in African States and its relations with the Government. Perhaps no more need really be said about this matter, but on the other hand it would be most convenient to put in a summary form in the concluding chapter the main objectives which it has been intended all along to put across. Unless the Civil Service and Civil Servants form a proper appreciation of the part they have to play in the revolution now taking place in contemporary Africa, they run the risk of forefeiting their right to survive in the form in which the service now exists and is likely to develop in the future.

The Civil Service in present-day Africa is faced with tasks and responsibilities which were not envisaged only a few years ago. Certainly, no one contemplated, before 1939, that there would be this rapid post-war acceleration of constitutional development. It caught the Civil Service completely unawares. The service was therefore not easily adjustable to the rapidly changing conditions. As stated earlier, the old colonial administrations and technical departments were concerned with such matters as maintenance of law and order, local administration, the provision of a moderate level of social services, elementary communications network and the husbanding of natural resources. There were no five or ten year development plans, no major policies on industrialization, no talk of providing economic infrastructure services, nor any full development of the economy, no balance of payment difficulties, no talk of deficit financing policies, no central banking nor the creation of money markets, and no external relations problems whether political, economic or commercial.

Now, however, all African States have got to concern themselves with major matters and problems of a variety and complexity that would test the abilities of the most mature Civil Servants of any country. All African governments promise to work for the raising of the standard of life of their peoples and they all, as a matter of priority, embark on the preparation and carrying out of comprehensive development plans. The preparation of such plans, which shall provide for balanced development in economic, social and cultural fields, so that the increase in the national income and therefore government revenue is able to pay for the non-productive services, is a very complicated matter and requires a degree of sophisticated economic, statistical and professional knowledge not easily available to African countries. Coupled with this programme of economic and social development planning is the need to establish a system for the regulation of the economic and financial structure of the particular State. This implies the modernization of budgeting policies and procedures, the creation of a central banking institution, the establishment of legislation, institutions or machinery to favour industrial and agricultural development, and the setting up of planning organizations or units, including machinery for manpower planning.

Closely related is the accelerated expansion of social and socio-economic services in such fields as health and nutrition, education, social development and community development. These used to be regarded as social services only, which should be maintained and expanded when the economic services could pay for them. It is now recognized that they have their significant contributions to make to economic development. Obviously for instance, the provision of health services and better nutrition in areas which are populated with men whose health is below the normal level, and who suffer from food deficiencies, would be bound to result in healthier workers and therefore higher productivity. It is recognized also that the educational system is the main instrument for the training of manpower and that social and community development provides positive means for mobilizing local available resources – including local manpower resources – for tackling some of the more immediate social and economic problems of the local areas. This recognition of the role of social and socio-economic services in the improvement of the well-being of the people has come at a time when new African governments are taking over. Even expatriate Civil Servants of ripe experience generally would have found it difficult to adjust their ideas to this new approach.

Furthermore, the establishment of external relations policies and organizations is something completely new to the experience of all who exercise some responsibilities for the affairs of government in African States. It is natural that external or foreign relations should come to new countries at the time of their independence, since only independent States could organize Ministries of External or Foreign Affairs, diplomatic services and diplomatic missions abroad. New policies in relation to the United Nations, the Commonwealth, the Afro-Asian bloc, apartheid, colonialism, the European Common Market, disarmament, the 'cold war' and other external matters have to be formulated, bearing in mind the safeguarding of the national interest. Policies and organizations have also to accommodate the rise of African politics and Pan-Africanism and moves towards the achievement of a political union of African States.

Again, there is the problem of the creation of a nation out of a conglomeration of tribes and communities and, in some instances, races who reside within the national boundaries. These were brought together and held together by the imperial power in the pre-independence days. The task before the new States is to create a national consciousness among these various peoples and a feeling of belonging to one nation whose interests should transcend all others, including tribal and communal interests. This is not an easy task to perform, and the objective of achieving a sense of nationhood by which citizenship is the best qualification for consideration in all national matters rather than tribe or religion or race is a hard one to attain.

All these matters – economic development planning, the provision of social and socio-economic services, the establishment of economic and financial services, external relations, African politics and the integration of all tribes, religions, communities and races into a sense of nationhood – are formidable matters for any Government to handle. They are even more formidable when they have to be tackled by governments whose members are new to these problems and whose Civil Services are being rapidly Africanized. Such men are carried forward into doing the best they can, under the circumstances, because of an almost missionary zeal which impels them to attempt to bring progress, prosperity and happiness to their peoples. Enthusiasm operates where experience is lacking or is insufficient. In most African States, Ministers and other members of the government have had comparatively recent experience of matters of policy of this nature. Certainly, a rapidly changing Civil Service which is being Africanized at an accelerated rate could not claim to have the experience for tackling these formidable programmes and problems. They could not have acquired this experience from their former expatriate colleagues since these themselves had not been through this experience, which is a function of independence.

The new African Civil Service has therefore the task of not only building itself up and placing itself as rapidly as possible on an indigenous basis but also of adapting itself to assist Ministers in tackling the major matters and problems mentioned above, as well as others not included. To this should be added the need to reform the orientation and structure of the Civil Service so that it is able to function in consonance with the government's political systems and policies. It should be emphasized that these responsibilities are either very new to the African situation or else they have to be discharged under conditions vastly different from those prevailing before independence. The experience that rested in the old Civil Service was therefore either irrelevant in some cases or else had to be considerably adapted to the contemporary situation. This adaptation and this orientation have to take place at a time when the service itself is going through a period of rapid turnover in personnel brought about by accelerated Africanization policies, and when inevitably there are lacking in the officials a wealth of ripe experience and adequate maturity. In the circumstances, therefore, it is most encouraging to find that there is a great awareness among African Civil Servants that they have a role to play in the contemporary African situation which must match the increased range of responsibilities that now devolve on them. In most cases, they have succeeded in providing, in understanding and enthusiasm, what they might have lacked in experience and maturity. There is no disguising the fact, however, that on the whole, the African Civil Service has not been prepared for its new role, through no fault of its own, and has therefore not been able to meet adequately, and in all respects, the challenge of the new age.

The task of the Civil Service has been made more difficult by a number of other factors which might account for the fact that the service has to go through a much longer period of adjustment before it settles down to the responsibilities thrust upon it. Far too often, African governments and their Ministers do not understand and appreciate the relative roles of themselves and the Civil Service. They either expect too much and are disappointed if they do not have performance matching up to expectations, or else they endeavour to by-pass their Civil Servants, which further complicates matters. This situation arises from a number of reasons. Ministers are impatient to get on with the programmes they have set before them in their election manifestos and Party pronouncements. Their people expect quick results and they themselves are anxious to demonstrate that independence means action for progress and the alleviation of some of the burdens and impediments of the past. They find, in the circumstances, that the Civil Service machinery is too ponderous for their purpose and too deliberate in its procedures for examining and implementing policies. They make no allowances for the fact that by their own policies, comparatively inexperienced persons have been placed in the key positions of Permanent Secretaries and Heads of Departments and that, even though these men are working long hours and with all their ability to keep up with the pile of responsibilities which confront them, they would necessarily take a much longer time to get through their tasks, since they have to work most things out from first principles and only a few can take things in the stride of experience. In such circumstances, patience and understanding is called for from both sides and this is not always forthcoming.

The situation is further complicated by attempts by Ministers to control or influence appointments, promotions and discipline in the Civil Service. This is an understandable desire since a Minister's responsibility for the management of the services and policies within his portfolio cannot be entirely divorced from those aspects of this management concerning the personnel executing these services and policies. This matter has been discussed at some length earlier but there is a tendency for Ministers to go beyond the point that is reasonable and they make it difficult to create the conditions for the establishment of those healthy conventions that are essential for ensuring morale, security and discipline in the Civil Service.

An aspect of this improper intervention in appointments and promotions is the intrusion of political appointments into the Civil Service. Where these are competent, they present no problem and in fact they might result in a net gain since, in the early stages of Africanization at any rate, there is normally so much vacant room that the interests of career Civil Servants are not at any serious risk. Very often, however, the main qualification of a political appointee is party political zeal and he does not have the ability, experience or competence to discharge the responsibilities of the post to which he is appointed. This sort of situation is bound to undermine confidence and efficiency in the service. The situation is worse where politically appointed officers are placed above career Civil Servants of greater experience and ability. A relevant example is the appointment of politicians to district administrative positions as District or Area Commissioners, in some cases over the heads of graduates or officials with long field experience.

Another factor in the situation is that all African governments adopt the policy of a welfare state in some form or other. This policy very often takes the form of socialism – African or democratic socialism, Nkrumahism or Ujamaa. Whether it is termed socialism or not, all new governments adopt a policy of State intervention and participation in the major economic and social programmes of development so as to accelerate the economic and social betterment of the people. They further endeavour to influence the political, social and cultural outlook of the people, particularly of the youth, as part of the programme for the transformation of the society into one which is indigenously based, whilst taking advantage of existing or future developments from overseas which would help to bring indigenous society into the modern world. This is an additional factor in making the task of the Civil Service more complex than it would normally be.

It is not surprising, therefore, that in nearly all the African States, the Civil Service no more has the initiative in the formulation of operational policies. It is, it has already been made clear, the responsibility of the Ministers to determine political policy but the programming of such policies should normally be left to the Civil Service. It is the usual situation nowadays, however, to see Ministers working out their own detailed programmes, supervising the execution of these programmes and generally carrying out functions which should properly be discharged by their officials. Admittedly there is nothing sacrosanct about the pattern of the past or the conventions in the relationship between Ministers and officials established elsewhere; it is entirely proper that African States should wish to establish their own patterns or conventions. But local and appropriate patterns and conventions have to be established and stabilized so that the Civil Service is in the position to form an appreciation of its role and to exercise full initiative within it. The object should be that operational policy is defined as the responsibility of the Civil Service, leaving political and broad policy to Ministers. In between there is always room for Civil Servants to assist Ministers with their policy formulation responsibilities and for Ministers to give clear indications, whenever necessary or appropriate, on how they wish particular policies to be carried out.

To recapture the initiative in exercising the right to formulate operational policy, and even to provide the lead in most of the major, sometimes political, policies, does mean both the establishment of the proper pattern or conventions in the relations between Minister and officials, and imaginative planning for the education and orientation of the Civil Service. The policies and detailed programmes required for these would vary from State to State according to the circumstances. But some or all of the programmes which will now be discussed would apply.

In the first place, it is important that there should be a programme of orientation training aimed at inculcating in all Civil Servants, particularly those in the higher ranks, as full an understanding as possible of the socio-economic policies of their governments. This understanding is essential if they are to be in the position to play a positive role in the affairs of their Governments, to advise on the formulation of political and major policies on economic and social matters and to be in the position to interpret in terms of operational policies and programmes, the policies of their Ministers.

Secondly, there is need also to educate the Civil Servants to understand and appreciate the politics of their country, and in particular, the politics of the Party in power. National politics provide the climate within which the whole government functions, and the highly placed official has got to become consciously aware of this if he is to operate within the context of what the political objectives of his government are. This is particularly important in new African States where politics are pursued with national fervour. Unless the Civil Service operates on the same wavelength as the Government, there cannot be harmonious relations or even efficiency. The Civil Service is not

Q

a mechanical system which merely responds to the whims and idiosyncrasies of Ministers. It is a living organism with a mind of its own which should endeavour to achieve a sympathy with the aspirations of the government if it is to be an effective partner in managing the affairs of the nation. The government, if it is a responsible government, would be glad to work with a service which has made a successful effort to achieve this degree of sympathy. On the other hand, a Civil Service which operates on its own chosen wavelength different from that of the government would cease to be effective, however well staffed and operationally efficient it might be, and would soon fall out with the government.

Thirdly, machinery should be provided for bringing about mutual understanding of each other's role between Ministers on the one hand, and the Civil Service on the other. This is really an aspect of the first two programmes discussed above. What is required here, however, is that there should be a conscious effort on the part of the head of Government and the head of the Civil Service to bring about a firm appreciation of each other's worth between these two groups. The establishment of mutual confidence upon which sound working relations will emerge cannot happen by chance. It has got to be worked for, and a further effort has to be expended to maintain a healthy state of affairs once this has been achieved. Seminars and conferences, whether of a general nature or on specific projects, should be arranged whenever the opportunity offers so that Ministers and officials could apply their minds and experience towards finding solutions to problems of mutual concern. There should be periodical and regular conferences between Ministers and their staffs for the discussion and consideration of major problems, or even for the purpose of talking generally about the general programmes of the particular Ministries. There should also be occasional meetings between the President or Prime Minister and Permanent Secretaries and heads of Departments so that the overall government policy can be understood against the background of discussion with the highest authority in the land and so also that the President or Prime Minister may come to hear the views of the top level officials concerned with operational policies and get to know them and their worth. Every possible opportunity for getting politicians and Civil Servants together, whether to work on projects of mutual concern or to get to know one another better, should be exploited. The object of all of these is to bring home to Ministers and officials alike the realization that they are all working for common objectives within the same regime and are not operating in separate watertight compartments.

The next practical programme is the provision of comprehensive and purposeful training facilities. All training should be orientated not only towards achieving operational efficiency but also towards educating Civil Servants on the 'facts of life' of the current situation in their country including its politics, economy, society and culture. The scope and programme of training have already been discussed and all that is necessary is to reiterate here that there should be a clear understanding among all those that have responsibility for the administration and management of the Civil Service at all levels that this training programme is a constant, never-ending and evolving process, and must be a permanent feature of any Civil Service. It is not enough to provide training in the techniques and routine responsibilities of particular classes or grades of posts. In addition, there must be a conscious inclusion in the syllabus of every training course the preparation and orientation of the minds and attitudes of all trainees to make them aware of the political, economic and social background against which they have to relate their day-to-day responsibilities. Only if there is a determined and planned effort to achieve this as part of the training process is it possible to make the Civil Service work in consonance with the policies and impetus of the Government.

The role of the Institutes or Schools of Public Administration and Staff Colleges has already been described. It is in these institutions that the study and research into administrative problems, the interpretation of the welfare state philosophy in terms of local circumstances, and the techniques that are relevant to the local situation could be carried out. It is also in these institutions, particularly the latter, that those officers who are going to influence policy by virtue of the key positions they hold, or are likely to hold, could be given an intimate appreciation of the factors that bear on national policy, including internal politics, finance, military potential both internal and external, world politics, security and industry. Particular emphasis should be laid on research into administrative problems and techniques, the organization of the structure of the government machinery required to respond to the new political patterns, manpower development problems, methodologies, the training materials and techniques suited to the social and psychological background of the people, and the methods of application of the results of research. The importance of research to the Civil Service is the same as relevant research is to industry. It provides, in its results, for economy in the use of resources and the most appropriate and relevant material for the ordering of government business, and the preparation through training, directed experience and orientation of Civil Servants for the effective discharge of their duties.

Fundamental to all these programmes is the endeavour to inculcate in Civil Servants the right ideas on the role of their service in the welfare state – or socialist state, as some would prefer to call it. This is necessary if they are to be effective as the executive arm of the government and, for those in the higher ranks, if they are to be in the position to help, counsel and advise their Governments in the formidable task of shaping the policies and hence the destiny, of the nation. The scope of this process of orientation is wide and embraces an appreciation and study of such matters as political science, economics, sociology, social psychology, law, and international relations in combinations as necessary for the particular situation. The process of orientation should also not only lay emphasis on professional training, efficient working methods and training in objectivity and analysis, but should also provide synthesis, common sense, power of judgement and reason and the ability to find out practical and positive solutions to various administrative problems.

On the Civil Servants in the higher ranks – the Senior Administrators in Ministries, in the Departments and Divisions and in the Regions or Provinces – lies the responsibility for providing the leadership in all these matters. In particular, in the present era of rapid economic and social change, they have the special responsibility for the management of the economic and social policies planned for their states – and the application of technology to this against the background of deliberate political and ideological policy. They should be able to identify the most urgent and priority targets of government in the social and economic fields, spearhead planning policy, be in the position to secure the implementation of plans and programmes and to arrange the evaluation of programmes completed or in progress. This implies ability to mobilize all the resources required for this purpose and to set the pace for other Civil Servants whom they lead.

Senior Administrators have therefore to be as professional in their role of policy formulators and managers as the specialist doctor, engineer, economist or technologist. They should also be innovators if they are to be able to operate on the frontiers of policy in partnership with Ministers and those responsible for other sectors of the economy. This implies sustained and systematic effort at preparation and training. It implies also continual review, not only of the structure of the Civil Service, but also of the machinery of government if the administration is to have the proper setting to fulfil its dynamic role.

The acceptance by all Civil Servants of the principle that their role is determined by the dynamics of change which apply in any particular period and in the peculiar situation of each state should impel them to adapt themselves so that they are able to fulfil the role expected of them. Unless they approach their tasks with a desire to bring themselves up to date, to adopt a professional approach to their responsibilities and to understand their proper place in the order of things, they might find that they have ceased to become effective instruments of change.

The Civil Service in its life and work should effectively and positively respond to the nation's will and be able to act in consonance with the urgency of the political and economic situation of all new countries. It should work to earn the trust and confidence of the government and people so that it is enabled to establish itself as the permanent stabilizing force necessary for orderly progress in the state and towards the well-being of the people.

APPENDIX I
DIAGRAMMATIC PRESENTATION OF THE STRUCTURE OF
THE GENERAL SERVICES BRANCH OF THE CIVIL SERVICE

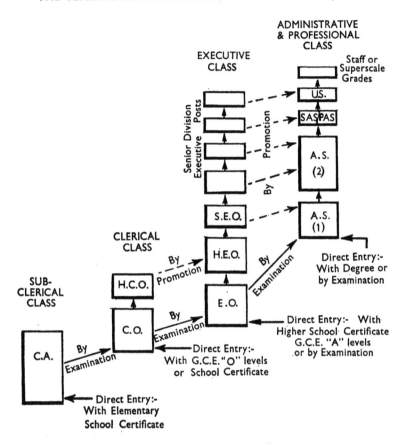

Legend

CA	...	Clerical Assistant
CO	...	Clerical Officer
HCO	...	Higher Clerical Officer
EO	...	Executive Officer
HEO	...	Higher Executive Officer
SEO	...	Senior Executive Officer
AS	...	Assistant Secretary
SAS	...	Senior Assistant Secretary
PAS	...	Principal Assistant Secretary
US	...	Under Secretary

APPENDIX II

SOME TYPICAL EXISTING SALARY STRUCTURES

	NIGERIA	GHANA	SIERRA LEONE	UGANDA	TANGANYIKA	KENYA AND E.A. COMMUNITY
Staff Grade/Superscale Posts	£3900—£1728	£3050—£1470	£3350—£1600	£3100—£1839	£2600—£1860	£2780—£1760
Administrative, Professional and Scientific Classes	£1368—£1890 £720—£1584	£1040—£1320 £680—£980	£1284—£1476 £684—£1236	£1026—£1791 £798—£975	£1014—£1830 £762—£966	£1020—£1710 £804—£976
Executive, Technical and Senior Secretarial Classes	£312—£1584	£265—£1450	£360—£1476	£416—£1671	£300—£1710	£380—£1598
Clerical, Junior Secretarial, Minor Technical and Artisan Classes	£174—£828	£175—£365	£168—£552	£210—£394	£174—£420	£236—£500
Sub-Clerical and Auxiliary Classes	£132—£371	£125—£185	£102—£237	£100—£193	£101—£190	£156—£254

APPENDIX III

ORGANISATIONAL STRUCTURE OF A MINISTRY OF AGRICULTURE AND NATURAL RESOURCES

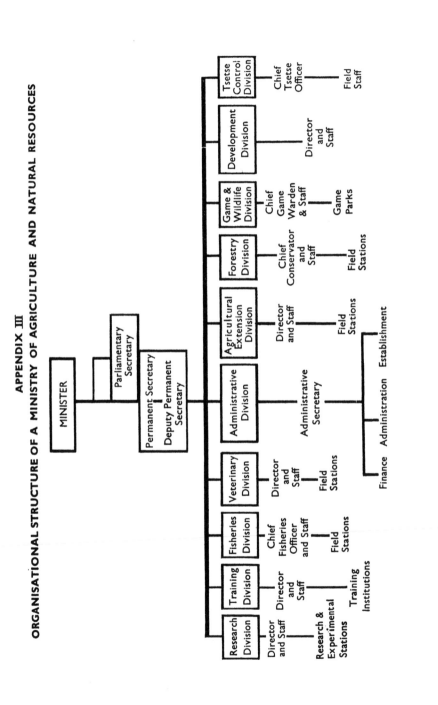

INDEX

For Product Safety Concerns and Information please contact our EU
representative GPSR@taylorandfrancis.com
Taylor & Francis Verlag GmbH, Kaufingerstraße 24, 80331 München, Germany